A NEW
UNIVERSITY ANTHOLOGY
Of ENGLISH POETRY

A NEW
UNIVERSITY
ANTHOLOGY
of ENGLISH
POETRY

Edited by
MC Andersen
SG Kossick
E Pereira

1993
Cape Town
Oxford University Press

Oxford University Press
Walton Street, Oxford OX2 6DP, United Kingdom

Oxford   New York   Toronto
Delhi   Bombay   Calcutta   Madras   Karachi
Kuala Lumpur   Singapore   Hong Kong   Tokyo
Nairobi   Dar es Salaam   Cape Town
Melbourne   Auckland   Madrid

and associated companies in
Berlin   Ibadan

A NEW UNIVERSITY ANTHOLOGY OF ENGLISH POETRY

IBSN 0 19 570 873 3

© Oxford University Press 1984
Third edition 1993

Oxford is a trademark of Oxford University Press

Cover design by Mara Singer

Published by Oxford University Press Southern Africa, Harrington
House, Barrack Street, Cape Town, 8001, South Africa.

Set in Sabon by Theiner Typesetting, Cape.
Printed by CTP Book Printers, Cape.

Preface

In the ten years since the first publication of *A University Anthology of English Poetry*, many important changes—social, political and cultural—have occurred, some of which have found expression in contemporary literature. Women's writing, for instance, has come strongly to the fore, and there has been an upsurge of creative work by South African writers in English, as well as a greater emphasis on our own literature in schools and universities. In order to reflect these developments and to meet the changing needs of our students, an extensively revised collection has become necessary. In keeping with recent trends in the teaching of literature, greater emphasis has been placed on the work of modern poets, though we have retained a basic selection of poems from the fourteenth to the nineteenth centuries. The process of revision has also enabled us to adapt our approach so as to offer more teaching support, for example, by the introduction of headnotes supplying contextual information about the poets and their poems.

The collection can be regarded as catering for first-year students of English at a tertiary level, providing, as it does, a chronological record from medieval verse to contemporary South African poetry. The poems selected are, for the most part, accessible, in that they do not assume a high level of erudition or scholarship on the part of the student. The wide range of poems and extracts selected—some 225 in all—allows tutors a considerable degree of flexibility in choosing specific works for teaching purposes. First-year students, too, will be able to acquaint themselves with the breadth and diversity of the poets and periods they will be examining in greater detail, should they select English as a major subject. The range and variety should, however, also appeal to those who do not intend to further their studies in English—and even to the general reader seeking guidance—as the anthology reflects much of the achievement of English poetry over some seven centuries.

Regrettably, some important but unduly long poems, such as Coleridge's *Rime of the Ancient Mariner*, have had to be omitted for reasons of space, while major works such as Chaucer's *Canterbury Tales* and Milton's *Paradise Lost* could be included only by way of brief extracts. (The editors were moreover restricted by such considerations as copyright and availability.) Old English was considered too difficult to master at first-year level, so our selection opens with examples of Middle English poetry. Because most first-year university syllabuses include at least one of Shakespeare's plays, we have offered a more limited selection of his verse than might otherwise be expected. While we have reduced the number of pre-twentieth century poems, the selection remains, we believe, fairly representative; on the other hand, as already mentioned, there has been a significant increase in the number of poets and poems of contemporary significance (in particular, works by South African and women writers.)

The arrangement of poems is chronological, the poet's date of birth being the criterion. We have deliberately chosen not to classify the poets according to period, as this not only presents an artificial (and distorted) view of the historical development of poetry, but inhibits an awareness of the continuity of the creative impulse and the overlapping of styles, periods and attitudes. The line numbering of extracts from long poems is continuous, with breaks and omissions indicated, and the original line or stanza numbers are given in the heading. Nouns have been kept to lower case lettering throughout, except where the words with a special or emblematic connotation retain an initial capital (for example, "Nature" in Wordsworth often indicates an almost religious significance).

As far as possible spelling has been modernized, an important feature in teaching first-year students. Sometimes, however, modernization was difficult, specifically where the rhythm of the poem required the original pronunciation (and consequently the original spelling). The only cases where we have not consistently attempted to modernize spelling—because we believe that the quality of diction would have suffered—was in dealing with Middle English poets and the Scottish poet Robert Burns; here glosses of difficult or elusive words are provided. We have kept glosses to a minimum: words which appear in the *Concise Oxford Dictionary* (eighth edition) have generally not been included, except where unusual forms or usages occur. Notes clarifying topical allusions and lengthy glosses which could not be accommodated at the side of the page, are supplied below the relevant poem. In addition, classical, mythological, historical and other references are given in the footnotes. Where the titles of poems are not supplied, the poem has been identified by a first-line quotation or, in the case of an extract, by a descriptive indicator (not italicized). The composite Index covers authors, titles and the first lines of all the poems.

Our aim, as noted above, is to make the poems as accessible as possible to first-year students. The textual aids we have included should facilitate understanding, without intruding between text and reader. The placing of contextual, explanatory and other supplementary material on the same page as the text, wherever possible, will, we hope, make for greater ease of reference and enable students to come more readily to terms with the text. And that, finally, is the purpose of this anthology: to promote understanding and appreciation of English poetry. Like all anthologies, this one will not please all its readers and may even appear arbitrary. What we can affirm is that the selection has not been compiled in the service of any specific literary doctrine. The investigation of critical attitudes seems to us to be part of the teaching process. We have, however, tried to stimulate interest in poetry and encourage readers to go further than the present book in their literary explorations.

The compilation of this anthology has mainly been a team effort. Members of the Department of English at the University of South

Africa were consulted concerning the scope and nature of the volume
and they submitted titles and authors of poems. The editors gratefully
acknowledge the assistance of their colleagues and, in particular, the
first-year poetry team. We also wish to record our thanks to our
proofreaders, and to the editorial staff at Oxford University Press
Southern Africa, for continuing interest and assistance.

Pretoria, 1993   M.C.A.
                                                              S.G.K.
                                                               E.P.

Contents

Blues for district six .
Theme for English B.

Acknowledgements

The editors and publisher gratefully acknowledge permission to reproduce copyright poems in this book. Every effort has been made to trace copyright holders, but where this has proved impossible, the publishers would be grateful for information which would enable them to amend any omissions in future editions.

Tatamkulu Afrika: "Waiting for Lazarus" from *New Coin Poetry*, Volume 27, Number 1, June 1991. Reprinted by permission of the author.

Maya Angelou: "Still I Rise" and "Woman Work". Reprinted by permission of Virago Press.

John Ashbery: "The Painter" and "Crazy Weather".

Farouk Asvat: "The Possibilities for a Man Hunted by SBs".

Margaret Atwood: "Earth" from *True Stories*, copyright © 1981 Margaret Atwood; "Habitation" from *Procedures for Underground* by Margaret Atwood, copyright © 1970 Oxford University Press Canada. Reprinted by permission of Oxford University Press Canada.

W.H. Auden: "Musée des Beaux Arts" and "The Unknown Citizen" from *Collected Poems* by W.H. Auden. Reprinted by permission of Faber and Faber Ltd.

shabbir banoobhaai: "The Border." Reprinted by permission of the author.

George Barker: "To My Mother" from *Collected Poems* by George Barker. Reprinted by permission of Faber and Faber Ltd.

Sujata Bhatt: "Muliebrity" from *Brunizem* by Sujata Bhatt. Reprinted by permission of Carcanet Press Ltd.

Elizabeth Bishop: "The Fish" and "In the Waiting Room" from *The Complete Poems 1927-1979* by Elizabeth Bishop, copyright © 1979, 1983 Alice Helen Methfessel. Reprinted by permission of Farrar, Straus & Giroux, Inc.

Herman Charles Bosman: "Seed" from *The Earth is Waiting* by Herman Charles Bosman. Reprinted by permission of Human & Rousseau (Pty) Ltd, Cape Town and the estate of Helena Lake.

Dennis Brutus: "On the Island" from *Letters to Martha and other Poems from a South African Prison* by Dennis Brutus.

Lynne Bryer: "Our One" from *A Time in the Country*, published by Carrefour Press. Reprinted by permission of the author.

Guy Butler: "Stranger to Europe" and "Myths" from *Collected Poems* by Guy Butler. Reprinted by permission of the author and Ad. Donker (Pty) Ltd.

Roy Campbell: "The Zulu Girl" and "Autumn" from *Selected Poems* by Roy Campbell. Reprinted by permission of Francisco Campbell Custodio and Ad. Donker (Pty) Ltd.

Sydney Clouts: "After the Poem" and "The Sleeper" from *One Life* by Sydney Clouts. Reprinted by permission of David Philip Publisher (Pty) Ltd.

Jeni Couzyn: "Spell for Birth".

E.E. Cummings: "anyone lived in a pretty how town", "Buffalo Bill's" and "the Cambridge ladies who live in furnished souls" from *The Complete Poems 1913-1962* by E.E. Cummings. Reprinted by permission of W.W. Norton & Company, Ltd.

R.N. Currey: "Durban Revisited" from *The Africa We Knew* by R.N. Currey. Reprinted by permission of David Philip Publisher (Pty) Ltd.

Ingrid de Kok: "Small Passing" from *Familiar Ground* by Ingrid de Kok, published by Ravan Press, 1988. Reprinted by permission of the author and Ravan Press (Pty) Ltd.

Anthony Delius: "The Gamblers" from *Wild Wave: An Anthology of Poetry* compiled by H.S. Houghton-Hawksley and A.B.S. Eaton. Reprinted by permission of Peter Delius.

H.I.E. Dhlomo: "Not For Me" from *The Return of the Amasi Bird: Black South African Poetry 1891-1981* ed. Tim Couzens and Essop Patel. Reprinted by permission of Professor Tim Couzens on behalf of the estate of H.I.E. Dhlomo.

Modike Dikobe: "Counter 14" from *The Return of the Amasi Bird: Black South African Poetry 1891-1981* ed. Tim Couzens and Essop Patel.

T.S. Eliot: "Macavity the Mystery Cat" from *Old Possum's Book of Practical Cats* by T.S. Eliot; "Preludes", "Rhapsody on a Windy Night", "The Hollow Men" and "Journey of the Magi" from *Collected Poems 1909-1962* by T.S. Eliot. Reprinted by permission of Faber and Faber Ltd.

D.J. Enright: "The Word" from *Collected Poems* by D.J. Enright. Reprinted by permission of Watson, Little Ltd.

Lawrence Ferlinghetti: "Constantly Risking Absurdity" from *A Coney Island of the Mind* by Lawrence Ferlinghetti, copyright © 1958 by Lawrence Ferlinghetti. Reprinted by permission of New Directions Publishing Corporation.

Robert Frost: "Out, Out—" and "Stopping by Woods on a Snowy Evening" from *The Poetry of Robert Frost* edited by Edward Connery Lathem. Reprinted by permission of the executors of the estate of the author and Jonathan Cape Publishers.

Nikki Giovanni: "Nikki Rosa".

Thom Gunn: "Memory Unsettled" from The Man with Night Sweats by Thom Gunn. Reprinted by permission of Faber and Faber Ltd.

Dorian Haarhoff: "Trader on the Namib Edge" from the collection *Bordering* by Dorian Haarhoff. Reprinted by permission of Justified Press, P.O. Box 5091, Rivonia, 2128, RSA.

Geoffrey Haresnape: "The Necklace". Reprinted by permission of the author and Justified Press, P.O. Box 5091, Rivonia, 2128, RSA.

Seamus Heaney: "Act of Union" from *North* by Seamus Heaney. Reprinted by permission of Faber and Faber Ltd.

Langston Hughes: "As I Grew Older" and "Theme for English B" from *Selected Poems* of Langston Hughes. Reprinted by permission of David Higham Associates Ltd.

Ted Hughes: "Pike" from *Lupercal*, "The Thought-Fox" from *The Hawk in the Rain* by Ted Hughes, "Thrushes" and "Night Jar" from *Selected Poems* by Ted Hughes and "Two Legends" from *Crow* by Ted Hughes. Reprinted by permission of Faber and Faber, Ltd.

Abdullah Ibrahim: "blues for district six" from *Africa, Music and Show Business* by Abdullah Ibrahim.

Wopko Jensma: "Misto 3" from *Sing for our Execution* by Wopko Jensma. Reprinted by permission of Ravan Press (Pty) Ltd.

Fhazel Johennesse: "thinking about a white christmas". Reprinted by permission of the author.

Solly Kaplinski: "In the Shoe Shop" and "Lublin—4th November 1943—2.30 p.m." Reprinted by permission of the author.

Daniel Kunene: "Do Not Ask Me" from *The Return of the Amasi Bird: Black South African Poetry 1891-1981* ed. Tim Couzens and Essop Patel.

L.R.: "'Civilised' Labour Policy" from *Umteteli wa Bantu*.

Philip Larkin: "Mr Bleaney" from *The Whitsun Weddings*. Reprinted by permission of Faber and Faber Ltd.

D.H. Lawrence: "Piano" and "Red Geranium and Godly Mignonette" from *The Complete Poems* ed. Vivian de Sola Pinto and Warren Roberts. Reprinted by permission of Laurence Pollinger Ltd. on behalf of the Estate of Frieda Lawrence Ravagli.

Douglas Livingstone: "There are Times" from *A Rosary of Bone*; "Gentling a Wildcat" from *Eyes Closed Against the Sun* © 1970 Oxford University Press Oxford; "Stormshelter" and "Sunstrike" from *Sjambok and other poems from Africa* © 1964 Oxford University Press Oxford, all by Douglas Livingstone. Reprinted by permission of, respectively, David Philip Publisher (Pty) Ltd and Oxford University Press Oxford.

Roger Mc Gough: "A Brown Paper Carrier Bag" from *In the Glassroom* by Roger Mc Gough. Reprinted by permission of Peters Fraser & Dunlop Group Ltd.

Archibald Macleish: "Ars Poetica" from *New and Collected Poems 1917-1976* by Archibald Macleish.

Louis Macneice: "Snow" from *The Collected Poems of Louis MacNeice*. Reprinted by permission of Faber and Faber Ltd.

Charles Madge: "The Apocalypse".

Gcina Mhlophe: "The Dancer". Reprinted by permission of the author.

Ruth Miller: "The Floating Island" from *The Floating Island*, "Penguin on the Beach" and "Submarine" from *Selected Poems*, both by Ruth Miller. Reprinted by permission of Lionel Abrahams on behalf of Mrs Pat Campbell and the estate of Ruth Miller.

Marianne Moore: "Poetry" from *The Collected poems of Marianne Moore*. Reprinted by permission of Faber and Faber Ltd.

Edwin Morgan: "Opening the Cage" from *The Second Life* by Edwin Morgan. Reprinted by permission of Edinburgh University Press.

Casey Motsisi: "The Efficacy of Prayer".

Oupa Thando Mthimkulu: "Nineteen Seventy-Six".

Mbuyiseni Oswald Mtshali: "An Abandoned Bundle", "The Master of the House" and "The Moulting Country Bird" from *Sounds of a Cowhide Drum* by Mbuyiseni Oswald Mtshali. Reprinted by permission of Oxford University Press Oxford.

Charles Mungoshi: "Burning Log."

N.S. Ndebele: "The Revolution of the Aged" from *The Return of the Amasi Bird: Black South African Poetry from 1891-1981* ed. Tim Couzens and Essop Patel. Reprinted by permission of the author.

Arthur Nortje: "Waiting" from *Dead Roots*.

Motshile wa Nthodi: "Standard Fifty-Eight".

Marge Piercy: "A Story Wet as Tears" from *Stone, Paper, Knife*.

Sylvia Plath: "Black Rook in Rainy Weather" from *Colossus* and "You're", "Sheep in Fog" and "Balloons" from *The Collected Poems*, both by Sylvia Plath. Reprinted by permission of Faber and Faber Ltd.

William Plomer: "The Wild Doves at Louis Trichardt" and "Namaqualand after Rain" from *Collected Poems* by William Plomer. Reprinted by permission of the estate of the author and Jonathan Cape.

Ezra Pound: "In a Station of the Metro" from *Collected Shorter Poems* by Ezra Pound. Reprinted by permission of Faber and Faber Ltd.

Ndaleni Radebi: "Woman".

John Crowe Ransome: "Bells for John Whiteside's Daughter" from *Selected Poems* by John Crowe Ransome. Reprinted by permission of Carcanet Press Ltd.

Malvinia Reynolds: "Little Boxes".

Adrienne Rich: "Your Small Hands", Part VI from "Twenty-one Love Poems" in *The Fact of a Doorframe, Poems Selected and New, 1950-1984* by Adrienne Rich. Reprinted by permission of W.W. Norton & Company, Inc.

Theodore Roethke: "My Pappa's Waltz" from *The Collected Poems of Theodore Roethke*. Reprinted by permission of Faber and Faber Ltd.

Siegfried Sassoon: "Attack". Reprinted by permission of George T. Sassoon.

Pete Seeger: "Where have all the flowers gone?"

Sipho Sepamla: "Come Duze Baby" and "The Blues is You in Me".

Mongane Wally Serote: "For Don M.—Banned", "The Clothes", "Alexandra", "City Johannesburg", "Burning Cigarette" and "Prelude". Reprinted by permission of Mongane Wally Serote and Ad. Donker (Pty) Ltd.

Anne Sexton: "The Starry Night" from *All My Pretty Ones* by Anne Sexton; copyright Anne Sexton 1961. Reprinted by permission of Sterling Lord Literistic, Inc.

F.C. Slater: "Lament for a Dead Cow" from *Collected Poems (1957)*. Reprinted by permission of Pillans and Wilson, previously Blackwoods, Edinburgh.

Stevie Smith: "Not Waving But Drowning" from *The Collected Poems of Stevie Smith* (Penguin 20th Century Classics). Reprinted by permission of James MacGibbon.

Dylan Thomas: "Fern Hill" and "Do not go gentle into that good night" from *The Poems* by Dylan Thomas. Reprinted by permission of David Higham Associates Ltd and Dent Publishers.

Charles Tomlinson: "Paring the Apple" from *Collected Poems* by Charles Tomlinson. Reprinted by permission of Oxford University Press Oxford.

Christopher van Wyk: "A Riot Policeman". Reprinted by permission of the author.

Alice Walker: "On Sight" from *Horses make a Landscape Look More Beautiful* by Alice Walker, first published in Great Britain by The Women's Press Ltd, 1985, 34 Great Sutton Street, London EC1V 0DX. Reprinted by permission of The Women's Press Ltd and David Higham Associates Ltd.

William Carlos Williams: "The Red Wheelbarrow" and "This is Just to Say" from *Collected Earlier Poems* by William Carlos Williams. Reprinted by permission of Carcanet Press Ltd.

David Wright: "Swift" from *Selected Poems* by David Wright. Reprinted by permission of David Philip Publisher (Pty) Ltd.

W.B. Yeats: "The Second Coming", "A Prayer for my Daughter" and "Leda and the Swan". Reprinted by permission of Macmillan Publishers, Ltd.

Anonymous

"Sumer is icumen in"
(Thirteenth Century)

Sumer° is icumen° in,[1]   *summer / is coming*
Lhude°[2] sing, cuccu!°   *loudly / cuckoo*
Groweth sed° and bloweth med°   *seed grows / meadow blooms*
And springth the wude nu.[3]
5   Sing, cuccu!

Awe° bleteth after lomb,°   *ewe / lamb*
Lhouth after calve cu,[4]
Bulluc sterteth°, bucke verteth.°   *leaps / breaks wind*
Murie° sing, cuccu!   *merrily*
10   Cuccu, cuccu,
Wel singes thu,° cuccu.   *you sing well*
Ne swik° thu naver° nu!   *cease / never*

Sing cuccu nu, sing cuccu!
Sing cuccu, sing cuccu nu!

"Swarte smekéd smethes"
(Fifteenth Century)

Swarte smekéd smethes, smattered with smoke,[1]
Drive me to deth with den° of here dintes!°   *din / blows*
Swech° nois° on nightes ne herd men never: *such / noise*
What knavene cry,° and clattering of knockes!   *workers' cries*
5   The cammede° kongons° crien after "Col,° col!"   *crooked / creatures / coal*
And blowen here bellewes that all here brain brestes.°   *bursts*
"Huff, puff!" seith that one; "Haff, paff!" that other.
They spitten° and sprawlen° and spellen° many spelles,   *spit / swear / tell*
They gnawen° and gnacchen,° they grones° togedere,   *gnash / grind / groan*
10   And holden hem hote° with here hard hammers.   *keep themselves hot*

---

1 *Difficult words, or words unfamiliarly spelt,*
   are explained or glossed only on their first
   appearance.
2 *As in Chaucer and much other Middle*
   English verse, the final "e" is sounded, except

when followed immediately by a vowel.
3 *The wood breaks into leaf now.*
4 *The cow lows after the calf.*
1 *Black-smoked smiths begrimed with smoke.*

Of a bole hide ben here barm-felles,[2]
Here schankes ben schakeled° for the fere-flunderes;°   *protected against / sparks*
Hevy hammeres they han that hard ben handled,
Stark° strokes they striken on a steled° stokke.°   *hard / steel / anvil*
15   "Luss, buss! lass, dass!" routen be rowe°—   *crash in turn*
Sweche dolful a dreme° the devil it to drive![3]   *din*
The maister longeth a litel and lascheth a lesse,[4]
Twineth hem twein, and toucheth a treble.[5]
"Tik, tak! hic, hac! tiket, taket! tik, tak!
20   Luss, buss! luss, dass!" swich lif° they leden!°   *life / lead*
Alle clothemeres,° Crist hem give sorwe,   *horse armourers*
May no man for brenwateres[6] on night han his rest!

Westron Winde
(Sixteenth Century)

Westron° winde, when will thou blow,   *western*
The smalle raine downe can raine?
Christ, if my love were in my armes,
And I in my bed againe.

Lord Randal[1]

"O where ha° you been, Lord Randal, my son?   *have*
And where ha you been, my handsome young man?"
"I ha been at the greenwood; mother, mak° my bed soon,   *make*
For I'm wearied wi° huntin, and fain wad° lie down."   *with / gladly would*

5   "And wha° met ye° there, Lord Randal, my son?   *who / you*
And wha met you there, my handsome young man?"
"O I met wi my true-love; mother, mak my bed soon,
For I'm wearied wi huntin, and fain wad lie down."

"And what did she give you, Lord Randal, my son?
10   And what did she give you, my handsome young man?"
"Eels fried in a pan; mother, mak my bed soon,
For I'm wearied wi huntin, and fain wad lie down."

2 *Their leather aprons are made of bull's hide.*
3 *May the devil take it.*
4 *Lengthens and beats small pieces of iron.*
5 *Twines them together and strikes a treble note.*

6 *Because of burning water.*
1 *There have been many versions of this ballad, dating from the late medieval period right up to the nineteenth century.*

"And wha gat° your leavins°, Lord Randal, my son?   *got / leavings (left-overs)*
And wha gat your leavins, my handsome young man?"
15 "My hawks and my hounds; mother, mak my bed soon,
For I'm wearied wi huntin, and fain wad lie down."

"And what becam° of them, Lord Randal, my son?   *became*
And what becam of them, my handsome young man?"
"They stretched their legs out an° died; mother, mak my bed soon,   *and*
20 For I'm wearied wi huntin, and fain wad lie down."

"O I fear you are poisoned, Lord Randal, my son!
I fear you are poisoned, my handsome young man!"
"O yes, I am poisoned; mother, mak my bed soon,
For I'm sick at the heart, and I fain wad lie down."

25 "What d' ye° leave to your mother, Lord Randal, my son?   *do you*
What d' ye leave to your mother, my handsome young man?"
"Four and twenty milk kye°; mother, mak my bed soon,   *cows*
For I'm sick at the heart, and I fain wad lie down."

"What d' ye leave to your sister, Lord Randal, my son?
30 What d' ye leave to your sister, my handsome young man?"
"My gold and my silver; mother, mak my bed soon,
For I'm sick at the heart, and I fain wad lie down."

"What d' ye leave to your brother, Lord Randal, my son?
What d' ye leave to your brother, my handsome young man?"
35 "My houses and my lands; mother, mak my bed soon,
For I'm sick at the heart, and I fain wad lie down."

"What d' ye leave to your true-love, Lord Randal, my son?
What d' ye leave to your true-love, my handsome young man?"
"I leave her hell and fire; mother, mak my bed soon,
40 For I'm sick at the heart, and I fain wad lie down."

Geoffrey Chaucer (c.1340 – 1400)

Geoffrey Chaucer, the son of a wine-merchant, was born in London in about 1340. Though at times he suffered financial constraints (see his amusing complaint to his empty purse), he led a most stimulating life. He was associated with the royal and aristocratic courts, was sent in a minor capacity on diplomatic missions to Europe and held various civil service posts such as Comptroller of Customs. In 1386 he became Knight of the Shire for Kent (more or less the equivalent of a Member of Parliament). Because of his position in society, Chaucer was at the centre of the events of his day and he came into contact with a wide cross-section of society. To these experiences he added his own gifts of wide reading, a keen visual sense and delightful humour—all of which are put to good use in his poetry, making him well worth reading, not only as a chronicler of his times but also as a discerning student of human nature.

From THE CANTERBURY TALES[1]

The General Prologue   *(extract: lines 1-41)*

	Whan that Aprill with his shoures soote°	*pleasant showers*
	The droghte° of March hath perced° to the roote,	*dryness / pierced*
	And bathed every veyne° in swich° licour°	*vein / such / sap*
	Of which vertu[2] engendred is the flour;°	*flower*
5	Whan Zephirus eek° with his sweete° breeth°	*also / sweet / breath*
	Inspired hath in every holt° and heeth°	*wood / plain*
	The tendre croppes°, and the yonge° sonne	*crops / youthful*
	Hath in the Ram[3] his halfe cours yronne,[4]	
	And smale° foweles° maken melodye,[5]	*small / birds*
10	That slepen° al the nyght with open eye—	*sleep*
	So priketh° hem nature in hir corages°—	*urges / hearts*
	Thanne longen° folk to goon on pilgrimages,	*long (yearn)*
	And palmeres° for to seken° straunge° strondes°	*pilgrims / seek / distant shores*
	To ferne° halwes,° kowthe in sondry londes;[6]	*far-off / shrines*

---

1 The Canterbury Tales, *Chaucer's best-known work, is a collection of tales told by a group of fictional pilgrims on their way to and from the shrine of St Thomas à Becket in Canterbury, south-eastern England.*

2 *Life-giving power.*

3 *The Ram—the zodiacal sign of Aries—includes the latter half of March and the first half of April.*

4 *Completed half of its cycle.*

5 *Make a melody: sing.*

6 *Famous in various lands.*

15 And specially from every shires ende
    Of Engelond to Caunterbury[7] they wende
    The hooly blisful martir[8] for to seke°   *seek*
    That hem hath holpen° whan that they were seeke.° *helped / sick*
    Bifil that in that seson on a day[9]
20 In Southwerk at the Tabard[1] as I lay
    Redy to wenden° on my pilgrymage   *go*
    To Caunterbury with ful° devout corage,°   *very / heart*
    At nyght was come into that hostelrye°   *inn*
    Wel nyne and twenty in a compaignye   *company*
25 Of sondry folk, by aventure° yfalle°   *chance / fallen*
    In felaweship,° and pilgrimes were they alle, *fellowship*
    That toward Caunterbury wolden ryde.° *wished to ride*
    The chambres° and the stables weren wyde,° *rooms / spacious*
    And wel we weren esed atte beste.[2]
30 And shortly, whan the sonne was to reste,°   *set*
    So hadde I spoken with hem everichon°   *everyone*
    That I was of hir felaweship anon,°   *immediately*
    And made forward° erly for to ryse,   *agreed*
    To take oure wey ther as I yow devyse.[3]
35   But nathelees,° whil I have tyme and space, *nevertheless*
    Er that I ferther in this tale pace,°   *proceed*
    Me thynketh it acordaunt° to resoun   *fitting*
    To telle yow al the condicioun°   *circumstances*
    Of ech of hem, so as it semed me,° *(to) me*
40 And whiche they weren, and of what degree,° *rank*
    And eek in what array° that they were inne.[4] *dress*

The Complaint of Chaucer to his Purse

    To yow, my purse, and to noon other wight°   *person*
    Complayne I, for ye be my lady dere!°   *dear*
    I am so sory,° now that ye been lyght;°   *sad / light*
    For certés,° but° ye make me hevy° chere, *certainly / unless / heavy*
5 Me were as leef[5] be layd upon my bere;°   *bier*
    For which unto your mercy thus I crye:
    Beth hevy ageyn,° or ellés° mot° I dye! *again / else / must*

7 *Canterbury: ecclesiastical capital of England and seat of the primate of all England, that is, the head of the Anglican Church.*

8 *St Thomas à Becket, martyred in 1170 in Canterbury Cathedral.*

9 *It happened one day.*

1 *The name of an inn in a London borough.*

2 *Entertained and accommodated in the best way.*

3 *As I shall tell you.*

4 *Chaucer goes on to describe such characters as the Prioress, the Wife of Bath and the Pardoner.*

5 *I would as soon.*

Now voucheth sauf° this day, er yt⁶ be nyght,   *vouchsafe (grant)*
That I of yow the blisful° soun° may here,   *blissful / sound*
10 Or see your colour lyk the sonné° bryght,   *sun*
That of yelownesse° hadde never pere.°   *yellowness / peer (equal)*
Ye be my lyf,° ye be myn hertés° stere,°   *life / heart's / helmsman*
Quene° of comfort and of good companye: *Queen*
Beth hevy ageyn, or ellés moot I dye!   *must*

15 Now purse, that ben to me my lyvés° lyght   *life's*
And saveour,° as doun° in this world here,   *saviour / down*
Out of this touné° helpe me thurgh° your myght,   *town / through*
Syn° that ye wole° nat ben my tresorere;   *since / will / treasurer*
For I am shave as nye° as any frere.°   *closely / friar*
20 But yet I pray unto your curtesye:°   *courtesy*
Beth hevy agen, or ellés moot I dye!

Lenvoy de Chaucer°   *Chaucer's appeal*

O conquerour of Brutes Albyon,⁷
Which that by lyne° and free eleccion°   *lineage / election*
Been verray° kyng, this song to yow I sende;   *true*
25 And ye, that mowen° alle oure harmes° amende,   *may / harms*
Have mynde upon my supplicacion!°   *consider / supplication*

6 *Before it.*
7 *Brutus's Britain. The legend was that*   *of Rome), brought the Trojans to Britain*
   Brutus, great-grandson of Aeneas (founder   *(Albion), founding the New Troy (London)*
                                                       as its capital.

William Dunbar (c.1460 – c.1521)

One of the most successful of the medieval Scottish poets, Dunbar is also one of the most versatile. He wrote in a number of stanza forms and in a variety of styles to accord with the diversity of his poetic output. This includes burlesque, comic verse, invective and satire, as well as secular and religious lyrics. "Sweit rois of vertew" is a testimony to his ability to create a beautiful, well-crafted love lyric. A noteworthy aspect of Dunbar's poetry is its use of "aureate diction"—a highly decorative and richly ornamental style. Dunbar has been described as one of the "Scottish Chaucerians". While he and Scottish contemporaries such as Robert Henryson (c.1425 – c.1505) have proved to be admirers of Chaucer and have clearly been influenced by him, the title is not entirely accurate. Both Dunbar and Henryson are valued as unique poets in their own right.

"Sweit rois of vertew"

Sweit rois° of vertew° and of gentilnes,	*rose / virtue*
Delytsum° lyllie of everie lustynes,°	*delightful / pleasure*
Richest in bontie° and in bewtie° cleir,°	*bounty / beauty / clear*
And everie vertew that is [held maist] deir,°	*[most] dear*
5 Except onlie that ye ar mercyles.	
In to your garthe° this day I did persew;°	*garden / made my way*
Thair saw I flowris° that fresche wer of hew,°	*flowers / hue*
Baith quhyte and reid moist lusty wer to seyne,[1]	
And halsum° herbis° upone stalkis° grene,	*wholesome / herbs / stalks*
10 Yit leif° nor flour° fynd could I nane of rew.[2]	*leaf / flower*
I dout° that Merche° with his caild blastis keyne[3]	*suspect / March*
Hes slane° this gentill herbe that I of mene,°	*slain / I refer to*
Quhois petewous deithe dois to my hart sic pane[4]	
That I wald° mak° to plant his rute° agane,	*would / make / root*
15 So confortand° his levis° unto me bene.°	*comforting / leaves / are*

1 *Both white and red were most lovely to see.*
2 *"Rue" means pity or compassion; it is also the name of a bitter herb with medicinal properties.*

3 *Keen, cold blasts.*
4 *Whose piteous death brings my heart such pain.*

Sir Thomas Wyatt (1503 – 1542)

Employed as a diplomat by Henry VIII, Wyatt visited both France and Italy in this capacity. Possibly because of a suspected liaison with Anne Boleyn, Henry's second wife, Wyatt also spent a considerable time in prison and was fortunate to escape with his life. The foremost poet of his time, Wyatt is noted for his unique renditions, in English, of Petrarchan sonnets. The concluding couplet—familiar to readers of Shakespeare's later sonnet sequences—is one of Wyatt's innovations. One of his major poetic achievements is perhaps the introduction of rhythms which are natural to the speaking voice and characterized by some roughness or irregularity. These elements are apparent in "They flee from me", a poem which suggests some knowledge of the intrigue of royal courts.

"They flee from me"

They flee from me, that sometime did me seek
With naked foot stalking in my chamber.
I have seen them gentle, tame, and meek
That now are wild, and do not remember
5 That sometime they put themself in danger
To take bread at my hand; and now they range,
Busily seeking with a continual change.

Thanked be fortune it hath been otherwise
Twenty times better, but once in special,
10 In thin array after a pleasant guise
When her loose gown from her shoulders did fall,
And she me caught in her arms long and small,
Therewithal sweetly did me kiss,
And softly said, "Dear heart, how like you this?"

15 It was no dream: I lay broad waking.
But all is turned thorough° my gentleness   *through*
Into a strange fashion of forsaking,
And I have leave to go of her goodness,
And she also to use newfangleness.
20 But since that I so kindly am served,
I would fain° know what she hath deserved.   *gladly*

Henry Howard, Earl of Surrey (1517 – 1547)

Son of the Duke of Norfolk, Surrey (like Wyatt) was attached to the court of Henry VIII. Together with his father, Surrey was imprisoned by the king on a charge of so-called treason and was executed (although the older man lived to tell the tale). In his poetry, Surrey was greatly influenced by the Italian Renaissance and, like Wyatt, was responsible for the English rendition of Italian poetic forms—the sonnet in particular. In his English translation of Virgil's Aeneid, Surrey initiates the use of unrhymed iambic pentameter, or blank verse, in English poetry. This is the verse-form that was ably to serve Shakespeare's dramatic purposes later in the century.

Night

Alas! so all things now do hold their peace,
Heaven and earth disturbed in no thing.
The beasts, the air, the birds their song do cease;
The nightés chare° the stars about doth bring;   *chariot*
5 Calm is the sea; the waves work less and less.
So am not I, whom love, alas! doth wring,
Bringing before my face the great increase
Of my desires, whereat I weep and sing,
In joy and woe, as in a doubtful ease:
10 For my sweet thoughts sometime do pleasure bring;
But by and by, the cause of my disease
Gives me a pang, that inwardly doth sting,
When that I think what grief it is again,
To live and lack the thing should rid my pain.

Sir Walter Raleigh (c.1552 – 1618)

*As with many of his contemporaries, Raleigh's biography is a dramatic
one. Educated at Oxford, he served in the Huguenot army on the con-
tinent, and undertook military expeditions to Cadiz and the Azores; he
also embarked on voyages of discovery and exploration to
Newfoundland, Virginia and Guiana. Raleigh found favour with
Elizabeth I, becoming, for a while, rich and powerful. He forfeited this
privileged status as a result of his involvement with her lady-in-waiting,
Elizabeth Throckmorton. Under James I, he was unjustly condemned
to death for treason, reprieved and imprisoned in the Tower of London
for thirteen years, where he wrote* A History of the World. *On his
release, Raleigh undertook an expedition to the Orinoco in search of
gold. The failure of this attempt contributed to the renewal of charges
against him. He was arrested and beheaded at Westminster. The little
of his poetry that survives demonstrates skilful use of contemporary
styles, as well the ability to poke gentle fun at some of these conven-
tions.*

"Nature, that washed her hands in milk"

Nature, that washed her hands in milk,
    And had forgot to dry them,
Instead of earth took snow and silk,
    At Love's request to try them,
5   If she a mistress could compose
To please Love's fancy out of those.

Her eyes he would should be of light,
    A violet breath, and lips of jelly;
Her hair not black, nor overbright,
10   And of the softest down her belly;
As for her inside he 'ld have it
Only of wantonness and wit.[1]

At Love's entreaty such a one
    Nature made, but with her beauty
15   She hath framed a heart of stone,
    So as Love, by ill destiny,
Must die for her whom Nature gave him
Because her darling would not save him.

---

1 *Lacking in virtue and dignity.*

But Time, which Nature doth despise
20   And rudely gives her love the lie,
Makes Hope a fool, and Sorrow wise,
        His hands do neither wash nor dry;
But being made of steel and rust,
Turns snow and silk and milk to dust.

25   The light, the belly, lips, and breath,
        He dims, discolours, and destroys;
With those he feeds but fills not Death,
        Which sometimes were the food of joys.
Yea, Time doth dull each lively wit,
30   And dries all wantonness with it.

Oh, cruel Time! which takes in trust
        Our youth, our joys, and all we have,
And pays us but with age and dust;
        Who in the dark and silent grave
35   When we have wandered all our ways
Shuts up the story of our days.

The Nymph's Reply to the Shepherd[2]

If all the world and love were young,
And truth in every shepherd's tongue,
These pretty pleasures might me move
To live with thee and be thy love.

5   Time drives the flocks from field to fold,
When rivers rage and rocks grow cold,
And Philomel[3] becometh dumb;
The rest complain of cares to come.

The flowers do fade, and wanton° fields   *profusely flourishing*
10   To wayward° winter reckoning yields;   *wilful*
A honey tongue, a heart of gall,°   *bitterness*
Is fancy's spring, but sorrow's fall.

2 *See Christopher Marlowe, "The Passionate Shepherd to his Love", p. 17.*
3 *A princess of Athens whose brother-in-law, Tereus, violated her and then cut out her tongue. When pursued by him, she was transformed into a bird (usually, in legend, a swallow or a nightingale).*

Thy gowns, thy shoes, thy beds of roses,
Thy cap, thy kirtle,° and thy posies   *skirt or gown*
15   Soon break, soon wither, soon forgotten,
In folly ripe, in reason rotten.

Thy belt of straw and ivy buds,
Thy coral clasps and amber studs,
All these in me no means can move
20   To come to thee and be thy love.

But could youth last and love still breed,
Had joys no date nor age no need,
Then these delights my mind might move
To live with thee and be thy love.

Edmund Spenser (c.1552 – 1599)

Unlike Wyatt and Surrey, Spenser was not born into high court circles (although his father is reputed to have been of noble origins). He was, instead, a product of the greater spread of education among the middle classes. The influential friends he made while studying at Cambridge helped him to embark on a career as a civil servant. He spent almost eighteen years working for Elizabeth I in Ireland, and it is there that he wrote most of The Faerie Queene. *Based on English legends, this is sometimes called the first truly national poem. It is a work of fantasy and adventure, intended to evoke the glory of the Queen's reign. The poem makes use of allegory in which characters representing various virtues do battle against figures of evil and temptation. His sequence of sonnets and songs, the* Amoretti, *apparently has its origin in his courtship of Elizabeth Boyle (who became his wife). Looking forward to a joyful consummation of love in marriage, it differs from many other sonnet sequences which tend to explore the pain of doomed or thwarted love.*

Sonnet: "One day I wrote her name"

One day I wrote her name upon the strand,
But came the waves and washéd it away:
Again I wrote it with a second hand,
But came the tide and made my pains his prey.
5 Vain man! said she, that dost in vain assay
A mortal thing so to immortalise;
For I myself shall like to this decay,
And eke° my name be wipéd out likewise.   *also*
Not so, quoth I; let baser things devise
10 To die in dust, but you shall live by fame;
My verse your virtues rare shall eternise,
And in the heavens write your glorious name.
Where, whenas death shall all the world subdue,
Our love shall live, and later life renew.

Sir Philip Sidney (1554 – 1586)

There is an aura of romance and gallantry about the life of the soldier-poet, Sir Philip Sidney: bleeding heavily from a wound received in battle, he gave his only bottle of water to a dying soldier. The words he is reported to have said to the soldier typify the Renaissance ideal of courtliness combined with charity: "Thy necessity is yet greater than mine". He developed gangrene and died three weeks later, at the age of thirty-one.

Sidney is best remembered for his book on literary theory, An Apology for Poetry. *In it he defended the creative writer's role in society, suggesting that poetry could create a golden world of the imagination, leading humankind to higher truths. Sidney's most significant contribution to English poetry is his sequence of sonnets and songs,* Astrophel and Stella *(star-lover and star). The woman to whom they are addressed is probably Penelope Devereux who had been proposed as his bride when they were very young. Nothing came of this suit, but after she had been promised to someone else, Sidney found himself, too late, in love with her. The resulting poems, although modelled on the sonnets of the Italian poet, Petrarch, ring with Sidney's own desires, regrets and conflicts.*

Sonnet: "With how sad steps"

With how sad steps, O Moon, thou climb'st the skies!
How silently, and with how wan a face!
What, may it be that even in heavenly place
That busy archer his sharp arrows tries![1]
5   Sure, if that long-with-love-acquainted eyes
Can judge of love, thou feel'st a lover's case,
I read it in thy looks; thy languished grace,
To me, that feel the like, thy state descries.
Then, even of fellowship, O Moon, tell me,
10 Is constant love deemed there but want of wit?
Are beauties there as proud as here they be?
Do they above love to be loved, and yet
Those lovers scorn whom that love doth possess?
Do they call virtue there ungratefulness?

---

1 *Reference to Cupid.*

Robert Southwell (1561 – 1595)

Robert Southwell was the most celebrated of the so-called recusant
poets. "Recusant" is a term used to describe those—especially Roman
Catholics—who, from the time of Elizabeth I's reign to about the end
of the eighteenth century, refused to attend the services of the Church
of England. He was born at Horsham St Faith, Norfolk, to a noble
Catholic family. Like many other Catholic boys, he was sent to Europe
at the age of fifteen to escape the religious persecution carried out by
the English Protestants. He was ordained a Jesuit priest and returned
secretly to England in 1586, on a hazardous mission to restore English
Catholics to their faith. While in hiding in London, he wrote a volume
of poetry in which he propagated the new Counter-Reformation
Catholic Church and encouraged the persecuted English Catholics.
"The Burning Babe" is, in fact, a Jesuit meditation on the Nativity, a
popular aspect of the life of Jesus at the time. Southwell was eventually
captured by Topcliffe, Elizabeth's notorious official employed to
pursue the recusants. In 1595, Southwell was declared a traitor to the
Queen and was publicly hanged, drawn and quartered.

The Burning Babe

As I in hoary winter's night stood shivering in the snow,
Surprised I was with sudden heat which made my heart to glow;
And lifting up a fearful eye to view what fire was near,
A pretty Babe all burning bright did in the air appear;
5   Who, scorched with excessive heat, such floods of tears did shed,
As though his floods should quench his flames which with his tears were fed.
"Alas!" quoth he, "but newly born in fiery heats I fry,
Yet none approach to warm their hearts or feel my fire but I.
My faultless breast the furnace is, the fuel wounding thorns;
10   Love is the fire, and sighs the smoke, the ashes shame and scorns;
The fuel justice layeth on, and mercy blows the coals;
The metal in this furnace wrought are men's defiled souls:
For which, as now on fire I am to work them to their good,
So will I melt into a bath to wash them in my blood."
15   With this he vanished out of sight and swiftly shrunk away,
And straight I called unto mind that it was Christmas day.

Michael Drayton (1563 – 1631)

Little is known about Drayton's early life in Warwickshire. It seems that he entered service as a page to Sir Henry Goodere, whose daughter he praised as "Idea" in many of his sonnets and poems. A prolific writer, his works patriotically celebrated English landscape and history in loving detail. In later life, Drayton became a member of the "tribe of Ben", a stimulating community of poets and writers presided over by Ben Jonson.

Sonnet: "Since there's no help"

Since there's no help, come let us kiss and part.
Nay, I have done; you get no more of me,
And I am glad, yea, glad with all my heart,
That thus so cleanly I myself can free;
5 Shake hands for ever, cancel all our vows,
And when we meet at any time again,
Be it not seen in either of our brows
That we one jot of former love retain.
Now at the last gasp of Love's latest breath,
10 When, his pulse failing, Passion speechless lies,
When Faith is kneeling by his bed of death,
And Innocence is closing up his eyes,
Now if thou wouldst, when all have given him over,
From death to life thou mightst him yet recover.

Christopher Marlowe (1564 – 1593)

Born in Canterbury, the son of a successful shoemaker, Marlowe was educated at King's School, Canterbury, and Corpus Christi College, Cambridge. He is probably best known as the author of the plays, Dr Faustus, The Jew of Malta *and* Tamburlaine. *Ben Jonson praised Marlowe's "mighty line"—his ability to control the rhythms of blank verse in his dramatic writing. His life suggests a colourful personality: there are reports of secret government service and rumours of attending a Catholic seminary; and assaults, duels and brawls seem to have been a regular feature of his life. In 1593, the dramatist, John Kyd, was arrested for possessing atheistic documents. He declared they belonged to Marlowe and also accused him of treason and sodomy. On the eve of a court investigation into these charges, Marlowe was stabbed to death in a tavern. It is still not certain whether this was simply a hot-headed quarrel over a bill, or a politically motivated cover-up.*

The Passionate Shepherd to his Love

Come live with me and be my love,
And we will all the pleasures prove,°   *try*
That hills and valleys, dales and fields,
And all the craggy mountains yields.

5   There we will sit upon the rocks,
And see the shepherds feed their flocks,
By shallow rivers to whose falls
Melodious birds sing madrigals.[1]

And I will make thee beds of roses
10 With a thousand fragrant posies,
A cap of flowers, and a kirtle°   *skirt or gown*
Embroidered all with leaves of myrtle;

A gown made of the finest wool
Which from our pretty lambs we pull;
15 Fair lined slippers for the cold,
With buckles of the purest gold;

1 *Unaccompanied songs for several voices.*

A belt of straw and ivy buds,
With coral clasps and amber studs:
And if these pleasures may thee move,
20   Come live with me and be my love.

The shepherds' swains° shall dance and sing   *country youths or lovers*
For thy delight each May morning:
If these delights thy mind may move,
Then live with me and be my love.

William Shakespeare (1564 – 1616)

Shakespeare was born at Stratford-upon-Avon in the sixth year of Elizabeth I's reign. His parents were prosperous citizens of this busy market town. Little is known about his early years, but it is usually assumed that he went to the local grammar school, but did not go on to university. At eighteen, he married Anne Hathaway, who bore him three children. There are reports of him in his twenties as an actor and playwright in London. He went on to become the western world's most famous playwright and poet. Among his thirty-seven plays are the tragedies, Macbeth, King Lear, *and* Hamlet, *the comedies,* A Midsummer Night's Dream *and* Twelfth Night, *and the romance,* The Tempest.*

By 1592, just as he was beginning to establish a reputation as a playwright, there was an outbreak of the plague, and theatres were closed. It is some time after this that his sonnets were written, although they were published only in 1609. It cannot be established to whom they are addressed: the dedication in the first edition is simply "W.H.". It is clear, however, that four figures are involved in the series of sonnets: the speaker himself; a young man (addressed in sonnets 1 – 126), who could be a patron or friend; a rival poet who seems to be making a play for the patronage or affection of the young man; and a "Dark Lady" who transfers her affections from the speaker to the young man. This is a tangled web, and there is much speculation and controversy about possible identities. Many of the sonnets deal with the ravages of time upon human beauty, human monuments, and the natural world. Set against this is the power of poetry to endure as a written testament to what would otherwise be lost.

Song: **"Fear no more"**[1]

Fear no more the heat o' the sun
    Nor the furious winter's rages;
Thou thy worldly task hast done,
    Home art gone and ta'en thy wages.
5 Golden lads and girls all must,
As chimney-sweepers, come to dust.

Fear no more the frown o' the great,
    Thou art past the tyrant's stroke;
Care no more to clothe and eat;
10   To thee the reed is as the oak.
The sceptre, learning, physic, must
All follow this, and come to dust.

Fear no more the lightning-flash,
    Nor the all-dreaded thunder-stone:°   *thunderbolt*
15 Fear not slander, censure rash;
    Thou hast finished joy and moan.
All lovers young, all lovers must
Consign to thee, and come to dust.

Sonnet: **"Let me not to the marriage"**

Let me not to the marriage of true minds
Admit impediments. Love is not love
Which alters when it alteration finds,
Or bends with the remover to remove.
5 O, no! it is an ever-fixéd mark,
That looks on tempests and is never shaken;
It is the star to every wandering bark,°   *sailing vessel*
Whose worth's unknown, although his height be taken.
Love's not Time's fool, though rosy lips and cheeks
10 Within his bending sickle's compass come;
Love alters not with his brief hours and weeks,
But bears it out even to the edge of doom,°   *Judgement Day*
If this be error, and upon me proved,
I never writ, nor no man ever loved.

---

1 *From* Cymbeline.

Sonnet: "My mistress' eyes"

My mistress' eyes are nothing like the sun
Coral is far more red, than her lips' red,
If snow be white, why then her breasts are dun;°   *dull, greyish brown*
If hairs be wires, black wires grow on her head:
I have seen roses damasked, red and white,
But no such roses see I in her cheeks,
And in some perfumes is there more delight,
Than in the breath that from my mistress reeks.
I love to hear her speak, yet well I know,
That music hath a far more pleasing sound:
I grant I never saw a goddess go,°   *walk*
My mistress when she walks treads on the ground.
And yet, by heaven, I think my love as rare,
As any she belied with false compare.°   *comparison*

Sonnet: "Shall I compare thee"

Shall I compare thee to a summer's day?
Thou art more lovely and more __temperate:__
Rough winds do shake the darling buds of May,
And summer's lease hath all too short a date:
Sometime too hot the eye of heaven shines,
And often is his gold complexion dimmed,
And every fair from fair sometimes declines,
By chance, or nature's changing course untrimmed:
But thy eternal summer shall not fade,
Nor lose possession of that fair thou ow'st,°   *possess*
Nor shall death brag thou wand'rest in his shade,
When in eternal lines to time thou grow'st:
So long as men can breathe or eyes can see,
So long lives this, and this gives life to thee.

John Donne (1572 – 1631)

Donne's family was Catholic at a time when adherents of that faith
were barred from taking degrees at university or assuming high public
office. Therefore, although Donne (pronounced "dun") entered univer-
sity at thirteen, he did not take a degree. He spent some years studying
law (and is rumoured to have been a great "visitor of ladies"). His
hopes of early worldly success were dampened by his secret marriage
to Ann More, a ward of Sir Thomas Egerton (who had employed
Donne as a secretary). Sir Thomas was so angry that he had Donne
briefly imprisoned. He became a Protestant and, under James I, his
career in the Church at last prospered. At the time of his death, he was
Dean of St Paul's Cathedral in London.

Donne's poetry is strikingly dramatic, often witty and argument-
ative. It seems to reflect the wide-ranging moods, hopes, and fears of a
speaker earnestly exploring the nature of relationships, both between
men and women, and human beings and God. Together with poets
such as Herbert and Marvell, he is classed as a "Metaphysical" poet.
These poets draw their imagery from the non-physical world of ideas,
and the geographical, cosmological and scientific discoveries of their
time, rather than from the immediate world of nature.

The Good-Morrow

I wonder by my troth, what thou, and I
Did, till we loved? were we not weaned till then?
But sucked on country pleasures, childishly?
Or snorted° we in the Seven Sleepers's den?[1]   *snored*
5   'Twas so; but° this, all pleasures fancies be.   *except for*
If ever any beauty I did see,
Which I desired, and got, 'twas but a dream of thee.

And now good morrow to our waking souls,
Which watch not one another out of fear;
10   For love, all love of other sights controls,
And makes one little room an everywhere.
Let sea-discoverers to new worlds have gone,
Let maps to others, worlds on worlds have shown,
Let us possess one world, each hath one, and is one.

1   *The legendary young men of Ephesus who,*   *cave, were entombed there and were found*
     persecuted by the Romans, took refuge in a   *alive over two centuries later.*

15 My face in thine eye, thine in mine appears,
And true plain hearts do in the faces rest.
Where can we find two better hemispheres[2]
Without sharp North, without declining West?
Whatever dies, was not mixed equally;[3]
20 If our two loves be one, or thou and I
Love so alike, that none do slacken, none can die.

A Valediction: Forbidding Mourning

As virtuous men pass mildly away,
    And whisper to their souls, to go,
Whilst some of their sad friends do say,
    The breath goes now, and some say, no:

5 So let us melt, and make no noise,
    No tear-floods, nor sigh-tempests move,
'Twere profanation° of our joys   *irreverent treatment*
    To tell the laity[4] our love.

Moving of th' earth° brings harms and fears,   *earthquakes*
10   Men reckon what it did and meant,
But trepidation of the spheres,[5]
    Though greater far, is innocent.

Dull sublunary[6] lovers' love
    (Whose soul is sense) cannot admit
15 Absence, because it doth remove
    Those things which elemented it.[7]

2 *Curved surface of the eye-balls, likened to halves of the world.*
3 *Unequal mixing suggests an absence of constancy. Only uncompounded things were believed to be free from corruption and so to be immortal.*
4 *Non-religious persons; laypeople.*
5 *Aberrations in the orbits of the celestial bodies. (In the Ptolemaic view the sun and planets revolved around the earth and, while earthquakes might cause alarm, the vaster "movements" of the planets were seen as harmless.)*
6 *Beneath the moon; earthly.*
7 *Constituted by the four elements: earth, air, fire and water.*

But we by a love, so much refined,
    That ourselves know not what it is,
Inter-assured of the mind,
20   Care less, eyes, lips, and hands to miss.

Our two souls therefore, which are one,
    Though I must go, endure not yet
A breach,° but an expansion,   *break*
    Like gold to airy thinness beat.

25 If they be two, they are two so
    As stiff twin compasses are two,
Thy soul the fixed foot, makes no show
    To move, but doth, if the other do.

And though it in the centre sit,
30   Yet when the other far doth roam,
It leans, and hearkens after it,
    And grows erect, as that comes home.

Such wilt thou be to me, who must
    Like th'other foot, obliquely run;
35 Thy firmness makes my circle just,
    And makes me end, where I begun.

Holy Sonnet: "Batter my heart"

Batter my heart, three-personed God;[8] for, you
As yet but knock, breathe, shine, and seek to mend;
That I may rise, and stand, o'erthrow me, and bend
Your force, to break, blow, burn and make me new.
5 I, like an usurped° town, to another due,   *conquered*
Labour to admit you, but Oh, to no end,
Reason your viceroy° in me, me should defend,   *deputy*
But is captived, and proves weak or untrue,

---

8 *An allusion to the Holy Trinity.*

Yet dearly I love you, and would be loved fain,°   *willingly*
10 But am betrothed unto your enemy,
Divorce me, untie, or break that knot again,
Take me to you, imprison me, for I
Except you enthrall me, never shall be free,
Nor ever chaste, except you ravish me.

Holy Sonnet: "Death be not proud"

Death be not proud, though some have called thee
Mighty and dreadful, for, thou art not so;
For those whom thou think'st, thou dost overthrow,
Die not, poor Death, nor yet canst thou kill me;
5   From rest and sleep, which but thy pictures be,
Much pleasure, then from thee, much more must flow,
And soonest our best men with thee do go,
Rest of their bones, and souls' delivery.
Thou art slave to fate, chance, kings, and desperate men,
10 And dost with poison, war, and sickness dwell,
And poppy,⁹ or charms can make us sleep as well,
And better than thy stroke; why swell'st¹ thou then?
One short sleep past, we wake eternally,
And death shall be no more; Death thou shalt die.

9 *The opium drug, derived from poppies,*   1 *Become inflated with pride.*
induces sleep.

Ben Jonson (1572 – 1637)

*After an unhappy apprenticeship to his stepfather, a bricklayer, Jonson
undertook military service before eventually joining Henslowe's com-
pany as an actor and playwright. Argumentative, hot-tempered and
fearless, he killed a fellow actor in a duel. While in prison for this deed,
he converted to Catholicism, but returned to the Anglican Church
twelve years later.*

*Jonson numbered among his friends Bacon, Donne, Shakespeare,
Herrick and Suckling, and presided over a literary circle known as the
"sons" or "tribe of Ben" (see Drayton above, p. 16). In addition to
several plays, he produced many masques (with music and spectacular
effects) for James I, and learned (not without mishap) to walk the
tricky line between pleasing and offending this unpredictable king.
Often classical in their inspiration, and plain in style, Jonson's poems
may sometimes appear a little cool and restrained to modern readers.*

On My First Son

Farewell, thou child of my right hand, and joy;
    My sin was too much hope of thee, loved boy,
Seven years thou'wert lent to me, and I thee pay,
    Exacted by thy fate, on the just day.
5   O, could I lose all father, now. For why
    Will man lament the state he should envy
To have so soon 'scaped° worlds, and flesh's rage,   *escaped*
    And, if no other misery, yet age?
Rest in soft peace, and, asked, say here doth lie
10   Ben Jonson his best piece of poetry.
For whose sake, henceforth, all his vows be such,
    As what he loves may never like too much.

Song to Celia (I)[1]

Come my Celia, let us prove,
While we may, the sports of love;
Time will not be ours for ever:
He, at length, our good will sever.
5   Spend not then his gifts in vain.
Suns that set, may rise again:
But, if once we lose this light,
'Tis with us perpetual night.
Why should we defer our joys?
10   Fame, and rumour are but toys.
Cannot we delude the eyes
Of a few poor household spies?
Or his easier ears beguile,[2]
So removed by our wile?
15   'Tis no sin, love's fruit to steal,
But the sweet theft to reveal:
To be taken, to be seen,
These have crimes accounted been.

1 *From* Volpone.   2 *The unsuspicious ears of Celia's husband.*

Robert Herrick (1591 – 1674)

Herrick completed his MA degree at Cambridge in 1620. There is evidence that he mixed in London literary circles, particularly Ben Jonson's group, and became well known as a poet. Ordained as an Anglican clergyman, he became a vicar in the village of Dean Prior in the Devonshire countryside where most of his poems were written. After he was stripped of this post for political reasons, he returned to London where he began publishing delightful love lyrics, some of them reflecting the licence and attitudes of the times rather than his own feelings. "To the Virgins, to Make Much of Time" is a classic example of the carpe diem *tradition. This phrase (Latin for "seize the day") occurs in an ode by the Roman writer, Horace, and means in essence "enjoy yourself while you can." In Herrick's poem, the young are urged to make the most of life before time robs them of beauty and vigour. Herrick was reinstated at Dean Prior in 1660 where he spent the rest of his life.*

To the Virgins, to Make Much of Time

Gather ye rosebuds while ye may,
    Old Time is still a-flying:
And this same flower that smiles to-day
    Tomorrow will be dying.

5   The glorious lamp of heaven, the Sun,
    The higher he's a-getting,
The sooner will his race be run,
    And nearer he's to setting.

That age is best which is the first,
10   When youth and blood are warmer;
But being spent, the worse, and worst
    Times still succeed the former.

Then be not coy, but use your time,
    And while ye may, go marry:
15 For having lost but once your prime[1]
    You may for ever tarry.

---

1 *Youth or foremost state: the prime of life.*

George Herbert (1593 – 1633)

Herbert was a Fellow of Trinity College, Cambridge, and was elected orator for the University. His wit was much appreciated by James I, who gave him a sinecure of £120 a year. When Charles I succeeded James, Herbert took holy orders and set about rebuilding the decayed church in the diocese of Lincoln. The last three years of his life, during which he was happily married, brought forth the volume of poems, The Temple: Sacred Poems and Private Ejaculations. In "The Collar" and "Love", he dramatizes the difficulty of cleaving to God, using Metaphysical images notable for their freshness, colloquial immediacy, simplicity, and harmony. In "Easter Wings" the shape of each stanza is suggestive of the bird-like wings of the spirit on which the poet desires to rise towards God.

The Collar[1]

	I struck the board,° and cried, No more.	*table*
	I will abroad.	
	What? shall I ever sigh and pine?	
	My lines and life are free; free as the road,	
5	Loose as the wind, as large as store.	
	Shall I be still in suit?	
	Have I no harvest but a thorn	
	To let me blood,° and not restore	*bleed*
	What I have lost with cordial° fruit?	*restorative*
10	Sure there was wine	
	Before my sighs did dry it: there was corn	
	Before my tears did drown it.	
	Is the year only lost to me?	
	Have I no bays[2] to crown it?	
15	No flowers, no garlands gay? all blasted?	
	All wasted?	
	Not so my heart: but there is fruit,	
	And thou hast hands.	
	Recover all thy sigh-blown age	
20	On double pleasures: leave thy cold dispute	
	Of what is fit, and not. Forsake thy cage,	
	Thy rope of sands,	

1 *The collar worn by members of the clergy.*
2 *The bay- or laurel-leaf was awarded for*   *talent in poetry.*

Which petty thoughts have made, and made to thee
    Good cable, to enforce and draw,
25   And be thy law,
While thou didst wink and wouldst not see.
        Away! Take heed:
        I will abroad.
Call in thy death's head[3] there: tie up thy fears.
30   He that forbears
    To suit and serve his need,
      Deserves his load.
But as I raved and grew more fierce and wild
      At every word,
35   Me thought I heard one calling, *Child!*
      And I replied, *My Lord.*

Easter Wings[4]

Lord, who createdst man in wealth and store,[5]
Though foolishly he lost the same,
Decaying more and more
Till he became
5 Most poor:
    With thee
O let me rise
As larks harmoniously,
And sing this day thy victories:
10 Then shall the fall[6] further the flight in me.

My tender age in sorrow did begin:
And still with sickness and shame
Thou didst so punish sin,
That I became
15 Most thin.
    With thee
Let me combine,
And feel this day thy victory:
For, if I imp my wing on thine,[7]
20 Affliction shall advance the flight in me.

3 *Human skull, reminder of mortality.*
4 *Printed vertically, as above, the shape of wings is easily appreciated.*
5 *Plenty, abundance.*
6 *A reference to Adam and Eve's fall from grace in consequence of which all humanity was condemned to die, until Jesus' saving death and resurrection made eternal life in the spirit possible.*
7 *To graft feathers onto a damaged wing in order to mend it.*

Love

Love bade me welcome: yet my soul drew back,
    Guilty of dust[8] and sin.
But quick-eyed Love, observing me grow slack
    From my first entrance in,
5 Drew nearer to me, sweetly questioning,
    If I lacked any thing.

A guest, I answered, worthy to be here:
    Love said, You shall be he.
I the unkind, ungrateful? Ah my dear,
10   I cannot look on thee.
Love took my hand, and smiling did reply,
    Who made the eyes but I?

Truth, Lord, but I have marred them: let my shame
    Go where it doth deserve.
15 And know you not, says Love, who bore the blame?
    My dear, then I will serve.
You must sit down, says Love, and taste my meat:[9]
    So I did sit and eat.

8 *The dust of mortality, as in Genesis 3:19.*   9 *The communion feast.*

Edmund Waller (1606 – 1687)

Edmund Waller's long life spanned a tumultuous period in English history marked by religious and political upheaval. Educated at Eton and King's College, Cambridge, he entered Parliament early, at first as an active member of the opposition. Later he was to become an ardent royalist during the Civil War between supporters and opponents of the British monarchy, and left for France after leading an unsuccessful plot to seize London for Charles I. After the Restoration of the monarchy in 1660, he was restored to favour by Charles II and served as an esteemed member of Parliament.

Waller is usually associated with the Cavalier poets (royalists were known as "Cavaliers"). The lyrics of these poets are light, witty, polished and largely concerned with courtship and gallantry. "Go lovely Rose", one of Waller's early poems, is typical of the carpe diem *theme, which derives from the realization of the brevity of beauty, youth and life, and the inevitability of death (see Herrick above, p. 27). In this poem, Waller uses the rose as the traditional symbol of the beauty and transitoriness of life, both to compliment and to appeal to his mistress.*

Song: "Go, lovely rose!"

    Go, lovely rose!
Tell her that wastes her time, and me,
    That now she knows,
When I resemble° her to thee,   *compare*
5 How sweet, and fair, she seems to be.

    Tell her that's young,
And shuns to have her graces spied,
    That hadst thou sprung
In deserts, where no men abide,
10 Thou must have uncommended° died.   *unpraised*

    Small is the worth
Of beauty from the light retired:
    Bid her come forth,
Suffer herself to be desired
15 And not blush so to be admired.

    Then die! that she
The common fate of all things rare
    May read in thee:
How small a part of time they share,
20 That are so wondrous sweet, and fair!

John Milton (1608 – 1674)

In 1625 Milton entered Christ's College, Cambridge, where he began to write poetry in English, Latin and Italian on both religious and secular themes. Although he considered himself destined for the ministry, after graduating he devoted some years to private study (which included an intellectually rewarding trip to Italy). The outbreak of the Civil War, marked by the beheading of Charles I, began the imposition of Cromwell's Puritan regime, which Milton supported.

As an artist, Milton transcends his Puritan background, blending paganism and Christianity, nature and religion, in poetry which is witty, visionary and unique. As an epic poet, he dominated English poetry until the Victorian age. Paradise Lost, published in 1667, dramatizes the Biblical story of humankind's loss of Eden and attempts to "justify the ways of God to men". Milton's portrayal of Satan is, however, so energetic that many (including the poet, William Blake) have thought Milton was of the "devil's party" rather than God's. In the sonnet "On his Blindness", the poet reflects on how the affliction of blindness hinders his attempts to serve God fully through poetry. In his conclusion, Milton accepts the burden placed on him by God, suggesting that great strength can lie in seeming weakness.

On his Blindness

When I consider how my light is spent,
    Ere half my days, in this dark world and wide,
    And that one talent[1] which is death to hide
    Lodged with me useless, though my soul more bent
5 To serve therewith my Maker, and present
    My true account, lest He returning chide;
    "Doth God exact day-labour, light denied?"
    I fondly° ask. But Patience, to prevent   *foolishly*
That murmur, soon replies, "God doth not need
10 Either man's work or his own gifts. Who best
    Bear His mild yoke, they serve Him best. His state
    Is kingly: thousands at His bidding speed
    And post o'er land and ocean without rest;
    They also serve who only stand and wait."

1 Milton possibly alludes to Jesus' parable of
the talents (see Matthew 25).

From PARADISE LOST[2]

Book I *(extracts: lines 1–26; 44–69)*

Of man's first disobedience, and the fruit
Of that forbidden tree, whose mortal taste
Brought death into the world, and all our woe,
With loss of Eden, till one greater Man
5 Restore us, and regain the blissful seat,
Sing heavenly muse, that on the secret top
Of Oreb[3] or of Sinai,[4] didst inspire
That shepherd, who first taught the chosen seed
In the beginning how the heavens and earth
10 Rose out of Chaos:[5] or if Sion Hill[6]
Delight thee more, and Siloa's brook that flowed
Fast by the oracle of God; I thence
Invoke thy aid to my adventurous song,
That with no middle flight intends to soar
15 Above the Aonian[7] mount, while it pursues
Things unattempted yet in prose or rhyme.
And chiefly thou, O Spirit, that dost prefer
Before all temples the upright heart and pure,
Instruct me, for thou know'st; thou from the first
20 Wast present, and with mighty wings outspread
Dove-like sat'st brooding on the vast abyss
And mad'st it pregnant: What in me is dark
Illumine, what is low, raise and support;
That to the height of this great argument
25 I may assert Eternal Providence,
And justify the ways of God to men.

2 *Milton's epic poem is concerned with the fall of Adam and God's plan for humanity's ultimate redemption through Christ. Initially, the poem concentrates on Satan's fall from grace and his establishing his own realm in hell from which he, heroically but futilely, opposes God. It is through Satan's scheming that human beings learn disobedience and sin. Once expelled from Paradise, Adam becomes the heroic figure who, with Christ's mercy promised to him, must expiate his sins through practising faith, virtue, patience, temperance and love.*

3 *Mount Horeb (see footnote 4).*

4 *Sinai was the peninsula of ancient Palestine,*

where Moses received the Ten Commandments (Exodus 19:20). God first spoke to him while he watched sheep on Mount Horeb (Exodus 3.1).

5 *Original Confusion in which earth, sea and air were mixed up together. It was personified by the Greeks as the most ancient of the gods.*

6 *A holy hill of ancient Jerusalem, symbolising the heavenly Jerusalem or kingdom of heaven. Of great significance to the Jewish— and some sects of the Christian—religion. Also known as Zion Hill.*

7 *Aonia is often used to denote the province of Boeotia in ancient Greece.*

Satan banished from Heaven

. . . Him the Almighty Power
Hurled headlong flaming from the ethereal sky
With hideous ruin and combustion down
30   To bottomless perdition, there to dwell
In adamantine chains and penal fire,
Who durst° defy the Omnipotent to arms.   *dared*
Nine times the space that measures day and night
To mortal men, he with his horrid crew
35   Lay vanquished, rowling° in the fiery gulf,   *rolling*
Confounded though immortal: But his doom
Reserved him to more wrath; for now the thought
Both of lost happiness and lasting pain
Torments him; round he throws his baleful eyes
40   That witnessed huge affliction and dismay
Mixed with obdurate pride and steadfast hate:
At once as far as angels' ken° he views   *sight*
The dismal situation waste and wild,
A dungeon horrible, on all sides round
45   As one great furnace flamed, yet from those flames
No light, but rather darkness visible
Served only to discover sights of woe,
Regions of sorrow, doleful shades, where peace
And rest can never dwell, hope never comes
50   That comes to all; but torture without end
Still urges, and a fiery deluge, fed
With ever-burning sulphur unconsumed.

Anne Bradstreet (c.1612 – 1672)

Anne Bradstreet was the daughter of Thomas Dudley, a Puritan, who educated her beyond the level enjoyed by most girls at the time. At sixteen she married a Cambridge graduate, Simon Bradstreet, and the couple set sail for the New World (America). At first Bradstreet disliked the barren, hard, new country, but her Puritan world-view soon persuaded her that God's will should prevail. Despite her rather frail health, she gave birth to eight children, and came to terms with her new life in a strange land. Her poems, the first to be published by a writer from North America, appeared in 1650 (her brother-in-law, apparently without her knowledge, had taken a copy of her poems to London for publication). Some of them are meditative; many are concerned with the details of daily existence. "The Author to her Book", in its metaphorical likening of the second edition of her book to an imperfect, but much-loved child, reveals Bradstreet's ability to transform domestic and intimate detail into poetic imagery.

The Author to Her Book

Thou ill-formed offspring of my feeble brain,
Who after birth didst by my side remain,
Till snatched from thence by friends, less wise than true,
Who thee abroad exposed to public view,
5 Made thee in rags,[1] halting° to th' press to trudge,   *limping*
Where errors were not lessened (all may judge).
At thy return my blushing was not small,
My rambling brat (in print) should mother call;
I cast thee by as one unfit for light,
10 Thy visage was so irksome in my sight;
Yet being mine own, at length affection would
Thy blemishes amend, if so I could:
I washed thy face, but more defects I saw,
And rubbing off a spot still made a flaw.
15 I stretched thy joints to make thee even feet,[2]
Yet still thou run'st more hobbling than is meet;
In better dress to trim thee was my mind,
But nought save homespun cloth i' th' house I find.
In this array 'mongst vulgars may'st thou roam;
20 In critic's hands beware thou dost not come,
And take thy way where yet thou are not known;
If for thy father asked, say thou hadst none;
And for thy mother, she alas is poor,
Which caused her thus to send thee out of door.

1 *Rags were used in the manufacture of paper.*   2 *Also an allusion to metrical feet.*

Andrew Marvell (1621 – 1678)

Marvell graduated with a BA from Trinity College, Cambridge, in 1638 and then travelled abroad for four years in Holland, France, Italy and Spain. In 1657, he became assistant-secretary to Milton who served on the Council of State. In "To his Coy Mistress", Marvell wittily develops the carpe diem *theme (see Herrick and Waller above, pp. 27 and 31), assuring his beloved that his love and respect for her would be given full expression only if time were less swift and merciless in destroying beauty and lust. He thus gives a clever twist to the traditional seduction argument.*

To His Coy Mistress

Had we but world enough, and time,
This coyness, Lady, were no crime.
We would sit down, and think which way
To walk, and pass our long love's day.
5   Thou by the Indian Ganges'[1] side
Should'st rubies find: I by the tide
Of Humber[2] would complain. I would
Love you ten years before the Flood:[3]
And you should, if you please, refuse
10 Till the conversion[4] of the Jews.
My vegetable° love should grow   *plant-like*
Vaster than empires, and more slow.
An hundred years should go to praise
Thine eyes, and on thy forehead gaze;
15 Two hundred to adore each breast:
But thirty thousand to the rest.
An age at least to every part,
And the last age should show your heart.
For Lady you deserve this state;
20 Nor would I love at lower rate.
     But at my back I always hear
Time's wingéd chariot hurrying near:
And yonder all before us lie
Deserts of vast eternity.

1 *One of the great rivers of India with deep religious significance.*
2 *Estuary on the east coast of England, lying between Yorkshire and Lincolnshire at the mouths of the Trent and Ouse rivers.*
3 *The deluge which submerged the then known world with the exception of Noah, his family, and the animals he took onto the ark he built.*
4 *To Christianity.*

25 Thy beauty shall no more be found;
    Nor, in thy marble vault, shall sound
    My echoing song: then worms shall try
    That long preserved virginity:
    And your quaint honour turn to dust;
30 And into ashes all my lust.
    The grave's a fine and private place,
    But none I think do there embrace.
         Now therefore, while the youthful hue
    Sits on thy skin like morning glew,°   *glow*
35 And while thy willing soul transpires°   *breathes out*
    At every pore with instant fires,
    Now let us sport us while we may;
    And now, like amorous birds of prey,
    Rather at once our time devour,
40 Than languish in his slow-chapt° power.   *slowly consuming*
    Let us roll all our strength, and all
    Our sweetness, up into one ball:
    And tear our pleasures with rough strife,
    Thorough° the iron gates of life.   *through*
45 Thus, though we cannot make our sun
    Stand still, yet we will make him run.

Henry Vaughan (1622 – 1695)

Vaughan was educated at Jesus College, Oxford, and became a country doctor. A Metaphysical poet (see Donne above, p. 21), he wrote love poems, but is more famous for his religious poetry. In his work Silex Scintillans *(published in two parts in 1650 and 1655), he perceives himself as a "flint", striking sparks of "fire" for God. In "The Retreat", the innocence of childhood is described in a manner which foreshadows the idealization of youth by the Romantic poets. "The World" suggests Eternity in expansive images of light, whereas the time-bound world is portrayed beneath "a vast shadow", with its inhabitants troubled by thoughts "like sad eclipses".*

The Retreat

Happy those early days, when I
Shined in my angel-infancy!
Before I understood this place
Appointed for my second race,[1]
5   Or taught my soul to fancy aught°   *anything*
But a white, celestial thought,
When yet I had not walked above
A mile, or two, from my first love,
And looking back, at that short space,
10   Could see a glimpse of his bright face;
When on some gilded cloud, or flower
My gazing soul would dwell an hour,
And in those weaker glories spy
Some shadows of eternity;
15   Before I taught my tongue to wound
My conscience with a sinful sound,
Or had the black art to dispense
A several° sin to every sense,   *separate*
But felt through all this fleshy dress°   *the human body*
20   Bright shoots of everlastingness.
      O how I long to travel back
And tread again that ancient track!
That I might once more reach that plain,
Where first I left my glorious train,°   *procession*
25   From whence the enlightened spirit sees
That shady city of palm trees;

1 *Life on earth, as opposed to the heavenly existence before birth.*

But ah! my soul with too much stay
Is drunk, and staggers in the way.
Some men a forward motion love,
30 But I by backward steps would move,
And when this dust falls to the urn
In that state I came, return.

The World

I saw Eternity[2] the other night
Like a great ring of pure and endless light,
    All calm as it was bright;
And round beneath it, Time in hours, days, years,
5   Driven by the spheres°   *heavenly bodies*
Like a vast shadow moved; in which the world
    And all her train° were hurled.   *followers*
The doting lover in his quaintest strain[3]
    Did there complain;
10 Near him, his lute, his fancy, and his flights,°   *of expression*
    Wit's sour delights;
With gloves and knots, the silly snares of pleasure,
    Yet his dear treasure,
All scattered lay, while he his eyes did pour°   *gazed intently*
15   Upon a flower.

The darksome statesman, hung with weights and woe
Like a thick midnight fog, moved there so slow,
    He did nor stay, nor go;
Condemning thoughts—like sad eclipses—scowl
20   Upon his soul,
And clouds of crying witnesses without
    Pursued him with one shout.
Yet digged the mole,[4] and lest his ways be found,
    Worked under ground,
25 Where he did clutch his prey; but one did see
    That policy:
Churches and altars fed him, perjuries
    Were gnats and flies;
It rained about him blood and tears, but he
30   Drank them as free.°   *freely*

2 *Reference, in Christian terms, to the*
   hereafter.

3 *Ornamented song or verse.*
4 *The metaphor refers to the statesman.*

The fearful miser on a heap of rust
Sat pining all his life there, did scarce trust
    His own hands with the dust,
Yet would not place one piece above, but lives
35   In fear of thieves.
Thousands there were as frantic as himself,
    And hugged each one his pelf;°   *wealth*
The downright epicure⁵ placed heaven in sense,
    And scorned pretence;
40 While others, slipped into a wide excess,
    Said little less;
The weaker sort slight, trivial wares enslave,
    Who think them brave;°   *admirable*
And poor, despisèd Truth sat counting by
45   Their victory.

Yet some, who all this while did weep and sing,
And sing and weep, soared up into the ring;
    But most would use no wing.
Oh fools, said I, thus to prefer dark night
50   Before true light!
To live in grots and caves, and hate the day
    Because it shows the way;
The way, which from this dead and dark abode
    Leads up to God;
55 A way where you might tread the sun, and be
    More bright than he!
But as I did their madness so discuss,
    One whispered thus,
"This ring the Bridegroom did for none provide,
60   But for His bride."⁶

5 *Generally taken as one who delights in the
pleasures of the flesh, especially food and
drink.*

6 *Reference to the bride of Christ—in
Christian terms, the Church, and the soul
that has earned its salvation.*

John Dryden (1631 – 1700)

*John Dryden was educated at Westminster School and Trinity College,
Cambridge. After the Civil War, Dryden converted to Catholicism, and
became a leading literary figure. He was appointed poet laureate in
1668, and historiographer royal in 1670. He lost these positions in
1688 when the Catholic James II was forced to flee and the Dutch
Protestant, William of Orange, was invited by Parliament to be king.*
 Dryden was a prolific writer, producing critical works (such as Of
Dramatic Poesy)*, satires (the most celebrated of which are* Absalom
and Achitophel *and* MacFlecknoe) *and plays, as well as poetry. His
work reflects his context of change and turbulence, as well as a fascina-
tion for the past.*

To the Memory of Mr Oldham[1]

Farewell, too little, and too lately known,
Whom I began to think and call my own:
For sure our souls were near allied, and thine
Cast in the same poetic mould with mine.
5 One common note on either lyre did strike,
And knaves and fools we both abhorred alike.
To the same goal did both our studies° drive;   *endeavours*
The last set out the soonest did arrive.
Thus Nisus[2] fell upon the slippery place,
10 While his young friend performed and won the race.
O early ripe! to thy abundant store
What could advancing age have added more?
It might (what nature never gives the young)
Have taught the numbers of thy native tongue.
15 But satire needs not those, and wit will shine
Through the harsh cadence of a rugged line.
A noble error, and but seldom made,
When poets are by too much force betrayed.
Thy generous fruits, though gathered ere their prime,
20 Still showed a quickness;° and maturing time   *life (vitality)*
But mellows what we write to the dull sweets of rhyme.

1 *John Oldham (1652–83), author of* Satires
upon the Jesuits, *won a reputation as an
outspoken writer of both odes and satires.
He met Dryden, who was some 20 years his
senior, shortly before his own early death.*

2 *Two entrants in a foot race were the
devoted friends, Nisus and Euryalus.
Although Nisus was the swifter runner, he
slipped when nearing the winning-post. As a
result Euryalus took the lead and won the
race (Virgil's* Aeneid, V).

Once more, hail and farewell; farewell, thou young,
But ah too short, Marcellus[3] of our tongue;
Thy brows with ivy, and with laurels[4] bound;
25   But fate and gloomy night encompass thee around.

Alexander Pope (1688 – 1744)

Alexander Pope's father was a prosperous London merchant who, in 1700, moved his family to the village of Binfield near Windsor Forest in order to escape persecution as Roman Catholics. Pope's lifelong suffering from tuberculosis of the spine deprived him of the opportunity of a formal education but, with the encouragement of his father, he successfully educated himself. He began writing poetry at the age of twelve and soon achieved a reputation as a poet with works such as The Rape of the Lock. *The publication of his translations of Homer's* Iliad *and* Odyssey *brought him both fame and fortune and enabled him to establish himself in a villa at Twickenham. Pope's wit and wisdom are seen to great effect in* The Dunciad, *a telling satire on stupidity. This poem, as well as earlier satires, earned him the enmity of his literary opponents whom he ridiculed mercilessly. He also had, however, a capacity for deep friendships and took comfort from the support of friends such as Jonathan Swift.* The Rape of the Lock, *a perceptive commentary on social superficiality, is one of the most sustained pieces of satire in literature and derives much of its impact from the mock-epic mode which Pope adopted.*

THE RAPE OF THE LOCK *(extracts)*

Canto I *(lines 1–14; 121–148)*

What dire offence from amorous causes springs,
What mighty contests rise from trivial things,
I sing—This verse to Caryll,[1] Muse![2] is due:
This, even Belinda may vouchsafe to view;

---

3 *Member of a Roman Patrician family. The conqueror and five times consul of Syracuse (a town in Sicily), he was later murdered by his personal attendant.*
4 *Wreaths honouring poetic fame.*

1 *Lord Petre had cut off a lock of Miss Arabella Fermor's hair. Pope's friend Lord Caryll asked the poet to turn the incident into a poem to help reconcile the families.*
2 *One of the Greek goddesses of inspiration.*

5   Slight is the subject, but not so the praise,
If she inspire, and he approve my lays.
      Say what strange motive, goddess! could compel
A well-bred lord to assault a gentle belle?
Oh say what stranger cause, yet unexplored,
10   Could make a gentle belle reject a lord?
In tasks so bold, can little men engage,
And in soft bosoms dwells such mighty rage?
      Sol° through white curtains shot a tim'rous ray,   *the sun*
And oped those eyes that must eclipse the day.

      *   *   *

15   And now, unveiled, the toilet° stands displayed,   *dressing table*
Each silver vase in mystic order laid.
First, robed in white, the nymph intent adores,
With head uncovered, the cosmetic powers.
A heavenly image in the glass appears,[3]
20   To that she bends, to that her eye she rears;
Th' inferior priestess, at her altar's side,
Trembling, begins the sacred rites of pride.
Unnumbered treasures ope at once, and here
The various offerings of the world appear;
25   From each she nicely culls with curious toil,
And decks the goddess with the glittering spoil.
This casket India's glowing gems unlocks,
And all Arabia° breathes from yonder box.   *exotic perfume*
The tortoise here and elephant unite,
30   Transformed to combs, the speckled and the white.
Here files of pins extend their shining rows,
Puffs, powders, patches,[4] Bibles, billet-doux.°   *love-letters*
Now awful beauty puts on all its arms;
The fair each moment rises in her charms,
35   Repairs her smiles, awakens every grace,
And calls forth all the wonders of her face:
Sees by degrees a purer blush arise,
And keener lightnings quicken in her eyes.
The busy sylphs° surround their darling care,   *guardian spirits*
40   These set the head, and those divide the hair,
Some fold the sleeve, while others plait the gown;
And Betty's° praised for labours not her own.   *Belinda's maid*

---

3 *The beautiful Belinda is reflected in the mirror.*   4 *Cosmetic patches applied to the face.*

Canto II *(lines 19–34)*

This nymph,° to the destruction of mankind,   *Belinda*
 Nourished two locks, which graceful hung behind
In equal curls, and well conspired to deck
With shining ringlets the smooth ivory neck.
5   Love in these labyrinths his slaves detains,
And mighty hearts are held in slender chains.
With hairy springes° we the birds betray,   *snares*
Slight lines of hair surprise the finny° prey,   *fishy*
Fair tresses man's imperial race ensnare,
10   And beauty draws us with a single hair.
      Th' adventurous baron the bright locks admired;
He saw, he wished, and to the prize aspired.
Resolved to win, he meditates the way,
By force to ravish, or by fraud betray;
15   For when success a lover's toils attends,
Few ask, if fraud or force attained his ends.

Canto III *(lines 105–178)*

For lo! the board with cups and spoons is crowned,
The berries° crackle, and the mill turns round: *coffee beans*
On shining altars of Japan° they raise   *lacquered tables*
The silver lamp; the fiery spirits blaze:
5   From silver spouts the grateful liquors glide,
While China's earth° receives the smoking tide: *porcelain cups*
At once they gratify their scent and taste,
And frequent cups prolong the rich repast.
Straight hover round the fair her airy band;
10   Some, as she sipped, the fuming liquor fanned,
Some o'er her lap their careful plumes displayed,
Trembling, and conscious of the rich brocade.
Coffee (which makes the politician wise,
And see through all things with his half-shut eyes)
15   Sent up in vapours to the baron's brain
New stratagems, the radiant lock to gain.
Ah cease, rash youth! desist ere 'tis too late,
Fear the just gods, and think of Scylla's⁵ fate!
Changed to a bird, and sent to flit in air,
20   She dearly pays for Nisus' injured hair!

5 *Daughter of Nisus, the king of Megara. His life, as well as the fate of the city, depended on the lock of red hair on his head. Scylla* *cut this lock off and betrayed the city to Minos, King of Crete.*

But when to mischief mortals bend their will,
How soon they find fit instruments of ill!
Just then, Clarissa drew with tempting grace
A two-edged weapon from her shining case:
25 So ladies, in romance, assist their knight,
Present the spear, and arm him for the fight.
He takes the gift with reverence and extends
The little engine on his fingers' ends;
This just behind Belinda's neck he spread,
30 As o'er the fragrant steams she bends her head.
Swift to the lock a thousand sprites repair,
A thousand wings, by turns, blow back the hair;
And thrice they twitched the diamond in her ear;
Thrice she looked back, and thrice the foe drew near.
35 Just in that instant, anxious Ariel sought
The close recesses of the virgin's thought:
As on the nosegay in her breast reclined,
He watched th' ideas rising in her mind,
Sudden he viewed in spite of all her art,
40 An earthly lover lurking at her heart.
Amazed, confused, he found his power expired,[6]
Resigned to fate, and with a sigh retired.
    The peer now spreads the glitt'ring forfex° wide,   *scissors*
T' enclose the lock; now joins it, to divide.
45 Even then before the fatal engine closed,
A wretched sylph too fondly interposed;
Fate urged the shears, and cut the sylph in twain,
(But airy substance soon unites again)[7]
The meeting points the sacred hair dissever
50 From the fair head, for ever, and for ever!
    Then flashed the living lightning from her eyes,
And screams of horror rend th' affrighted skies.
Not louder shrieks to pitying Heaven are cast,
When husbands or when lap-dogs breathe their last;
55 Or when rich China vessels, fallen from high,
In glittering dust and painted fragments lie!
    "Let wreaths of triumph now my temples twine,"
(The victor cried) "the glorious prize is mine!
While fish in streams, or birds delight in air,
60 Or in a coach and six the British fair,
As long as *Atalantis*[8] shall be read,
Or the small pillow grace a lady's bed,

6 *Because Belinda has an earthly lover in*
  attendance.
7 *Being without substance, the sylphs are in*
  no physical danger.

8 "The New Atalantis", *a famous*
  contemporary book by Mrs Manley (and full
  of court scandal).

While visits shall be paid on solemn days,
When numerous wax-lights in bright order blaze,
65   While nymphs take treats, or assignations give,
So long my honour, name, and praise shall live!"
What Time would spare, from steel receives its date,
And monuments, like men, submit to fate!
Steel could the labour of the gods destroy,
70   And strike to dust th' imperial towers of Troy;[9]
Steel could the works of mortal pride confound,
And hew triumphal arches to the ground.
What wonder then, fair nymph! thy hairs should feel
The conquering force of unresisted steel?

Canto IV *(lines 143–176)*

Then see! the nymph in beauteous grief appears,
Her eyes half-languishing, half-drowned in tears;
On her heaved bosom hung her drooping head,
Which, with a sigh, she raised; and thus she said:
5   "For ever cursed be this detested day,
Which snatched my best, my favourite curl away!
Happy! ah ten times happy had I been,
If Hampton Court[1] these eyes had never seen!
Yet am not I the first mistaken maid,
10   By love of courts to numerous ills betrayed,
Oh had I rather unadmired remained
In some lone isle, or distant northern land;
Where the gilt chariot never marks the way,
Where none learn ombre,° none e'er taste bohea!°   *a card game / tea*
15   There kept my charms concealed from mortal eye,
Like roses that in deserts bloom and die.
What moved my mind with youthful lords to roam?
Oh had I stayed, and said my prayers at home!
'Twas this the morning omens seemed to tell:
20   Thrice from my trembling hand the patch-box[2] fell;
The tott'ring china shook without a wind;
Nay, Poll sat mute, and Shock[3] was most unkind!

9 *Located in Asia Minor, scene of the Trojan War, caused by the abduction of Helen by Paris and associated with Trojan heroes such as Hector, Greek heroes such as Achilles, and generals such as Agamemnon and Ulysses. The gods took sides and intervened actively in the Trojan War.*

1 *A royal palace close to London, and scene of the theft of Belinda's lock.*
2 *See footnote 4, p. 43.*
3 *"Poll" and "Shock" are Belinda's parrot and her lap-dog. (Both were popular names for such pets.)*

A sylph too warned me of the threats of Fate,
In mystic visions, now believed too late!
25 See the poor remnants of these slighted hairs!
My hands shall rend what e'en thy rapine spares:
These in two sable ringlets taught to break,
Once gave new beauties to the snowy neck;
The sister-lock now sits uncouth, alone,
30 And in its fellow's fate foresees its own;
Uncurled it hangs, the fatal shears demands,
And tempts, once more, thy sacrilegious hands.
Oh hadst thou, cruel! been content to seize
Hairs less in sight, or any hairs but these!"

Canto V *(lines 141–150)*

Then cease, bright nymph! to mourn thy ravished hair,
Which adds new glory to the shining sphere!
Not all the tresses that fair head can boast
5 Shall draw such envy as the lock you lost.
For, after all the murders of your eye,
When, after millions slain, yourself shall die;
When those fair suns shall set, as set they must,
And all those tresses shall be laid in dust;
10 This lock, the Muse shall consecrate to fame,
And 'midst the stars inscribe Belinda's name.

Samuel Johnson (1709 – 1784)

The son of a poor bookseller, Johnson received a traditional classical education and attended Pembroke College, Oxford, before poverty forced him to withdraw. In 1737, accompanied by one of his pupils, David Garrick, he set out for London, to try to earn a living in Grub Street. After ten years of badly-paid journalism and intermittent ventures in publishing, he achieved a measure of recognition for his moral essays in The Rambler, *a periodical written almost entirely by himself. In the 1750s, with the publication of his great* Dictionary of the English Language *and his philosophical novel,* Rasselas, *he began to be recognized as one of the most important writers of his time.*

A profoundly humble man, gifted with vigorous intellectual powers, Johnson was also recognized as a poet of distinction. In his long poem, The Vanity of Human Wishes *(a free adaptation of the tenth satire of Juvenal, a Roman satirist), he applies his trenchant good sense and rugged honesty to the problem of evil inherent in the material world, urging the reader to attain a realistic and responsible grasp of ethical standards, to convert hatred into compassion, and to search for what is consistent with truth and probability.*

THE VANITY OF HUMAN WISHES
(extracts: lines 135–190; 343–368)

. . . When first the college rolls receive his name,
The young enthusiast quits his ease for fame;
Through all his veins the fever of renown
Burns from the strong contagion of the gown;
5   O'er Bodley's dome[1] his future labours spread,
And Bacon's[2] mansion trembles o'er his head.
Are these thy views? proceed, illustrious youth,
And Virtue guard thee to the throne of Truth!
Yet should thy soul indulge the generous heat,
10   Till captive Science yields her last retreat;
Should Reason guide thee with her brightest ray,
And pour on misty Doubt resistless day;
Should no false Kindness lure to loose delight,
Nor Praise relax, nor Difficulty fright;

1 *"Bodley's dome" refers to the Bodleian Library, Oxford; "dome" is used in the architectural sense.*
2 *Roger Bacon (c. 1214–c.1292) was an* Oxford philosopher and scientist. It was believed that if a greater man than he passed under Bacon's study (which was constructed on an arch over a bridge), it would collapse.

15   Should tempting Novelty thy cell refrain,
       And Sloth effuse her opiate fumes in vain;
       Should Beauty blunt on fops her fatal dart,
       Nor claim the triumph of a lettered heart;
       Should no Disease thy torpid veins invade,
20   Nor Melancholy's phantoms haunt thy shade;
       Yet hope not life from grief or danger free,
       Nor think the doom of man reversed for thee:
       Deign on the passing world to turn thine eyes,
       And pause awhile from letters to be wise;
25   There mark what ills the scholar's life assail,
       Toil, envy, want, the patron, and the jail.
       See nations slowly wise, and meanly just,
       To buried merit raise the tardy bust.
       If dreams yet flatter, once again attend,
30   Hear Lydiat's[3] life, and Galileo's[4] end.
          Nor deem, when learning her last prize bestows,
       The glittering eminence exempt from foes;
       See when the vulgar 'scape, despised or awed,
       Rebellion's vengeful talons seize on Laud.[5]
35   From meaner minds, though smaller fines content,
       The plundered palace or sequestered rent;
       Marked out by dangerous parts he meets the shock,
       And fatal Learning leads him to the block:
       Around his tomb let Art and Genius weep,
40   But hear his death, ye blockheads, hear and sleep.
          The festal blazes, the triumphal show,
       The ravished standard, and the captive foe,
       The senate's thanks, the gazette's[6] pompous tale,
       With force resistless o'er the brave prevail.
45   Such bribes the rapid Greek[7] o'er Asia whirled,
       For such the steady Romans shook the world;
       For such in distant land the Britons shine,
       And stain with blood the Danube or the Rhine;
       This power has praise that virtue scarce can warm,
50   Till fame supplies the universal charm.
       Yet Reason frowns on War's unequal game,
       Where wasted nations raise a single name,

---

3 *Thomas Lydiat (1572–1646). Although a brilliant mathematician and an Oxford don, he lived and died a poor man.*

4 *Galileo Galilei (1564–1642), Italian astronomer and physicist, was declared a heretic and imprisoned by the Inquisition in 1633. He maintained that the earth moved around the sun, but was forced to recant.*

5 *William Laud, Archbishop of Canterbury under Charles I, was executed by the Puritans in 1645.*

6 *Official court record.*

7 *Alexander the Great.*

And mortgaged states their grandsire's wreaths regret,
From age to age in everlasting debt;
55 Wreaths which at last the dear-bought right convey
To rust on medals, or on stones decay.

*   *   *

... Where then shall Hope and Fear their objects find?
Must dull Suspense corrupt the stagnant mind?
Must helpless man, in ignorance sedate,
60 Roll darkling down the torrent of his fate?
Must no dislike alarm, no wishes rise,
No cries attempt the mercies of the skies?
Enquirer, cease, petitions yet remain,
Which heaven may hear; nor deem religion vain.
65 Still raise for good the supplicating voice,
But leave to heaven the measure and the choice,
Safe in his power, whose eyes discern afar
The secret ambush of a specious prayer.
Implore his aid, in his decisions rest,
70 Secure whate'er he gives, he gives the best.
Yet when the sense of sacred presence fires,
And strong devotion to the skies aspires,
Pour forth thy fervours for a healthful mind,
Obedient passions, and a will resigned;
75 For love, which scarce collective man can fill;
For patience sovereign o'er transmuted ill;
For faith, that panting for a happier seat,
Counts death kind Nature's signal of retreat:
These goods for man the laws of heaven ordain,
80 These goods he grants, who grants the power to gain;
With these celestial wisdom calms the mind,
And makes the happiness she does not find.

Thomas Gray (1716 – 1771)

For much of his life, Gray was a scholarly recluse, following the quiet routine of a Cambridge academic. A professor of Modern History, his wide interests also included pre-Elizabethan poetry and old Welsh and Norse literature—fields which were not well known at the time. He was a fine judge of music and painting and expressed a keen apprecia-tion of nature.

Gray's concern for perfection, balance and simplicity of style is evident in his famous "Elegy Written in a Country Churchyard". Although almost every line in the Elegy has a classical parallel, Gray's subtle art and patient craftsmanship ensure that it speaks to common humanity. In the neo-classical period, public utterance was often cha-racterized by learned allusions and elaborate language, rather than con-cise and elegant expressions, and Gray's work occasionally falls into this category. However, in his "Ode on the Death of a Favourite Cat Drowned in a Tub of Gold Fishes", he successfully deflates overblown writing by using mock-heroic conventions to mourn a drowned cat.

Elegy Written in a Country Churchyard

The curfew tolls the knell of parting day,
    The lowing herd wind slowly o'er the lea,
The ploughman homeward plods his weary way,
    And leaves the world to darkness and to me.

5   Now fades the glimmering landscape on the sight,
    And all the air a solemn stillness holds,
Save where the beetle wheels his droning flight,
    And drowsy tinklings lull the distant folds.

Save that from yonder ivy-mantled tower
10   The moping owl does to the moon complain
Of such, as wandering near her secret bower,
    Molest her ancient solitary reign.

Beneath those rugged elms, that yew-tree's shade,
    Where heaves the turf in many a mouldering heap,
15 Each in his narrow cell forever laid,
    The rude forefathers of the hamlet sleep.

The breezy call of incense-breathing morn,
    The swallow twittering from the straw-built shed,
The cock's shrill clarion or the echoing horn,
20   No more shall rouse them from their lowly bed.

For them no more the blazing hearth shall burn,
    Or busy housewife ply her evening care;
No children run to lisp their sire's return,
    Or climb his knees the envied kiss to share.

25 Oft did the harvest to their sickle yield;
    Their furrow oft the stubborn glebe° has broke;   *pasture*
How jocund did they drive their team afield!
    How bowed the woods beneath their sturdy stroke!

Let not Ambition mock their useful toil,
30   Their homely joys and destiny obscure;
Nor Grandeur hear with a disdainful smile
    The short and simple annals of the poor.

The boast of heraldry, the pomp of power,
    And all that beauty, all that wealth e'er gave,
35 Awaits alike the inevitable hour:
    The paths of glory lead but to the grave.

Nor you, ye proud, impute to these the fault,
    If Memory o'er their tomb no trophies raise,
Where through the long-drawn aisle and fretted vault
40   The pealing anthem swells the note of praise.

Can storied urn or animated bust
    Back to its mansion call the fleeting breath?
Can Honour's voice provoke the silent dust,
    Or Flattery soothe the dull cold ear of Death?

45 Perhaps in this neglected spot is laid
    Some heart once pregnant with celestial fire;
Hands that the rod of empire might have swayed,
    Or waked to ecstasy the living lyre.

But Knowledge to their eyes her ample page,
50   Rich with the spoils of time, did ne'er unroll;
Chill Penury repressed their noble rage,
    And froze the genial current of the soul.

Full many a gem of purest ray serene,
    The dark unfathomed caves of ocean bear;
55 Full many a flower is born to blush unseen,
    And waste its sweetness on the desert air.

Some village Hampden,[1] that with dauntless breast
    The little tyrant of his fields withstood;
Some mute inglorious Milton[2] here may rest,
60   Some Cromwell,[3] guiltless of his country's blood.

The applause of listening senates to command,
    The threats of pain and ruin to despise,
To scatter plenty o'er a smiling land,
    And read their history in a nation's eyes,

65 Their lot forbade; nor circumscribed alone
    Their growing virtues, but their crimes confined.
Forbade to wade through slaughter to a throne,
    And shut the gates of mercy on mankind;

The struggling pangs of conscious truth to hide,
70   To quench the blushes of ingenuous shame.
Or heap the shrine of Luxury and Pride
    With incense kindled at the Muse's[4] flame.

Far from the madding crowd's ignoble strife,
    Their sober wishes never learned to stray;
75 Along the cool sequestered vale of life
    They kept the noiseless tenor of their way.

Yet even these bones from insult to protect,
    Some frail memorial still erected nigh,
With uncouth rhymes and shapeless sculpture decked,
80   Implores the passing tribute of a sigh.

Their name, their years, spelt by the unlettered muse,
    The place of fame and elegy supply;
And many a holy text around she strews,
    That teach the rustic moralist to die.

85 For who, to dumb Forgetfulness a prey,
    This pleasing anxious being e'er resigned,
Left the warm precincts of the cheerful day,
    Nor cast one longing lingering look behind?

1 *John Hampden (1594–1643) refused to submit to a special tax levied by Charles I in 1636 and, as a Member of Parliament, he defended the rights of the people.*
2 *John Milton (1608–1674), author of* Paradise Lost; *see p. 32.*

3 *Oliver Cromwell (1599–1658) was commander of the Parliamentarian forces in the Civil War against Charles I. He later acted as Lord Protector of the Realm (1653–8) in place of a king.*
4 *One of the Greek goddesses of inspiration.*

On some fond breast the parting soul relies,
90   Some pious drops the closing eye requires;
Even from the tomb the voice of Nature cries,
      Even in our ashes live their wonted fires.

For thee, who mindful of the unhonoured dead
      Dost in these lines their artless tale relate;
95 If chance, by lonely contemplation led,
      Some kindred spirit shall inquire thy fate,

Haply some hoary-headed swain may say,
      "Oft have we seen him at the peep of dawn
Brushing with hasty steps the dews away
100   To meet the sun upon the upland lawn.

"There at the foot of yonder nodding beech
      That wreathes its old fantastic roots so high,
His listless length at noon tide would he stretch,
      And pore upon the brook that babbles by.

105 "Hard by yon wood, now smiling as in scorn,
      Muttering his wayward fancies he would rove;
Now drooping, woeful-wan, like one forlorn,
      Or crazed with care, or crossed in hopeless love.

"One morning I missed him on the customed hill,
110   Along the heath and near his favourite tree;
Another came; nor yet beside the rill,
      Nor up the lawn, nor at the wood was he;

"The next, with dirges due, in sad array,
      Slow through the church-way path we saw him borne.
115 Approach and read (for thou canst read) the lay,
      'Graved on the stone beneath yon aged thorn."

The Epitaph

Here rests his head upon the lap of earth,
      A youth to Fortune and to Fame unknown;
Fair Science frowned not on his humble birth,
120   *And Melancholy marked him for her own.*

Large was his bounty and his soul sincere;
      Heaven did a recompense as largely send:
He gave to Misery all he had, a tear;
      He gained from Heaven ('twas all he wished) a friend.

125 No *farther seek his merits to disclose,*
    Or draw his frailties from their dread abode,
  (There they alike in trembling hope repose)
    The bosom of his Father and his God.

Ode on the Death of a Favourite Cat,
Drowned in a Tub of Gold Fishes

'Twas on a lofty vase's side,
Where China's gayest art had dyed
    The azure flowers, that blow;°   *bloom*
Demurest of the tabby kind,
5 The pensive Selima reclined,
    Gazed on the lake below.

Her conscious tail her joy declared;
The fair round face, the snowy beard,
    The velvet of her paws,
10 Her coat, that with the tortoise vies,
Her ears of jet, and emerald eyes,
    She saw; and purred applause.

Still had she gazed; but 'midst the tide
Two angel forms were seen to glide,
15   The Genii° of the stream: *presiding spirits*
Their scaly armour's Tyrian⁵ hue
Through richest purple to the view
    Betrayed a golden gleam.

The hapless nymph with wonder saw:
20 A whisker first and then a claw,
    With many an ardent wish,
She stretched in vain to reach the prize.
What female heart can gold despise?
    What cat's averse to fish?

25 Presumptuous maid! with looks intent
Again she stretched, again she bent,
    Nor knew the gulf between.
(Malignant Fate sat by, and smiled)
The slippery verge her feet beguiled,
30   She tumbled headlong in.

---

5 *Dye made in Tyre (an ancient city on the*   *used to adorn royal garments.*
   Mediterranean) called Tyrian purple, was

Eight times emerging from the flood
She mewed to every watery God,
    Some speedy aid to send.
No dolphin came, no Nereid[6] stirred:
35 Nor cruel Tom, nor Susan heard.
    A favourite has no friend!

From hence, ye Beauties, undeceived,
Know, one false step is ne'er retrieved,
    And be with caution bold.
40 Not all that tempts your wandering eyes
And heedless hearts, is lawful prize;
    Nor all, that glisters, gold.

George Crabbe (1754 – 1832)

Crabbe was born to a poor family in the village of Aldeburgh in Suffolk. After sampling the careers of doctor and apothecary, he was ordained and returned to Aldeburgh in the capacity of curate. He later served as a cleric in other country parishes. The Village, The Parish Register *and* The Borough *are the most significant of Crabbe's many volumes of poetry. As seen in the extract below, Crabbe uses the heroic couplet favoured by Dryden and Pope, but with his own unique idiom. The rural life described in this poem bears little resemblance to the idealized scene portrayed in either Marlowe's "The Passionate Shepherd to his Love" or Raleigh's "The Nymph's Reply to the Shepherd". Crabbe's version of life in the country is informed by his experience of poverty and the dire need to work in order to survive.*

From THE VILLAGE

Book I *(extract: lines 1–62)*

The village life, and every care that reigns
O'er youthful peasants and declining swains;°   *country youths or lovers*
What labour yields, and what, that labour past,
Age, in its hour of languor, finds at last;
5 What form the real picture of the poor,
Demand a song—the Muse[1] can give no more.

6 *In Greek mythology, Nereids are the daughters of the sea god, Nereus.*

1 *One of the Greek goddesses of inspiration.*

Fled are those times, when, in harmonious strains,
The rustic poet praised his native plains:
No shepherds now, in smooth alternate verse,
10 Their country's beauty or their nymphs'° rehearse;   *shepherdesses*
Yet still for these we frame the tender strain,
Still in our lays fond Corydons² complain,
And shepherds' boys their amorous pains reveal,
The only pains, alas! they never feel.
15   On Mincio's³ banks, in Caesar's bounteous reign,
If Tityrus⁴ found the Golden Age again,
Must sleepy bards the flattering dream prolong,
Mechanic echoes of the Mantuan⁵ song?
From Truth and Nature shall we widely stray,
20 Where Virgil, not where Fancy, leads the way?
        Yes, thus the Muses sing of happy swains,
Because the Muses never knew their pains:
They boast their peasants' pipes;° but peasants now   *reed instrument*
Resign their pipes and plod behind the plough:
25 And few, amid the rural-tribe, have time
To number syllables, and play with rhyme;
Save honest Duck,⁶ what son of verse could share
The poet's rapture and the peasant's care?
Or the great labours of the field degrade,
30 With the new peril of a poorer trade?
        From this chief cause these idle praises spring,
That themes so easy few forbear to sing;
For no deep thought the trifling subjects ask;
To sing of shepherds is an easy task:
35 The happy youth assumes the common strain,
A nymph his mistress, and himself a swain;
With no sad scenes he clouds his tuneful prayer.
But all, to look like her, is painted fair.
        I grant indeed that fields and flocks have charms
40 For him that grazes or for him that farms;
But when amid such pleasing scenes I trace
The poor laborious natives of the place,
And see the mid-day sun, with fervid ray,
On their bare heads and dewy temples play;

2 *A common name for a shepherd in pastoral poetry.*
3 *The Mincio River in Italy. This is its ancient Roman name.*
4 *A shepherd in Virgil's* Eclogues I.
5 *Virgilian. (Virgil, the Roman poet, was born near Mantua in Cisalpine Gaul.)*
6 *The poet, Stephen Duck (1705-1756), favoured by Queen Caroline, wife of George IV.*

45   While some, with feebler heads and fainter hearts,
    Deplore their fortune, yet sustain their parts:
    Then shall I dare these real ills to hide
    In tinsel trappings of poetic pride?
        No; cast by Fortune on a frowning coast,
50   Which neither groves nor happy valleys boast;
    Where other cares than those the Muse relates,
    And other shepherds dwell with other mates;
    By such examples taught, I paint the Cot,[7]
    As truth will paint it, and as bards will not:
55   Nor you, ye poor, of letter'd scorn complain,
    To you the smoothest song is smooth in vain;
    O'ercome by labour, and bow'd down by time,
    Feel you the barren flattery of a rhyme?
    Can poets soothe you, when you pine for bread,
60   By winding myrtles round your ruin'd shed?
    Can their light tales your weighty griefs o'erpower,
    Or glad with airy mirth the toilsome hour?

---

7 *Portray cottage life.*

William Blake (1757 – 1827)

Blake was passionately concerned with social issues. His Lambeth resi-dence was within sight of the poor-houses, where destitute adults and children were housed in appalling conditions, while being put to work almost as slave-labour, supposedly for their moral improvement, but in fact for the material benefit of society in the name of Christian charity. Blake felt these and other social injustices keenly. Poems such as "London" in the Songs of Experience *express the poet's outrage at the perversion and corruption in his society, and call for far-ranging reform at all levels of life. For Blake, the fault permeated the deepest reaches of human existence, including the state, educational and religious sys-tems, and sexual and spiritual mores.*

Blake's primary concern as a poet was to provide an inspired vision of divine love which might lead people from the folly of this world (which he perceived as a fallen one) and guide them to a true perception of God and their own divine humanity. In his poems, he symbolizes the contrary spiritual states of the soul, those of "Innocence" and "Experience".

In his poetry, Blake uses relatively simple diction but with sym-bolic overtones that expand the meaning of the text. The "worm" in "The Sick Rose" could be anything which defiles and destroys what is beautiful and expansive of spirit. In "The Tiger", the fierce animal is symbolic of all that is contrary to the spirit of the "lamb", which rep-resents selfless love and forgiveness. The poet perceives the creator of the universe as struggling to contain the energies represented by the "tiger", such as, perhaps, selfishness, cruelty, blood lust and revenge-fulness—whatever feeds like a devourer on what is gentle, meek, forgiving and generous of spirit.

The Clod and the Pebble

"Love seeketh not itself to please,
"Nor for itself hath any care,
"But for another gives its ease,
"And builds a Heaven in Hell's despair."

5 So sang a little clod of clay
Trodden with the cattle's feet,
But a pebble of the brook
Warbled out these metres meet:

"Love seeketh only self to please,
10 "To bind another to its delight,
"Joys in another's loss of ease,
"And builds a Hell in Heaven's despite."

The Little Black Boy

My mother bore me in the southern wild,
And I am black, but O! my soul is white;
White as an angel is the English child,
But I am black, as if bereaved of light.

5 My mother taught me underneath a tree,
And sitting down before the heat of day,
She took me on her lap and kissed me,
And pointing to the east, began to say:

"Look on the rising sun: there God does live,
10 "And gives his light, and gives his heat away;
"And flowers and trees and beasts and men receive
"Comfort in morning, joy in the noon day.

"And we are put on earth a little space,
"That we may learn to bear the beams of love;
15 "And these black bodies and this sunburnt face
"Is but a cloud, and like a shady grove.

"For when our souls have learned the heat to bear,
"The cloud will vanish; we shall hear his voice,
"Saying: 'Come out from the grove, my love and care,
20 'And round my golden tent like lambs rejoice.'"

Thus did my mother say, and kissed me;
And thus I say to little English boy.
When I from black and he from white cloud free,
And round the tent of God like lambs we joy,

25 I'll shade him from the heat, till he can bear
To lean in joy upon our father's knee;
And then I'll stand and stroke his silver hair,
And be like him, and he will then love me.

London

I wander through each chartered[1] street,
Near where the chartered Thames[2] does flow,
And mark in every face I meet
Marks of weakness, marks of woe.

5   In every cry of every man,
In every infant's cry of fear,
In every voice, in every ban,[3]
The mind-forged manacles I hear.

How the chimney-sweeper's cry
10   Every black'ning church appalls;
And the hapless soldier's sigh
Runs in blood down palace walls.

But most through midnight streets I hear
How the youthful harlot's curse[4]
15   Blasts the new born infant's tear,
And blights with plagues the marriage hearse.

The Sick Rose

O Rose, thou art sick!
The invisible worm
That flies in the night,
In the howling storm,

5   Has found out thy bed
Of crimson joy:
And his dark secret love
Does thy life destroy.

1 *To charter is to grant privileges or contracts to certain companies or individuals, thus imposing restrictions on others.*
2 *Principal river in England, flowing east from Oxford and passing through London. It provides one of Britain's largest ports.*
3 *Prohibition or curse, with a suggested allusion to the marriage bann.*
4 *The prostitute's uttering of maledictions and swear-words.*

The Tiger

Tiger! Tiger! burning bright
In the forests of the night,
What immortal hand or eye
Could frame thy fearful symmetry?

5   In what distant deeps or skies
Burnt the fire of thine eyes?
On what wings dare he aspire?
What the hand dare seize the fire?

And what shoulder, and what art,
10 Could twist the sinews of thy heart?
And when thy heart began to beat,
What dread hand? and what dread feet?

What the hammer? what the chain?
In what furnace was thy brain?
15 What the anvil? what dread grasp
Dare its deadly terrors clasp?

When the stars threw down their spears,
And watered heaven with their tears,
Did he smile his work to see?
20 Did he who made the Lamb make thee?

Tiger! Tiger! burning bright
In the forests of the night,
What immortal hand or eye
Dare frame thy fearful symmetry?

Robert Burns (1759 – 1796)

Robert Burns is one of the most famous Scottish poets, and his birth-
day on 25 January is still commemorated as "Burns Night". He was the
son of a poor tenant-farmer in Ayrshire, and spent a considerable part
of his life living and working on farms. Some of his poems were writ-
ten in "standard" English, but he is perhaps chiefly remembered for the
poetry written in the Scottish dialect. His writings brought him consi-
derable fame in his own lifetime and gave him access to fashionable
Edinburgh society. "A Red, Red Rose" is one of his best-known lyrics.

A Red, Red Rose[1]

O my love's like a red, red rose,
    That's newly sprung in June;
O my love's like the melody
    That's sweetly played in tune.

5   As fair art thou, my bonny lass,
    So deep in love am I;
And I will love thee still, my dear,
    Till a'° the seas gang° dry.   *all / run (go)*

    Till a' the seas gang dry, my dear,
10   And the rocks melt wi'° the sun: *with*
I will love thee still, my dear,
    While the sands o' life shall run.

And fare thee weel,° my only love!   *well*
    And fare thee weel, a while!
15   And I will come again, my love,
    Tho' it were ten thousand mile!

1 *Burns's poem is in Scottish dialect; the*   *there is no loss to the spirit of the original.*
  spelling has been Anglicized only where

William Wordsworth (1770 – 1850)

*Wordsworth spent his childhood among the mountains, lakes and val-
leys of the English Lake District. After attending St John's College,
Cambridge, he went on a walking tour of the Alps, and observed
France at the height of its revolutionary optimism. In 1791 he returned
to France, where he saw some of the after-effects of the French
Revolution. He returned to England in 1792, deeply troubled by regret
and doubt, not only about the course of the Revolution, but concern-
ing his vocation as a poet. In 1795 he settled at Racedown, Dorset,
with his sister Dorothy. Her presence, and his new friendship with
Coleridge, helped him to recover from his long crisis of faith.*

*Wordsworth's poetry argues that there is a bond between the
human mind and the external universe. His autobiographical poem,
The Prelude, is a detailed record of the tensions, perplexities and pro-
gressions in the growth of a poet's mind. In the "boat-stealing" episode
of The Prelude, he seems to show that nature is responsible for awa-
kening a moral sense in the growing mind. In "Composed upon
Westminster Bridge", his imagination is roused by the presence of
nature at the centre of a great civilization. The city, momentarily trans-
formed into a natural spectacle, seems to prove that there is an inti-
mate relationship between people and the created world.*

*Wordsworth regarded poetry as the natural utterance of a "man
speaking to men". Instead of eighteenth-century poetic diction, he used
ordinary language to reflect the vitality and integrity of apparently
commonplace incidents.*

Composed upon Westminster Bridge,[1] September 3, 1802

Earth has not anything to show more fair:
Dull would he be of soul who could pass by
A sight so touching in its majesty:
This city now doth, like a garment, wear
5   The beauty of the morning; silent, bare,
Ships, towers, domes, theatres, and temples lie
Open unto the fields, and to the sky;
All bright and glittering in the smokeless air.
Never did sun more beautifully steep
10 In his first splendour, valley, rock, or hill;
Ne'er saw I, never felt, a calm so deep!
The river glideth at his own sweet will:
Dear God! the very houses seem asleep;
And all that mighty heart is lying still!

1 *A bridge in central London.*

"She dwelt among the untrodden ways"

She dwelt among the untrodden ways
    Beside the springs of Dove,[2]
A maid whom there were none to praise
    And very few to love:

5   A violet by a mossy stone
    Half hidden from the eye!
—Fair as a star, when only one
    Is shining in the sky.

She lived unknown, and few could know
10   When Lucy ceased to be;
But she is in her grave, and, oh,
    The difference to me!

From THE PRELUDE

    Book 1 *(extract: lines 357–400)*

[handwritten annotation: Wordsworth own moral growth. He becomes aware of the need for moral conscience — Spirited nature]

    One summer evening (led by her)[3] I found
A little boat tied to a willow tree
Within a rocky cave, its usual home.
Straight I unloosed her chain, and stepping in
5 Pushed from the shore. It was an act of stealth *[handwritten: knows he's done wrong.]*
And troubled pleasure, nor without the voice
Of mountain–echoes did my boat move on;
Leaving behind her still, on either side,
Small circles glittering idly in the moon,
10 Until they melted all into one track
Of sparkling light. But now, like one who rows, *[handwritten: becoming good at ROWING.]*
Proud of his skill, to reach a chosen point
With an unswerving line, I fixed my view
Upon the summit of a craggy ridge,
15 The horizon's utmost boundary; far above
Was nothing but the stars and the grey sky.
She was an elfin pinnace;° lustily   *small boat*
I dipped my oars into the silent lake,
And, as I rose upon the stroke, my boat
20 Went heaving through the water like a swan;

2 *River in Derbyshire, England, well known to Wordsworth (whose home was—and still is—called Dove Cottage).*

3 *Led by the spirit of nature. "Her" in line 4, however, refers to the boat.*

Theme · Nature can teach us a lesson – with help of conscience.

When, from behind that craggy steep till then
The horizon's bound, a huge peak, black and huge, *cliff; rocky hillside*
As if with voluntary power instinct,°   *charged with power*
Upreared its head. I struck and struck again, *rowing frantically*
25 And growing still in stature the grim shape
Towered up between me and the stars, and still,
For so it seemed, with purpose of its own *pursuing him as he has done*
And measured motion like a living thing, *wrong. (guilty conscience).*
Strode after me. With trembling oars I turned,
30 And through the silent water stole my way *stealth ¦ stole same word in dif-*
Back to the covert of the willow tree; *erent context.*
There in her mooring-place I left my bark,—
And through the meadows homeward went, in grave
And serious mood; but after I had seen
35 That spectacle, for many days, my brain
Worked with a dim and undetermined sense
Of unknown modes of being; o'er my thoughts
There hung a darkness, call it solitude
Or blank desertion. No familiar shapes *End effect – very little joy gained*
40 Remained, no pleasant images of trees, *out of his misdoing. /threat of*
Of sea or sky, no colours of green fields; *punishment overwhelms any*
But huge and mighty forms, that do not live *prior joy gained.*
Like living men, moved slowly through the mind
By day, and were a trouble to my dreams.

Sonnet: "The world is too much with us"

The world is too much with us; late and soon,
Getting and spending, we lay waste our powers:
Little we see in Nature that is ours;
We have given our hearts away, a sordid boon!
5 This sea that bares her bosom to the moon;
The winds that will be howling at all hours,
And are up-gathered now like sleeping flowers;
For this, for everything we are out of tune;
It moves us not.—Great God! I'd rather be
10 A pagan suckled in a creed outworn;
So might I, standing on this pleasant lea,°   *meadow*
Have glimpses that would make me less forlorn;
Have sight of Proteus[4] rising from the sea;
Or hear old Triton[5] blow his wreathéd horn.

4 *The prophetic old man of the sea, who
tended the flocks of the seagod Poseidon
(Neptune).*
5 *Son of Poseidon, who lived in a golden*
*palace on the sea floor. Often (in the plural),
described as sea monsters, human in the
upper part of their bodies, fish in the lower.*

Samuel Taylor Coleridge (1772 – 1834)

Coleridge's few poems of superlative quality were mostly written within a single year, 1797-8, known as his Annus Mirabilis. *It was in the course of that year that Coleridge established his memorable friendship with Wordsworth with whom he shared a love of poetry and hillwalking. The two poets influenced each other greatly, in their poetry as well as their critical opinions. The publication of their joint work,* Lyrical Ballads, *is a landmark in English literary history, and gave the early Romantic movement in England its strongest impetus.*

The poems of the Annus Mirabilis *fall readily into two distinct groups, those dealing with visionary experience, and those that are reflective in tone. While it is the former group that has justly established Coleridge's reputation, with poems such as "The Rime of the Ancient Mariner" and "Kubla Khan", the latter group, of which "This Lime-Tree Bower my Prison" is one of the best known, links Coleridge with Wordsworth as one of the most important practitioners of reflective verse of the period. Close thematic similarities exist between the two groups of Coleridge's poems, despite their obvious differences in form and mode of presentation. There is in both the same predominant concern with the achievement of a unified vision of humankind and nature. The reflective poems present a subjective appraisal of common, everyday experience, while the visionary poems emphasize the strange and unfamiliar by means of an impersonal representation of reality.*

Kubla Khan[1]

In Xanadu[2] did Kubla Khan
A stately pleasure-dome decree:
Where Alph,[3] the sacred river, ran
Through caverns measureless to man
5   Down to a sunless sea.
So twice five miles of fertile ground
With walls and towers were girdled round:
And there were gardens bright with sinuous rills,
Where blossomed many an incense-bearing tree;
10   And here were forests ancient as the hills,
Enfolding sunny spots of greenery.

1 *Khan was a title given to Asian rulers. In Coleridge's poem,* Kubla Khan *is a legendary prince. The historical Kubla Khan united China and founded the Mongol Empire in the thirteenth century. He was highly praised by Marco Polo in his account of the travels of the Polo family.*

2 *Shang-tu, or K'ai-p'ing, Kubla Khan's residence in south-eastern Mongolia.*

3 *A river of the Peloponnesian Peninsula (Greece), which flows into the Ionian Sea. It is now known as the Rufia.*

But oh! that deep romantic chasm which slanted
Down the green hill athwart a cedarn cover!°   *cedar grove*
A savage place! as holy and enchanted
15 As e'er beneath a waning moon was haunted
By woman wailing for her demon-lover!
And from this chasm, with ceaseless turmoil seething,
As if this earth in fast thick pants were breathing,
A mighty fountain momently was forced:
20 Amid whose swift half-intermitted burst
Huge fragments vaulted like rebounding hail,
Or chaffy grain beneath the thresher's flail:
And 'mid these dancing rocks at once and ever
It flung up momently the sacred river.
25 Five miles meandering with a mazy motion
Through wood and dale the sacred river ran,
Then reached the caverns measureless to man,
And sank in tumult to a lifeless ocean:
And 'mid this tumult Kubla heard from far
30 Ancestral voices prophesying war!

The shadow of the dome of pleasure
Floated midway on the waves;
Where was heard the mingled measure
From the fountain and the caves.
35 It was a miracle of rare device,
A sunny pleasure-dome with caves of ice!

A damsel with a dulcimer
In a vision once I saw:
It was an Abyssinian maid,
40 And on her dulcimer she played,
Singing of Mount Abora.⁴
Could I revive within me
Her symphony and song,
To such a deep delight 'twould win me,
45 That with music loud and long,
I would build that dome in air,
That sunny dome! those caves of ice!
And all who heard should see them there,
And all should cry, Beware! Beware!
50 His flashing eyes, his floating hair!

4 Possibly a modification of an exotic   course of reading travel books and tales of
   geographical name Coleridge noted in the   exploration.

Weave a circle round him thrice,
And close your eyes with holy dread,
For he on honey-dew hath fed,
And drunk the milk of Paradise.

This Lime-Tree Bower my Prison[5]

Well, they are gone, and here must I remain,
This lime-tree bower my prison! I have lost
Beauties and feelings, such as would have been
Most sweet to my remembrance even when age
5 Had dimmed mine eyes to blindness! They, meanwhile,
Friends, whom I never more may meet again,
On springy heath, along the hill-top edge,
Wander in gladness, and wind down, perchance,
To that still roaring dell, of which I told;
10 The roaring dell, o'erwooded, narrow, deep,
And only speckled by the mid-day sun;
Where its slim trunk the ash from rock to rock
Flings arching like a bridge; that branchless ash,
Unsunned and damp, whose few poor yellow leaves
15 Ne'er tremble in the gale, yet tremble still,
Fanned by the water-fall! and there my friends
Behold the dark green file of long lank weeds,
That all at once (a most fantastic sight!)
Still nod and drip beneath the dripping edge
20 Of the blue clay-stone.
               Now, my friends emerge
Beneath the wide wide heaven—and view again
The many-steepled tract magnificent
Of hilly fields and meadows, and the sea,
With some fair bark, perhaps, whose sails light up
25 The slip of smooth clear blue betwixt two isles
Of purple shadow! Yes! they wander on
In gladness all; but thou, methinks, most glad,
My gentle-hearted Charles![6] for thou hast pined
And hungered after Nature, many a year,
30 In the great city pent, winning thy way
With sad yet patient soul, through evil and pain
And strange calamity! Ah! slowly sink
Behind the western ridge, thou glorious Sun!

5 *An injured foot kept Coleridge confined to his home while his friends Charles Lamb, William and Dorothy Wordsworth walked* *about the Somersetshire countryside.*
6 *Charles Lamb.*

Shine in the slant beams of the sinking orb,
35 Ye purple heath-flowers! richlier burn, ye clouds!
Live in the yellow light, ye distant groves!
And kindle, thou blue ocean! So my friend
Struck with deep joy may stand, as I have stood,
Silent with swimming sense; yea, gazing round
40 On the wide landscape, gaze till all doth seem
Less gross than bodily; and of such hues
As veil the Almighty Spirit, when yet he makes
Spirits perceive his presence.
                    A delight
Comes sudden on my heart, and I am glad
45 As I myself were there! Nor in this bower,
This little lime-tree bower, have I not marked
Much that has soothed me. Pale beneath the blaze
Hung the transparent foliage; and I watched
Some broad and sunny leaf, and loved to see
50 The shadow of the leaf and stem above
Dappling its sunshine! And that walnut-tree
Was richly tinged, and a deep radiance lay
Full on the ancient ivy, which usurps
Those fronting elms, and now, with blackest mass
55 Makes their dark branches gleam a lighter hue
Through the late twilight: and though now the bat
Wheels silent by, and not a swallow twitters,
Yet still the solitary humble-bee
Sings in the bean-flower! Henceforth I shall know
60 That nature ne'er deserts the wise and pure;
No plot so narrow, be but Nature there,
No waste so vacant, but may well employ
Each faculty of sense, and keep the heart
Awake to love and beauty! and sometimes
65 'Tis well to be bereft of promised good,
That we may lift the soul, and contemplate
With lively joy the joys we cannot share.
My gentle-hearted Charles! when the last rook
Beats its straight path along the dusky air
70 Homewards, I blest it! deeming its black wing
(Now a dim speck, now vanishing in light)
Had crossed the mighty orb's dilated glory,
While thou stood'st gazing; or, when all was still,
Flew creeking o'er thy head, and had a charm
75 For thee, my gentle-hearted Charles, to whom
No sound is dissonant which tells of life.

George Gordon, Lord Byron (1788 – 1824)

Byron was of English and Scottish ancestry. After studying at Cambridge, he embarked on a tour of Europe at a time when that continent was embroiled in the Napoleonic wars. He was in Spain and Portugal while the Peninsula war was in progress, later visiting Greece and Turkey which were not then part of a usual tourist itinerary. On his return to London he established his reputation as a poet of the exotic with the publication of Childe Harold's Pilgrimage *in 1812 and, in the years that followed, with oriental tales such as* The Giaour *and* Lara. *Much of his poetry was based on the rich experiences of his travels. As well as being a writer of considerable lyric intensity, demonstrated in such pieces as "She walks in beauty" and "So we'll go no more a-roving", he wrote a number of poetic dramas. He also developed a strongly articulated opposition to tyranny. This can be seen in the "Sonnet on Chillon" and in his parliamentary speeches delivered in the House of Lords. His most famous poem is* Don Juan, *an acerbic and amusing satire on contemporary society. Byron was that rare example of a poet widely read and translated in his own life-time. He died of fever at Missolonghi in Greece while helping to organize resistance to Turkish rule.*

"She walks in beauty"

She walks in beauty, like the night
    Of cloudless climes and starry skies;
And all that's best of dark and bright
    Meet in her aspect and her eyes:
5 Thus mellowed to that tender light
    Which heaven to gaudy day denies.

One shade the more, one ray the less,
    Had half impaired the nameless grace
Which waves in every raven tress,
10   Or softly lightens o'er her face;
Where thoughts serenely sweet express
    How pure, how dear their dwelling-place.

And on that cheek, and o'er that brow,
    So soft, so calm, yet eloquent,
15 The smiles that win, the tints that glow,
    But tell of days in goodness spent,
A mind at peace with all below,
    A heart whose love is innocent!

Sonnet on Chillon[1]

Eternal Spirit of the chainless Mind!
Brightest in dungeons, Liberty! thou art,
For there thy habitation is the heart—
The heart which love of thee alone can bind;
5   And when thy sons to fetters are consigned—
To fetters, and the damp vault's dayless gloom,
Their country conquers with their martyrdom,
And Freedom's fame finds wings on every wind.
Chillon! thy prison is a holy place,
10   And thy sad floor an altar—for 'twas trod,
Until his very steps have left a trace
Worn, as if thy cold pavement were a sod,
By Bonnivard![2] May none those marks efface!
For they appeal from tyranny to God.

"So, we'll go no more a-roving"

So, we'll go no more a-roving
    So late into the night,
Though the heart be still as loving,
    And the moon be still as bright.

5   For the sword outwears its sheath,
    And the soul wears out the breast,
And the heart must pause to breathe,
    And love itself have rest.

Though the night was made for loving,
10   And the day returns too soon,
Yet we'll go no more a-roving
    By the light of the moon.

1 *The name of a castle in Switzerland. The sonnet prefaces Byron's poem "The Prisoner of Chillon", which deals with the physical, mental, and psychological effects of confinement.*

2 *Francois Bonnivard (1493–1570) was a priest who was imprisoned in the Castle of Chillon for seven years, because of his strong revolutionary and democratic leanings.*

Percy Bysshe Shelley (1792 – 1822)

Shelley was born in Sussex, England, into an aristocratic family. A young man of unconventional ideas, he was expelled from Oxford University in 1811 for his pamphlet entitled The Necessity of Atheism. *During the same year he eloped with Harriet Westbrook but their marriage came to an end when he left her for Mary Wollstonecraft Godwin, daughter of the revolutionary thinker, William Godwin, and the feminist, Mary Wollstonecraft. The couple settled in Italy and were married after the suicide of Shelley's first wife. Shelley was opposed to oppressive government, so that he sympathized strongly with the cause that overthrew the French monarchy during the French Revolution in 1789. He drowned, at the age of twenty-nine, in a sailing accident off the Italian coast.*

Along with Keats and Byron, Shelley is generally regarded as a "second generation" Romantic poet, which means that their poetry shares some of the main ideas and features found in the work of such major first-generation Romantic poets as Blake, Wordsworth and Coleridge. The Romantic aspects of Shelley's writing include his enjoyment and celebration of nature, the special place he gives to the individual, and the revolutionary trend of his writing. Shelley's poetry bears testimony to his beliefs that individuals have to find their own way to truth and that this is done by casting off outworn, conventional ideas and allowing the creative imagination complete freedom. This conviction unites with Shelley's passion for natural phenomena in "Ode to the West Wind", one of his best-known poems.

Ode to the West Wind

I

O wild West Wind, thou breath of Autumn's being,
Thou, from whose unseen presence the leaves dead
Are driven, like ghosts from an enchanter fleeing.

Yellow, and black, and pale, and hectic° red,[1]   *wasting, consuming*
5 Pestilence-stricken multitudes: O Thou,
Who chariotest to their dark wintry bed

---

1 *These colours possibly represent the*   American Indian races.
Mongoloid, Negroid, Caucasian and

The winged seeds, where they lie cold and low,
Each like a corpse within its grave, until
Thine azure sister of the Spring shall blow

10 Her clarion° o'er the dreaming earth, and fill   *trumpet*
(Driving sweet buds like flocks to feed in air)
With living hues and odours plain and hill:

Wild Spirit, which art moving everywhere;
Destroyer and Preserver:[2] hear, O hear!

II

15 Thou on whose stream, mid the steep sky's commotion,
Loose clouds like earth's decaying leaves are shed,
Shook from the tangled boughs of Heaven and Ocean,

Angels° of rain and lightning: there are spread   *messengers*
On the blue surface of thine aery surge,
20 Like the bright hair uplifted from the head

Of some fierce Maenad,[3] even from the dim verge
Of the horizon to the zenith's height,
The locks of the approaching storm. Thou Dirge

Of the dying year, to which this closing night
25 Will be the dome of a vast sepulchre,
Vaulted with all thy congregated might

Of vapours, from whose solid atmosphere
Black rain and fire and hail will burst: O hear!

III

Thou who didst waken from his summer dreams
30 The blue Mediterranean where he lay,
Lulled by the coil of his chrystalline streams,

---

2 *A reference to the Hindu gods: Siva, the Destroyer, and Vishnu, the Preserver.*
3 *One of the Maenades or Bacchae, who were the female companions of Dionysus or Bacchus, a Greek god associated with hedonistic rites.*

Beside a pumice° isle on Baiae's bay,[4]   *porous lava*
And saw in sleep old palaces and towers[5]
Quivering within the wave's intenser day,

35 All overgrown with azure moss and flowers
So sweet, the sense faints picturing them! Thou
For whose path the Atlantic's level powers

Cleave themselves into chasms, while far below
The sea-blooms and the oozy woods which wear
40 The sapless foliage of the ocean, know

Thy voice, and suddenly grow grey with fear,
And tremble and despoil themselves: O hear!

    IV

If I were a dead leaf thou mightest bear;
If I were a swift cloud to fly with thee;
45 A wave to pant beneath thy power, and share

The impulse of thy strength, only less free
Than thou, O Uncontrollable! If even
I were as in my boyhood, and could be

The comrade of thy wanderings over Heaven,
50 As then, when to outstrip thy skiey speed
Scarce seemed a vision; I would ne'er have striven

As thus with thee in prayer in my sore need.
Oh, lift me as a wave, a leaf, a cloud!
I fall upon the thorns of life! I bleed!

55 A heavy weight of hours has chained and bowed
 One too like thee: tameless,° and swift, and proud.   *untameable*

    V

Make me thy lyre, even as the forest is:
What if my leaves are falling like its own!
The tumult of thy mighty harmonies

---

4 *Town on a small bay near Naples,*   *emperors and nobles.*
    abounding in warm mineral springs, and   5 *Ruins of villas from the days of imperial*
    frequented as a watering place by Roman   *Rome.*

60 Will take from both a deep, autumnal tone,
    Sweet though in sadness. Be thou, Spirit fierce,
    My spirit! Be thou me, impetuous one!

    Drive my dead thoughts over the universe
    Like withered leaves to quicken a new birth!
65 And, by the incantation of this verse,

    Scatter, as from an unextinguished hearth
    Ashes and sparks, my words among mankind!
    Be through my lips to unawakened Earth

    The trumpet of a prophecy! O Wind,
70 If Winter comes, can Spring be far behind?

Ozymandias[6]

    I met a traveller from an antique land,
    Who said—"Two vast and trunkless legs of stone
    Stand in the desert . . . Near them, on the sand,
    Half sunk, a shattered visage lies, whose frown,
5   And wrinkled lip, and sneer of cold command,
    Tell that its sculptor well those passions read
    Which yet survive, stamped on these lifeless things,
    The hand that mocked them, and the heart that fed;
    And on the pedestal these words appear:
10 My name is Ozymandias, King of Kings:
    Look on my Works, ye Mighty, and despair!
    Nothing beside remains. Round the decay
    Of that colossal wreck, boundless and bare
    The lone and level sands stretch far away."

6 *This was another name for the Egyptian
   king Rameses II, whose tomb near Thebes
   was in the form of a huge sculpted sphinx.
   The Sphinx was a composite figure* *consisting of a lion's body with human head,
   and was commonly used to represent the
   Egyptian king. It was an image to be
   revered.*

To a Sky–lark[7]

Hail to thee, blithe Spirit!
  Bird thou never wert—
That from Heaven, or near it,
  Pourest thy full heart
5 In profuse strains of unpremeditated art.

  Higher still and higher
  From the earth thou springest
Like a cloud of fire;
  The blue deep thou wingest,
10 And singing still dost soar, and soaring ever singest.

In the golden lightning
  Of the sunken Sun—
O'er which clouds are brightning,
  Thou dost float and run;
15 Like an unbodied joy whose race is just begun.

The pale purple even
  Melts around thy flight;
Like a star of Heaven,[8]
  In the broad daylight
20 Thou art unseen, but yet I hear thy shrill delight,

Keen as are the arrows
  Of that silver sphere,[9]
Whose intense lamp narrows
  In the white dawn clear
25 Until we hardly see—we feel that it is there.

All the earth and air
  With thy voice is loud,
As, when night is bare
  From one lonely cloud
30 The moon rains out her beams—and Heaven is overflowed.

What thou art we know not;
  What is most like thee?
From rainbow clouds there flow not
  Drops so bright to see
35 As from thy presence showers a rain of melody.

---

7 Alauda arrensis: *a small European bird that sings only in flight, usually when it is too high to be clearly visible.*

8 *Venus, as the evening star.*

9 *Venus, as the morning star.*

Like a Poet hidden
In the light of thought,
Singing hymns unbidden,
Till the world is wrought
40 To sympathy with hopes and fears it heeded not:

Like a high-born maiden
In a palace-tower,
Soothing her love-laden
Soul in secret hour
45 With music sweet as love—which overflows her bower:

Like a glow-worm golden
In a dell of dew,
Scattering unbeholden°   *unobserved*
Its aerial hue
50 Among the flowers and grass, which screen it from the view:

Like a rose embowered
In its own green leaves—
By warm winds deflowered—
Till the scent it gives
55 Makes faint with too much sweet those heavy-wingéd thieves:

Sound of vernal showers
On the twinkling grass,
Rain-awakened flowers,
All that ever was
60 Joyous, and clear and fresh, thy music doth surpass:

Teach us, Sprite or Bird,
What sweet thoughts are thine;
I have never heard
Praise of love or wine
65 That panted forth a flood of rapture so divine:

Chorus Hymeneal,[1]
Or triumphal chant,
Matched with thine would be all
But an empty vaunt,
70 A thing wherein we feel there is some hidden want.

---

1 *Hymen was the classical god of marriage,*   *name also denoted a marriage song of the*
  carrying a bridal torch and yellow robe. The   *ancient Greeks.*

What objects are the fountains
　　Of thy happy strain?
What fields, or waves, or mountains?
　　What shapes of sky or plain?
75　What love of thine own kind? what ignorance of pain?

With thy clear keen joyance°　　　　　　　　　　　　*delight*
　　Languour cannot be—
Shadow of annoyance
　　Never came near thee;
80　Thou lovest—but ne'er knew love's sad satiety.

Waking or asleep,
　　Thou of death must deem
Things more true and deep
　　Than we mortals dream,
85　Or how could thy notes flow in such a chrystal stream?

We look before and after,
　　And pine for what is not—
Our sincerest laughter
　　With some pain is fraught—
90　Our sweetest songs are those that tell of saddest thought.

Yet if we could scorn
　　Hate and pride and fear;
If we were things born
　　Not to shed a tear,
95　I know not how thy joy we ever should come near.

Better than all measures
　　Of delightful sound—
Better than all treasures
　　That in books are found—
100　Thy skill to poet were, thou scorner of the ground!

Teach me half the gladness
　　That thy brain must know,
Such harmonious madness
　　From my lips would flow
105　The world should listen then—as I am listening now.

John Keats (1795 – 1821)

Keats was born in London and, although he studied medicine, he devoted his brief life to the writing of poetry. After nursing his brother, Tom, who died of tuberculosis, Keats found himself infected with the disease and finally travelled to Italy in a vain attempt to restore his health. He died at the age of twenty-six and was buried in Rome.

Keats, like Shelley, is often referred to as a "second generation" Romantic poet. Certainly his poetry is concerned with revising and recasting the role and nature of poetry, as is the work of Shelley, Coleridge, Wordsworth and Byron. Keats's thought and poetry also bear traces of affiliation with classical Greek writers and with Shakespeare and Milton.

Keats's brief poetic career is remarkable, not only for the quality of his output, but also for the poetic evolution it embodies. He experimented with a wide range of verse-forms, including sonnets, classical epics and odes. His best work was the product of only one year: among other works, "The Eve of St Agnes", "La Belle Dame sans Merci" and the great odes were written in 1819. It is in the latter that Keats confronts and becomes reconciled to some of the more painful realities of life.

La Belle Dame sans Merci[1]

Oh, what can ail thee, knight-at-arms,
    Alone and palely loitering?
The sedge has withered from the lake,
    And no birds sing!

5 Oh, what can ail thee, knight-at-arms,
    So haggard and so woe-begone?
The squirrel's granary is full,
    And the harvest's done.

I see a lily on thy brow,
10   With anguish moist and fever-dew,
And on thy cheek a fading rose
    Fast withereth too.

I met a lady in the meads,
    Full beautiful, a fairy's child,
15 Her hair was long, her foot was light,
    And her eyes were wild.

---

1 *"The beautiful lady without mercy".*

I made a garland for her head,
    And bracelets too, and fragrant zone;
She looked at me as she did love,
20   And made sweet moan.

I set her on my pacing steed,
    And nothing else saw all day long;
For sidelong would she bend, and sing
    A fairy's song.

25 She found me roots of relish sweet,
    And honey wild, and manna dew;[2]
And sure in language strange she said,
    "I love thee true".

She took me to her elfin grot,
30   And there she wept, and sighed full sore,
And there I shut her wild, wild eyes
    With kisses four.

And there she lulléd me asleep,
    And there I dreamed—Ah! woe betide!—
35 The latest dream I ever dreamed
    On the cold hill side.

I saw pale kings, and princes too,
    Pale warriors, death-pale were they all;
They cried—"La belle dame sans merci
40   Hath thee in thrall!"

I saw their starved lips in the gloam°   *twilight*
    With horrid warning gapéd wide,
And I awoke, and found me here
    On the cold hill's side.

45 And this is why I sojourn here,
    Alone and palely loitering,
Though the sedge is withered from the lake,
    And no birds sing.

2 *Sweet juice from plants.*

Ode to a Nightingale

My heart aches, and a drowsy numbness pains
   My sense, as though of hemlock I had drunk,
Or emptied some dull opiate to the drains°   *dregs*
   One minute past, and Lethe-wards[3] had sunk.
5 'Tis not through envy of thy happy lot,
   But being too happy in thine happiness—
      That thou, light-wingéd Dryad[4] of the trees,
        In some melodious plot
   Of beechen green, and shadows numberless,
10   Singest of summer in full-throated ease.

Oh, for a draught of vintage! that hath been
   Cooled a long age in the deep-delvéd earth,
Tasting of Flora[5] and the country green,
   Dance, and Provençal[6] song, and sunburnt mirth!
15 Oh, for a beaker full of the warm South,
   Full of the true, the blushful Hippocrene,[7]
      With beaded bubbles winking at the brim,
        And purple-stainéd mouth,
   That I might drink, and leave the world unseen,
20   And with thee fade away into the forest dim—

Fade far away, dissolve, and quite forget
   What thou among the leaves hast never known,
The weariness, the fever, and the fret
   Here, where men sit and hear each other groan;
25 Where palsy shakes a few, sad, last grey hairs,
   Where youth grows pale, and spectre-thin, and dies;
      Where but to think is to be full of sorrow
        And leaden-eyed despairs;
   Where Beauty cannot keep her lustrous eyes,
30   Or new Love pine at them beyond to-morrow.

3 *In classical mythology the Lethe is a river of the lower world, bestowing forgetfulness on those who drink of its waters.*
4 *A nymph of the woods.*
5 *Roman goddess of flowers and spring.*

6 *Provençe is a southern province of France.*
7 *The fountain of the Horse, a place sacred to the Muses (goddesses of inspiration) on Mount Helicon in Boeotia (a state in ancient Greece).*

Away! away! For I will fly to thee,
    Not charioted by Bacchus[8] and his pards,°   *leopards*
But on the viewless° wings of Poesy;   *invisible*
    Though the dull brain perplexes and retards.
35 Already with thee! Tender is the night,
        And haply the Queen-Moon is on her throne,
            Clustered around by all her starry fays;
                But here there is no light,
        Save what from heaven is with the breezes blown
40   Through verdurous glooms and winding mossy ways.

I cannot see what flowers are at my feet,
    Nor what soft incense hangs upon the boughs,
But, in embalméd° darkness, guess each sweet   *fragrant*
    Wherewith the seasonable month endows
45 The grass, the thicket, and the fruit-tree wild—
        White hawthorn, and the pastoral eglantine;
            Fast-fading violets covered up in leaves;
                And mid-May's eldest child,
        The coming musk-rose, full of dewy wine,
50   The murmurous haunt of flies on summer eves.

Darkling, I listen; and, for many a time
    I have been half in love with easeful Death,
Called him soft names in many a muséd rhyme,
    To take into the air my quiet breath;
55 Now more than ever seems it rich to die,
        To cease upon the midnight with no pain,
            While thou art pouring forth thy soul abroad
                In such an ecstasy!
        Still wouldst thou sing, and I have ears in vain—
60   To thy high requiem become a sod.

Thou wast not born for death, immortal bird!
    No hungry generations tread thee down;
The voice I hear this passing night was heard
    In ancient days by emperor and clown:

8 *The Roman god of wine whose festival was*   *he was crowned with ivy-berries and*
   celebrated with frenzied orgies and dances;   *adorned with ivy. (Greek: Dionysus.)*

65   Perhaps the self-same song that found a path
        Through the sad heart of Ruth,⁹ when, sick for home,
           She stood in tears amid the alien corn;
             The same that oft-times hath
        Charmed magic casements, opening on the foam
70   Of perilous seas in fairy lands forlorn.

    Forlorn! The very word is like a bell
        To toll me back from thee to my sole self!
    Adieu! The fancy cannot cheat so well
        As she is famed to do, deceiving elf.
75   Adieu! adieu! Thy plaintive anthem fades
        Past the near meadows, over the still stream,
           Up the hill-side; and now 'tis buried deep
             In the next valley-glades:
    Was it a vision, or a waking dream?
80   Fled is that music:—Do I wake or sleep?

To Autumn

    Season of mists and mellow fruitfulness,
        Close bosom friend of the maturing sun,
    Conspiring with him how to load and bless
        With fruit the vines that round the thatch-eaves run:
5   To bend with apples the mossed cottage-trees,
        And fill all fruit with ripeness to the core;
           To swell the gourd, and plump the hazel shells
    With a sweet kernel; to set budding more,
        And still more, later flowers for the bees,
10   Until they think warm days will never cease,
           For summer has o'er-brimmed their clammy cells.

    Who hath not seen thee oft amid thy store?
        Sometimes whoever seeks abroad may find
    Thee sitting careless on a granary floor,
15   Thy hair soft-lifted by the winnowing wind;
    Or on a half-reaped furrow sound asleep,
        Drowsed with the fume of poppies,¹ while thy hook
           Spares the next swath and all its twinéd flowers;
    And sometimes like a gleaner thou dost keep
20   Steady thy laden head across a brook;
        Or by a cider-press, with patient look,
           Thou watchest the last oozings hours by hours.

9 *Famous figure in the Bible who followed her*   *and shared her tribulations.*
  mother-in-law Naomi on her wanderings   1 *Sleep-inducing opium is made from poppies.*

Where are the songs of spring? Aye, where are they?
    Think not of them, thou hast thy music too—
25 While barréd° clouds bloom the soft-dying day,   *striated*
    And touch the stubble-plains with rosy hue.
    Then in a wailful choir the small gnats mourn
        Among the river sallows,° borne aloft   *willows*
            Or sinking as the light wind lives or dies;
30 And full-grown lambs loud bleat from hilly bourn;°   *domain*
    Hedge-crickets sing; and now with treble soft
    The red-breast whistles from a garden-croft;
        And gathering swallows twitter in the skies.

On First Looking into Chapman's Homer[2]

Much have I travelled in the realms of gold,
And many goodly states and kingdoms seen;
Round many western islands have I been
Which bards in fealty to Apollo[3] hold.
5   Oft of one wide expanse had I been told
That deep-browed Homer[4] ruled as his demesne;°   *domain*
Yet did I never breathe its pure serene
Till I heard Chapman speak out loud and bold.
Then felt I like some watcher of the skies
10 When a new planet swims into his ken;
Or like stout Cortez[5] when with eagle eyes
He stared at the Pacific, and all his men
Looked at each other with a wild surmise—
Silent, upon a peak in Darien.[6]

2 In October 1816 Keats and a friend had the loan of George Chapman's translation of Homer—a vigorous blank-verse rendering by the Elizabethan poet and dramatist. Until then, Keats's only acquaintance with Homer had been via Pope's translation, in heroic couplets.

3 Apollo, the god of music, prophecy, and philosophy, is often seen as the "patron" or lord of poetry.

4 The greatest epic poet of ancient Greece, author of the Iliad (a record of the Trojan War) and the Odyssey (a record of the voyages and adventures of Ulysses, or Odysseus).

5 Spanish conqueror of Mexico in the early sixteenth century. (Keats confused him with Balboa, who was in fact the first European to see the Pacific.)

6 The isthmus of Darien, a strip of land 95 kilometres wide linking the continents of North and South America, was the place from which Balboa first saw the Pacific Ocean. Keats has perhaps confused Balboa's account with Cortez's of his feelings on seeing Mexico City for the first time.

Elizabeth Barrett Browning (1806 – 1861)

*The facts of Elizabeth Barrett Browning's life are so shrouded in myth
as a result of over-romanticized plays and novels about her, that it is
worth demystifying the legend and taking note of the facts. She was
educated in the conventional fashion for girls, learning drawing, music,
and needlework, but she also had private tutors in classical and other
languages. She was intellectually inclined from an early age, writing her
first poem at the age of four. Contrary to the legends about her oppres-
sive, cruel father, he was proud of her early achievements, and became
possessive only later. Nor was she always a bed-ridden, chronic invalid,
as the myth would persuade us. After the family moved to Wimpole
Street in 1838, she lived a socially full life, and studied, wrote poetry
and corresponded with many friends.*

*She was an established poet by the time she met Robert Browning,
who declared his love for her in a now-famous letter. The couple
eloped, to avoid Mr Barrett's inevitable opposition, and went to Italy,
where they lived, for the most part, until her death. In 1849, she pre-
sented her husband with her* Sonnets from the Portuguese, *a record of
their relationship. The sequence tells the story of their love and the
emotions they experienced. The spectrum of human feelings from joy
to grief, pain to delight, withdrawal to complete giving, is contained in
the poems. Barrett Browning died unexpectedly in 1861 and was
buried in Florence.*

Sonnet: "Go from me"

Go from me. Yet I feel that I shall stand
Henceforward in thy shadow. Nevermore
Alone upon the threshold of my door
Of individual life I shall command
5   The uses of my soul, nor lift my hand
Serenely in the sunshine as before,
Without the sense of that which I forbore—
Thy touch upon the palm. The widest land
Doom takes to part us, leaves thy heart in mine
10 With pulses that beat double. What I do
And what I dream include thee, as the wine
Must taste of its own grapes. And when I sue
God for myself, He hears that name of thine,
And sees within my eyes the tears of two.

Sonnet: "When our two souls"

When our two souls stand up erect and strong,
Face to face, silent, drawing nigh and nigher,
Until the lengthening wings break into fire
At either curvéd point,—what bitter wrong
5   Can the earth do to us, that we should not long
Be here contented? Think. In mounting higher,
The angels would press on us, and aspire
To drop some golden orb of perfect song
Into our deep, dear silence. Let us stay
10 Rather on earth, Beloved,—where the unfit
Contrarious moods of men recoil away
And isolate pure spirits, and permit
A place to stand and love in for a day,
With darkness and the death-hour rounding it.

Edgar Allan Poe (1809 – 1849)

*Poe was born in Boston. By the time he was three years old, his father
had abandoned the family and his mother had died. He was raised by
foster parents, and shortage of funds ultimately prevented him from
completing a university course. He succeeded, nevertheless, in becom-
ing one of the western world's more influential literary figures.
Journalist, poet and critic, Poe is perhaps best known for his short
stories, many of which show a morbid interest in disaster, premature
burial and death. It is in his role as literary critic, however, that he is
most significant. For Poe, beauty is the major criterion in art and he
strongly rejects didacticism. He attracted such disciples as Wilde,
Swinburne and D.G. Rossetti in Victorian England, and the Symbolists
in France. The South African writer, Herman Charles Bosman, was
also greatly influenced by Poe's theory and practice.*

Annabel Lee

It was many and many a year ago,
   In a kingdom by the sea,
That a maiden there lived whom you may know
   By the name of Annabel Lee;
5 And this maiden she lived with no other thought
   Than to love and be loved by me.

She was a child and *I* was a child,
    In this kingdom by the sea,
But we loved with a love that was more than love—
10   I and my Annabel Lee—
With a love that the wingéd seraphs° of Heaven   *angels*
    Coveted her and me.

And this was the reason that, long ago,
    In this kingdom by the sea,
15   A wind blew out of a cloud by night
        Chilling my Annabel Lee;
So that her highborn kinsmen came
    And bore her away from me,
To shut her up in a sepulchre
20   In this kingdom by the sea.

The angels, not half so happy in Heaven,
    Went envying her and me:
Yes! that was the reason (as all men know,
    In this kingdom by the sea)
25   That the wind came out of the cloud, chilling
        And killing my Annabel Lee.

But our love it was stronger by far than the love
    Of those who were older than we—
    Of many far wiser than we—
30   And neither the angels in Heaven above
        Nor the demons down under the sea,
Can ever dissever° my soul from the soul   *separate*
    Of the beautiful Annabel Lee:

For the moon never beams without bringing me dreams
35   Of the beautiful Annabel Lee;
And the stars never rise but I see the bright eyes
        Of the beautiful Annabel Lee;
And so, all the night-tide, I lie down by the side
Of my darling, my darling, my life and my bride,
40   In her sepulchre there by the sea—
        In her tomb by the side of the sea.

Alfred, Lord Tennyson (1809 – 1892)

Immensely popular in his time, Tennyson is one of the most representative poets of Victorian England. He was the son of a rector of a country parish and was educated at home and at a local school. Shy and sensitive, he was sent to Cambridge in 1827 where he formed a deep friendship with the charismatic and brilliantly intellectual Arthur Henry Hallam. This was to be the most profound relationship of Tennyson's life. Hallam encouraged and guided the young poet's talent, stimulated his creativity through positive criticism and comforted him when his early volumes (1830 and 1832) received hostile reviews. It is hardly surprising that Tennyson was devastated when his friend died in 1833 of a cerebral haemorrhage. In attempting to rise above his grief, Tennyson began what is often regarded as one of the greatest elegies in English, In Memoriam A.H.H. *After seventeen years' work on this collection of 131 interlinked poems,* In Memoriam A.H.H. *was published in 1850. Thereafter Tennyson married, was made poet laureate, and in 1884 accepted a barony. Some critics feel that his popularity was detrimental to his writing, as the bulk of his most important work was completed before 1850.*

Tennyson's work shows a mastery of imagery and rhythm, and skilfully explores the evocative quality of word sounds. For all his technical accomplishments in poetry, he sometimes wondered whether language could actually express the depth of human emotions such as his grief at Hallam's death (see poem 5). Such humility is reflected in the starkly simple and haunting seventh poem ("Dark house"). "Morte d'Arthur", another early work, reflects the Victorian revival of interest in the Arthurian legends, which Tennyson transformed into a powerful form of moral commentary. "Ulysses", written soon after Hallam's death, explores the need to go forward and brave the struggles of life.

The Eagle

He clasps the crag with crooked hands;
Close to the sun in lonely lands,
Ringed with the azure world, he stands.

The wrinkled sea beneath him crawls;
5   He watches from his mountain walls,
And like a thunderbolt he falls.

IN MEMORIAM A. H. H. *(Poems 5; 7; 11; 106; 128)*

I sometimes hold it half a sin
    To put in words the grief I feel;
    For words, like nature, half reveal
And half conceal the soul within.

5   But, for the unquiet heart and brain,
    A use in measured language lies;
    The sad mechanic exercise,
Like dull narcotics, numbing pain.

In words, like weeds, I'll wrap me o'er,
10   Like coarsest clothes against the cold;
    But that large grief which these enfold
Is given in outline and no more.

    *   *   *

Dark house, by which once more I stand
    Here in the long unlovely street,
15   Doors, where my heart was used to beat
So quickly, waiting for a hand,

A hand that can be clasped no more—
    Behold me, for I cannot sleep,
    And like a guilty thing I creep
20 At earliest morning to the door.

He is not here; but far away
    The noise of life begins again
    And ghastly thro' the drizzling rain
On the bald street breaks the blank day.

    *   *   *

25 Calm is the morn without a sound,
    Calm as to suit a calmer grief,
    And only through the faded leaf
The chestnut pattering to the ground:

Calm and deep peace on this high wold,
30   And on these dews that drench the furze,
    And all the silvery gossamers
That twinkle into green and gold:

Calm and still light on yon great plain
    That sweeps with all its autumn bowers,
35   And crowded farms and lessening towers,
To mingle with the bounding main:

Calm and deep peace in this wide air,
    These leaves that redden to the fall;
    And in my heart, if calm at all,
40 If any calm, a calm despair:

Calm on the seas, and silver sleep,
    And waves that sway themselves in rest,
    And dead calm in that noble breast
Which heaves but with the heaving deep.

        *   *   *

45 Ring out, wild bells, to the wild sky,
    The flying cloud, the frosty light:
    The year is dying in the night;
Ring out, wild bells, and let him die.

Ring out the old, ring in the new,
50   Ring, happy bells, across the snow:
    The year is going, let him go;
Ring out the false, ring in the true.

Ring out the grief that saps the mind,
    For those that here we see no more;
55   Ring out the feud of rich and poor,
Ring in redress to all mankind.

Ring out a slowly dying cause,
    And ancient forms of party strife;
    Ring in the nobler modes of life,
60 With sweeter manners, purer laws.

Ring out the want, the care, the sin,
    The faithless coldness of the times;
    Ring out, ring out my mournful rhymes,
But ring the fuller minstrel in.

65 Ring out false pride in place and blood,
    The civic slander and the spite;
    Ring in the love of truth and right,
Ring in the common love of good.

Ring out old shapes of foul disease;
70   Ring out the narrowing lust of gold;
    Ring out the thousand wars of old,
Ring in the thousand years of peace.

Ring in the valiant man and free,
    The larger heart, the kindlier hand;
75   Ring out the darkness of the land,
Ring in the Christ that is to be.

      *   *   *

The love that rose on stronger wings,
    Unpalsied when he met with death,
    Is comrade of the lesser faith
80 That sees the course of human things.

No doubt vast eddies in the flood
    Of onward time shall yet be made,
    And throned races may degrade;
Yet O ye mysteries of good,

85 Wild hours that fly with hope and fear,
    If all your office had to do
    With old results that look like new;
If this were all your mission here,

To draw, to sheathe a useless sword,
90   To fool the crowd with glorious lies,
    To cleave a creed in sects and cries,
To change the bearing of a word,

To shift an arbitrary power,
    To cramp the student at his desk,
95   To make old bareness picturesque
And tuft with grass a feudal tower;

Why then my scorn might well descend
    On you and yours. I see in part
    That all, as in some piece of art,
100 Is toil co-operant to an end.

Morte d'Arthur *(extract, lines 1–51)*[1]

So all day long the noise of battle rolled
Among the mountains by the winter sea;
Until King Arthur's table, man by man,
Had fallen in Lyonnesse[2] about their Lord,
5 King Arthur: then, because his wound was deep,
The bold Sir Bedivere uplifted him,
Sir Bedivere, the last of all his knights,
And bore him to a chapel nigh the field,
A broken chancel with a broken cross,
10 That stood on a dark strait of barren land.
On one side lay the ocean, and on one
Lay a great water, and the moon was full.

Then spake King Arthur to Sir Bedivere:
"The sequel of today unsolders all
15 The goodliest fellowship of famous knights
Whereof this world holds record. Such a sleep
They sleep—the men I loved. I think that we
Shall never more, at any future time,
Delight our souls with talk of knightly deeds,
20 Walking about the gardens and the halls
Of Camelot,[3] as in the days that were.
I perish by this people which I made,—
Though Merlin[4] sware° that I should come again   *swore*
To rule once more—but let what will be, be,
25 I am so deeply smitten through the helm
That without help I cannot last till morn.
Thou therefore take my brand° Excalibur,   *sword*
Which was my pride: for thou rememberest how
In those old days, one summer noon, an arm
30 Rose up from out the bosom of the lake,
Clothed in white samite, mystic, wonderful,
Holding the sword—and how I rowed across
And took it, and have worn it, like a king:
And, wheresoever I am sung or told
35 In aftertime, this also shall be known:
But now delay not: take Excalibur,
And fling him far into the middle mere:°   *lake*
Watch what thou seest, and lightly° bring me word."   *swiftly*

---

1 *The death of King Arthur, legendary ruler of*
Britain and creator of the knightly
fellowship of the Round Table.
2 *A mythical country supposedly situated off*
the coast of Cornwall.
3 *The seat of King Arthur's court.*
4 *Magician who guided the destiny of Arthur.*

To him replied the bold Sir Bedivere:
40 "It is not meet, Sir King, to leave thee thus,
Aidless, alone, and smitten through the helm.
A little thing may harm a wounded man.
Yet I thy hest° will all perform at full,   command
Watch what I see, and lightly bring thee word."

45 So saying, from the ruined shrine he stepped
And in the moon athwart the place of tombs,
Where lay the mighty bones of ancient men,
Old knights, and over them the sea-wind sang
Shrill, chill, with flakes of foam. He, stepping down
50 By zig-zag paths, and juts of pointed rock,
Came on the shining levels of the lake.

Ulysses[5]

It little profits that an idle king,
By this still hearth, among these barren crags,
Matched with an aged wife, I mete and dole
Unequal laws unto a savage race,
5 That hoard, and sleep, and feed, and know not me.
I cannot rest from travel: I will drink
Life to the lees: all times I have enjoyed
Greatly, have suffered greatly, both with those
That loved me, and alone; on shore, and when
10 Through scudding drifts the rainy Hyades[6]
Vexed the dim sea: I am become a name;
For always roaming with a hungry heart
Much have I seen and known; cities of men
And manners, climates, councils, governments,
15 Myself not least, but honoured of them all;
And drunk delight of battle with my peers,
Far on the ringing plains of windy Troy.[7]

5 Roman name for the Greek general
Odysseus, who took part in the siege of
Troy (as told in Homer's Iliad) and whose
voyages and adventures in returning home
form the substance of Homer's Odyssey.
Aeneas features as the hero of Virgil's epic
poem, which combines many of the episodes
related in the two Homeric epics.
6 Nymphs who were nurses of the infant
Bacchus. For their care, they were rewarded
by being placed in the heavens as a cluster
of stars. Their rising at the same time as the
sun was thought to portend rainy weather.
7 Located in Asia Minor, scene of the Trojan
War caused by the abduction of Helen by
Paris. Associated with Trojan heroes such as
Hector, Greek heroes such as Achilles, and
generals such as Agamemnon and Ulysses
(the Greek Odysseus).

I am part of all that I have met;
Yet all experience is an arch wherethrough
20 Gleams that untravelled world, whose margin fades
For ever and for ever when I move.
How dull it is to pause, to make an end,
To rust unburnished, not to shine in use!
As tho' to breathe were life. Life piled on life
25 Were all too little, and of one to me
Little remains: but every hour is saved
From that eternal silence, something more,
A bringer of new things; and vile it were
For some three suns to store and hoard myself,
30 And this grey spirit yearning in desire
To follow knowledge like a sinking star,
Beyond the utmost bound of human thought.
    This is my son, mine own Telemachus,
To whom I leave the sceptre and the isle—
35 Well-loved of me, discerning to fulfil
This labour, by slow prudence to make mild
A rugged people, and through soft degrees
Subdue them to the useful and the good.
Most blameless is he, centred in the sphere
40 Of common duties, decent not to fail
In offices of tenderness, and pay
Meet° adoration to my household gods,   *appropriate*
When I am gone. He works his work, I mine.
    There lies the port; the vessel puffs her sail:
45 There gloom the dark broad seas. My mariners,
Souls that have toiled, and wrought, and thought with me—
That ever with a frolic welcome took
The thunder and the sunshine, and opposed
Free hearts, free foreheads—you and I are old;
50 Old age hath yet his honour and his toil;
Death closes all: but something ere the end,
Some work of noble note, may yet be done,
Not unbecoming men that strove with gods.[8]
The lights begin to twinkle from the rocks:
55 The long day wanes: the slow moon climbs: the deep
Moans round with many voices. Come, my friends,
'Tis not too late to seek a newer world.
Push off, and sitting well in order smite
The sounding furrows; for my purpose holds
60 To sail beyond the sunset, and the baths
Of all the western stars, until I die.

8 *As described by Homer in* The Iliad. *(The*   *the Trojan War.)*
   gods took sides and intervened actively in

It may be that the gulfs will wash us down:
It may be we shall touch the Happy Isles,⁹
And see the great Achilles,¹ whom we knew.
65 Though much is taken, much abides; and though
We are not now that strength which in old days
Moved earth and heaven; that which we are, we are;
One equal temper of heroic hearts,
Made weak by time and fate, but strong in will
70 To strive, to seek, to find, and not to yield.

9 *Islands of the Blessed. In Homer, not part of
the realms of the dead (Hades), but situated
in the far west on the banks of Oceanus, a
land of pure happiness reserved for heroes
who were transported there alive and*
endowed with immortality.
1 *Hero made invulnerable except for one of
his heels (hence "Achilles heel"). He was one
of the bravest and most handsome of the
Greeks besieging Troy, where he was killed.*

Robert Browning (1812 – 1889)

Robert Browning was the son of a clerk of the Bank of England. His father was a keen book-lover who amassed a library which fed the poet's lively imagination. Much of his life-history is familiar because the details of his clandestine relationship with Elizabeth Barrett and their elopement to Italy have become well known. Although Browning was reputed to be far more fond of Italy than of England, after his death in Venice in 1889, his body was brought back to the land of his birth, and he was buried in the poets' corner of Westminster Abbey.

Browning's reputation for "oddness", as the novelist Henry James termed it, stems largely from those of his poems whose sense is obscure and difficult, and in which he experimented with intricate form and expression. It can be argued, however, that Browning's fame is more appropriately ensured by his development of the dramatic monologue, of which "My Last Duchess" is a notable example. While he was by no means the only poet to use this form, he is certainly the most noteworthy. Briefly stated, the dramatic monologue is a device whereby the poet invents a character (or chooses one from history) to provide the voice and opinions represented in the text. Browning's particular contribution to the dramatic monologue was his ability to create a clear distinction between the poet and the speaker, a distinction which frequently causes an ironic light to be shed on the speaker—as is the case in "My Last Duchess". Here, the speaker, a manipulator par excellence, is in turn manipulated by the poet to reveal things about himself that he would prefer to keep concealed.

My Last Duchess

Ferrara

That's my last Duchess painted on the wall,
Looking as if she were alive. I call
That piece a wonder, now: Frà Pandolf's[1] hands
Worked busily a day, and there she stands.
5 Will 't please you sit and look at her? I said
"Frà Pandolf" by design, for never read
Strangers like you that pictured countenance,
The depth and passion of its earnest glance,

---

1 *Like Claus of Innsbruck (see line 56), a fictitious character (Pandolfi was a common name). In making Pandolf a friar, Browning*

possibly meant to preclude the implication of an affair between the artist and the Duchess.

But to myself they turned (since none puts by
10 The curtain I have drawn for you, but I)
And seemed as they would ask me, if they durst,
How such a glance came there; so, not the first
Are you to turn and ask thus. Sir, 'twas not
Her husband's presence only, called that spot
15 Of joy into the Duchess' cheek: perhaps
Frà Pandolf chanced to say, "Her mantle laps
Over my lady's wrist too much," or "Paint
Must never hope to reproduce the faint
Half-flush that dies along her throat:" such stuff
20 Was courtesy, she thought, and cause enough
For calling up that spot of joy. She had
A heart—how shall I say?—too soon made glad,
Too easily impressed; she liked whate'er
She looked on, and her looks went everywhere.
25 Sir, 'twas all one! My favour at her breast,
The dropping of the daylight in the west,
The bough of cherries some officious fool
Broke in the orchard for her, the white mule
She rode with round the terrace—all and each
30 Would draw from her alike the approving speech,
Or blush, at least. She thanked men,—good! but thanked
Somehow—I know not how—as if she ranked
My gift of a nine-hundred-years-old name
With anybody's gift. Who'd stoop to blame
35 This sort of trifling? Even had you skill
In speech—(which I have not)—to make your will
Quite clear to such an one, and say, "Just this
Or that in you disgusts me; here you miss,
Or there exceed the mark"—and if she let
40 Herself be lessoned so, nor plainly set
Her wits to yours, forsooth, and made excuse,
—E'en then would be some stooping; and I choose
Never to stoop. Oh sir, she smiled, no doubt,
Whene'er I passed her; but who passed without
45 Much the same smile? This grew; I gave commands;
Then all smiles stopped together. There she stands
As if alive. Will 't please you rise? We'll meet
The company below, then. I repeat,
The Count your master's known munificence
50 Is ample warrant that no just pretence

money as part of marriage settlement.

Of mine for <u>dowry</u> will be disallowed;
Though his fair daughter's self, as I <u>avowed</u>
At starting, is my object. Nay, we'll go
Together down, sir. Notice <u>Neptune</u>,[2] though, *god of the sea*
55   Taming a sea-horse, thought a rarity,
Which Claus of Innsbruck cast in bronze for me!

Should only be happy because of him.

→ *outraged: she should be grateful that he gave
her his aristocratic name in marriage and
behave accordingly, yet she is made equally
happy by other events / people like riding a
white mule!*

✓ *The word stoop - lower yourself to her
level - sees himself higher, more respectable
more important than him here. She should
have had the wits to see what she was
doing wrong; approached him. - he is the "hero"
His dignity would not permit him to approach
his lesser - she owed him.*

2 *The Roman name for the Greek god
Poseidon, the god of the sea.*

Emily Brontë (1814 – 1848)

*The Brontë sisters, Charlotte, Emily and Anne, and their brother
Branwell, lived with their father in the parsonage at Haworth,
Yorkshire. Their story, like that of Elizabeth Barrett Browning, has
become mythologized, owing to its qualities of strangeness and isola-
tion. All three sisters wrote fiction and poetry, but, of the three,
Emily—the author of the novel* Wuthering Heights—*is indisputably the
greatest poet. As a person, she was extremely antisocial and disliked
strangers, withdrawing completely if any were present. She could not
bear to leave her home, so integral to her existence were the bleak
moors and the gloomy parsonage. As children, Emily and her sisters
invented mythical worlds called Gondal and Angria and these fantasy
kingdoms later served as sources of poetic inspiration. Gondal, the
mythical land of anarchy, politics and sexual exploits, largely informs
Brontë's poetic thought. Add to this a love of solitude and introspec-
tion, and the reader has some major keys to her themes. She presents
the outside world as a threat to the integrity of solitude, and misery
seems to be an inseparable part of her vision. But, as she expresses in
"Remembrance", control must be exercised in the face of whatever fate
befalls one.*

Remembrance

Cold in the earth, and the deep snow piled above thee!
Far, far removed, cold in the dreary grave!
Have I forgot, my Only Love, to love thee,
Severed at last by Time's all-wearing wave?

5   Now, when alone, do my thoughts no longer hover
Over the mountains on Angora's[1] shore;
Resting their wings where heath and fern-leaves cover
That noble heart for ever, ever more?

Cold in the earth, and fifteen wild Decembers
10 From those brown hills have melted into spring;
Faithful indeed is the spirit that remembers
After such years of change and suffering!

---

1 *Earlier name of Ankara, Turkey, situated in
the vicinity of the confluence of the Çubuk*
*and Ankara rivers. Angora was so called
because of the goats of the region.*

Sweet Love of youth, forgive if I forget thee
While the World's tide is bearing me along:
15 Sterner desires and darker hopes beset me,
Hopes which obscure but cannot do thee wrong.

No other Sun has lightened up my heaven;
No other Star has ever shone for me:
All my life's bliss from thy dear life was given—
20 All my life's bliss is in the grave with thee.

But when the days of golden dreams had perished
And even Despair was powerless to destroy,
Then did I learn how existence could be cherished,
Strengthened and fed without the aid of joy;

25 Then did I check the tears of useless passion,
Weaned my young soul from yearning after thine;
Sternly denied its burning wish to hasten
Down to that tomb already more than mine!

And even yet, I dare not let it languish,
30 Dare not indulge in Memory's rapturous pain;
Once drinking deep of that divinest anguish,
How could I seek the empty world again?

Walt Whitman (1819 – 1892)

Walt Whitman was born in Huntingdon, a small town on Long Island, New York, but grew up in Brooklyn where he worked from his mid-teens as an office boy, printer, and journalist. From 1846 he edited the Brooklyn Eagle, which he made a mouthpiece for the anti-slavery movement. In 1848, after a disagreement with the proprietors of the paper, he resigned and travelled to New Orleans, before returning to New York through the mid-West. During the next seven years he read widely, particularly the works of Homer and Shakespeare, as well as the Bible.

In 1855, he published twelve poems under the title Leaves of Grass. *His intention with this collection was to place "a Person, a human being (myself in the latter half of the nineteenth century in America) freely, fully and truly on record". In the years that followed he added numerous poems to the subsequent edition. The themes of these poems are social, political and moral; and he treats topics such as beauty, death, war and sex in frank and natural language. His poetry was denounced as immoral and its publication cost him his clerkship in the US Government. Today he is celebrated as the first great poet whose work is distinctly American. Whitman died after a long period of illness in Camden, New Jersey.*

Sparkles from the Wheel

Where the city's ceaseless crowd moves on the livelong day,
Withdrawn I join a group of children watching, I pause aside with them.

By the curb toward the edge of the flagging,
A knife-grinder works at his wheel sharpening a great knife,
5 Bending over he carefully holds it to the stone, by foot and knee,
With measured tread he turns rapidly, as he presses with light but firm hand,
Forth issue then in copious golden jets,
Sparkles from the wheel.

The scene and all its belongings, how they seize and affect me,
10 The sad sharp-chinned old man with worn clothes and broad shoulder-band of leather,
Myself effusing and fluid, a phantom curiously floating, now here absorbed and arrested,
The group (an unminded point set in a vast surrounding),
The attentive, quiet children, the loud, proud, restive base of the streets,
The low hoarse purr of the whirling stone, the light–pressed blade,
15 Diffusing, dropping, sideways-darting, in tiny showers of gold,
Sparkles from the wheel.

"A sight in camp in the daybreak grey and dim"

A sight in camp in the daybreak grey and dim,
As from my tent I emerge so early sleepless,
As slow I walk in the cool fresh air the path near by the hospital tent,
Three forms I see on stretchers lying, brought out there untended lying,
5 Over each the blanket spread, ample brownish woollen blanket,
Grey and heavy blanket, folding, covering all.

Curious I halt and silent stand,
Then with light fingers I from the face of the nearest the first just lift the
    blanket;
Who are you elderly man so gaunt and grim with well-greyed hair, and flesh
    all sunken about the eyes?
10 Who are you my dear comrade?
Then to the second I step—and who are you my child and darling?
Who are you sweet boy with cheeks yet blooming?

Then to the third—a face nor child nor old, very calm, as of beautiful
    yellow-white ivory:
Young man I think I know you—I think this face is the face of the Christ
    himself,
15 Dead and divine and brother of all, and here again he lies.

"When I heard the learn'd astronomer"

When I heard the learn'd astronomer,
When the proofs, the figures, were ranged in columns before me,
When I was shown the charts and diagrams, to add, divide, and measure them,
When I sitting heard the astronomer where he lectured with much applause in
    the lecture-room,
5 How soon unaccountable I became tired and sick,
Till rising and gliding out I wandered off by myself,
In the mystical moist night air, and from time to time,
Looked up in perfect silence at the stars.

Matthew Arnold (1822 – 1888)

*Son of Thomas Arnold, who was headmaster of Rugby and a clergy-
man, Matthew Arnold served as professor of poetry at Oxford
University from 1857 to 1867. He was also one of the foremost poets
and critics of his time. The decline of religious faith and the accompa-
nying moral malaise that characterizes Victorian times is examined in
"Dover Beach" which, with its elegiac "note of sadness", highlights
both Arnold's regret concerning the diminishing "sea of Faith" and his
melancholy appraisal of the frailty of love. In his critical work, The
Study of Poetry, Arnold sums up his belief that it is "in poetry, as a
criticism of life . . . that the spirit of our race will find . . . as time goes
on and as other helps fail, its consolation and stay".*

Dover Beach[1]

The sea is calm to-night.
The tide is full, the moon lies fair
Upon the straits;—on the French coast the light
Gleams and is gone; the cliffs of England stand,
5   Glimmering and vast, out in the tranquil bay.
Come to the window, sweet is the night-air!
Only, from the long line of spray
Where the sea meets the moon-blanch'd land,
Listen! you hear the grating roar
10   Of pebbles which the waves draw back, and fling,
At their return, up the high strand,
Begin, and cease, and then again begin,
With tremulous cadence slow, and bring
The eternal note of sadness in.

15   Sophocles[2] long ago
Heard it on the Aegean,[3] and it brought
Into his mind the turbid ebb and flow
Of human misery; we
Find also in the sound a thought,
20   Hearing it by this distant northern sea.

---

1 *Dover is an English port on the Channel
coast, closest to France. The white cliffs on
the shore are a famous landmark.*
2 *Athenian tragedian and dramatist, author of*
plays such as Antigone *and* Oedipus.
3 *The part of the Mediterranean Sea on the*
eastern shores of Greece.

The Sea of Faith
Was once, too, at the full, and round earth's shore
Lay like the folds of a bright girdle furled.
But now I only hear
25 Its melancholy, long, withdrawing roar,
Retreating, to the breath
Of the night-wind, down the vast edges drear
And naked shingles of the world.

Ah, love let us be true
30 To one another! for the world, which seems
To lie before us like a land of dreams,
So various, so beautiful, so new,
Hath really neither joy, nor love, nor light,
Nor certitude, nor peace, nor help for pain;
35 And we are here as on a darkling plain
Swept with confused alarms of struggle and flight,
Where ignorant armies clash by night.

Emily Dickinson (1830 – 1886)

Like Anne Bradstreet, Emily Elizabeth Dickinson was reared in the Puritan tradition. She lived all her life in Amherst, Massachusetts, did not marry, and never left the house where she had grown up. For no apparent reason, she gradually withdrew from society, refusing to attend the First Baptist Church with which her family had always been closely associated, narrowing down her circle of acquaintances to a few dear and very select relatives and friends, and writing what amounted to a poem a day—1 775 in all. She was not a recluse in the usual sense of the word; she certainly had friendships of varying intensity with a few people, but realized that to marry would mean death to her valued individuality.

Dickinson was as selective in her reading as she was in her acquaintances. She seems to have decided that depth was more valuable than variety, so preferred to immerse herself in the work of only a few authors such as Shakespeare, Keats, Tennyson and the Brontës. Her own poems are characterized by intense experiences, thoughts and feelings. They are unmistakably influenced by the Baptist hymns she sang in her youth and often reflect the same form. They cover a vast range of concerns including nature, love, death and immortality. Dickinson was certainly preoccupied with death, as some of the following poems show, but she was usually unorthodox in her treatment of the topic. After her death, her poems were found lovingly sewn up in groups known as fascicles. Only about seven of the poems were published (anonymously) during her lifetime.

"After great pain, a formal feeling comes"

After great pain, a formal feeling comes—
The nerves sit ceremonious, like tombs—
The stiff heart questions was it He, that bore,
And yesterday, or centuries before?

5 The feet, mechanical, go round—
Of ground, or air, or ought—
A wooden way
Regardless grown,
A Quartz contentment, like a stone—

10 This is the hour of lead—
Remembered, if outlived,
As freezing persons, recollect the snow—
First—chill—then stupor—then the letting go—

"As imperceptibly as grief"

As imperceptibly as grief
The summer lapsed away,—
Too imperceptible at last
To seem like perfidy—
5 A quietness distilled,
As twilight long begun,
Or nature, spending with herself
Sequestered afternoon—
The dusk drew earlier in—
10 The morning foreign shone,—
A courteous, yet harrowing grace,
As guest that would be gone—
And thus, without a wing,
Or service of a keel,
15 Our summer made her light escape
Into the beautiful.

"I felt a funeral, in my brain"

I felt a funeral, in my brain,
And mourners to and fro
Kept treading—treading—till it seemed
That sense was breaking through—
5

And when they all were seated,
A service, like a drum—
Kept beating—beating—till I thought
My mind was going numb—

10 And then I heard them lift a box
And creak across my soul
With those same boots of lead, again,
Then space—began to toll,

As all the heavens were a bell,
15 And being, but an ear,
And I, and silence, some strange race
Wrecked, solitary, here—

And then a plank in reason, broke,
And I dropped down, and down—
20 And hit a world, at every plunge,
And finished knowing—then—

"Because I could not stop for Death"

Because I could not stop for Death—
He kindly stopped for me—
The carriage held but just ourselves—
And Immortality.

5 We slowly drove—he knew no haste,
And I had put away
My labour and my leisure too,
For his civility—

We passed the school where children strove
10 At recess—in a ring—
We passed the fields of gazing grain—
We passed the setting sun—

Or rather—he passed us—
The dews drew quivering and chill—
15 For only gossamer, my gown—
My tippet°—only tulle—   *shoulder cape*

We paused before a house that seemed
A swelling of the ground—
The roof was scarcely visible—
20 The cornice but a mound—

Since then—'tis centuries—but each
Feels shorter than the day
I first surmised the horses' heads
Were toward eternity—

"I heard a fly buzz—when I died"

I heard a fly buzz—when I died—
The stillness in the room
Was like the stillness in the air—
Between the heaves of storm—

5   The eyes around—had wrung them dry
And breaths were gathering firm
For that last onset—when the King
Be witnessed—in the room—

I willed my keepsakes—signed away
10 What portion of me be
Assignable—and then it was
There interposed a fly—

With blue—uncertain stumbling buzz—
Between the light—and me—
15 And then the windows failed—and then
I could not see to see—

Christina Rossetti (1830 – 1894)

*Christina Rossetti was born into the artistic Rossetti family two years
after her brother, Dante Gabriel. Her father was an Italian immigrant
who earned his living by teaching Italian. Like Elizabeth Barrett
Browning, Christina wrote poetry from an early age, but did not earn
public acclaim until the publication of the famous "Goblin Market" in
1862. Like her sister, Maria, who became a nun, Christina was mysti-
cally inclined, and much of her poetry is religious. While she was still
in her teens, Dante Gabriel, an artist and poet, and some of his friends,
including the artists Millais and Holman Hunt, founded the Pre-
Raphaelite Brotherhood. They proposed to return to the styles and
colours used by the artists prior to Raphael in their paintings, and
these artistic principles were evident also in their poetry. Christina was
popular as a model for some of these young artists and her face
appears in several of their now-famous paintings.*

*As a result of Victorian attitudes to women, Christina was unfor-
tunately marginalized by the Brotherhood, and they never really re-
cognized the worth of her work. Initially her poetry seems simple, and
the structure is close to that of hymnody, as is the case in Emily
Dickinson's poems. However, its subtleties are now being recognized.
There are sensual, even sexual, undertones in her writing, as is evident
in "Goblin Market". Towards the end of her life, Christina became
more reclusive and more religious, finally dying of cancer in 1894.*

Remember

Remember me when I am gone away,
    Gone far away into the silent land;
    When you can no more hold me by the hand,
Nor I half turn to go, yet turning stay.
5 Remember me when no more day by day
    You tell me of our future that you planned:
    Only remember me; you understand
It will be late to counsel then or pray.
Yet if you should forget me for a while
10   And afterwards remember, do not grieve:
    For if the darkness and corruption leave
A vestige of the thoughts that once I had,
Better by far you should forget and smile
    Than that you should remember and be sad.

Algernon Charles Swinburne (1837 – 1909)

Swinburne was born into a wealthy family of aristocratic origin. After completing his school education at Eton, he went to Oxford, where he came into contact with the poetic circle headed by Dante Gabriel Rossetti. Swinburne was much influenced by an approach to literature that stressed beauty as the supreme value. Simply put, poetic form was more important than its content or truth value: in fact, poetic form was the purpose of poetry. It is therefore not surprising that Swinburne devoted himself to a dazzling display of technical virtuosity in his pursuit of creating aesthetically impressive poetry.

Perhaps Swinburne's poetry should be seen against the background of the late-Victorian breakdown of moral certainties and conventional standards. Beauty seemed able to transcend doubts about society, human relationships and beliefs. However, some critics assert that in its pursuit of beauty, Swinburne's poetry often lacks genuine presence of thought and feeling. This is evident in the extract "Man" from his play Atalanta in Calydon, *which attempts to create the forms of Greek drama in human life. Here, because attention is given to beautiful diction, smoothly flowing rhythms and a delicate rhyme scheme, what emerges is well-written and technically superb poetry rather than any confrontation with the human condition.*

Man[1]

Before the beginning of years,
    There came to the making of man
Time, with a gift of tears;
    Grief, with a glass that ran;
5 Pleasure, with pain for leaven;
    Summer, with flowers that fell;
Remembrance fallen from heaven,
    And madness risen from hell;
Strength without hands to smite;
10   Love that endures for a breath;
Night, the shadow of light,
    And life, the shadow of death.
And the high gods took in hand
    Fire, and the falling of tears,
15 And a measure of sliding sand
    From under the feet of the years;

---

1 *From* Atalanta in Calydon.

And froth and drift of the sea;
And dust of the labouring earth;
And bodies of things to be
20   In the houses of death and of birth;
And wrought with weeping and laughter,
      And fashioned with loathing and love,
With life before and after
      And death beneath and above,
25 For a day and a night and a morrow,
      That his strength might endure for a span
With travail and heavy sorrow,
      The holy spirit of man.
From the winds of the north and the south
30   They gathered as unto strife;
They breathed upon his mouth,
      They filled his body with life;
Eyesight and speech they wrought
      For the veils of the soul therein,
35 A time for labour and thought,
      A time to serve and to sin;
They gave him light in his ways,
      And love, and a space for delight,
And beauty and length of days,
40   And night, and sleep in the night.
His speech is burning fire;
      With his lips he travaileth;
In his heart is a blind desire,
      In his eyes foreknowledge of death;
45 He weaves, and is clothed with derision;
      Sows, and he shall not reap;
His life is a watch or a vision
      Between a sleep and a sleep.

Thomas Hardy (1840 – 1928)

*Hardy was trained as an architect but was led by his imagination and
natural taste to become a poet and novelist. He wrote at the end of the
nineteenth century, a period known as the* fin de siécle *which, in litera-
ture, was often associated with a mood of pessimism or nostalgia. A
sense of tragedy is felt in his poems as well as his novels (such as* The
Mayor of Casterbridge *and* Tess of the D'Urbervilles*). In the poem
"Neutral Tones", nature seems muted and enervated; and a similar
emotional deadness is projected into nature in "The Darkling Thrush",
but this is transformed by the ecstatic singing of the bird, whose song
seems indicative of some hope that the desires of humankind will not
necessarily be crushed and disappointed.*

Neutral Tones

We stood by a pond that winter day,
And the sun was white, as though chidden° of God.   *rebuked*
And a few leaves lay on the starving sod;
    —They had fallen from an ash, and were grey.

5   Your eyes on me were as eyes that rove
Over tedious riddles of years ago;
And some words played between us to and fro
    On which lost the more by our love.

The smile on your mouth was the deadest thing
10   Alive enough to have strength to die;
And a grin of bitterness swept thereby
    Like an ominous bird a-wing . . .

Since then, keen lessons that love deceives,
And wrings with wrong, have shaped to me
15   Your face, and the God-cursed sun, and a tree,
    And a pond edged with greyish leaves.

The Darkling Thrush

I leant upon a coppice gate
    When frost was spectre-grey,
And winter's dregs made desolate
    The weakening eye of day.
5 The tangled bine-stems scored the sky
    Like strings of broken lyres,
And all mankind that haunted nigh
    Had sought their household fires.

The land's sharp features seemed to be
10   The century's corpse outleant,°   *stretched out*
His crypt the cloudy canopy,
    The wind his death-lament.
The ancient pulse of germ and birth
    Was shrunken hard and dry,
15 And every spirit upon earth
    Seemed fervourless as I.

At once a voice arose among
    The bleak twigs overhead
In a full-hearted evensong
20   Of joy illimited;
An aged thrush, frail, gaunt, and small,
    In blast-beruffled plume,
Had chosen thus to fling his soul
    Upon the growing gloom.

25 So little cause for carolings
    Of such ecstatic sound
Was written on terrestrial things
    Afar or nigh around,
That I could think there trembled through
30   His happy good-night air
Some blessed hope, whereof he knew
    And I was unaware.

Gerard Manley Hopkins (1844 – 1889)

*Gerard Manley Hopkins was born in Essex, the eldest son in a fairly
wealthy family, and gained a place at Balliol College, Oxford. Not only
was his academic performance brilliant, but he was already writing
poetry. Oxford was at this time alive with religious controversy. John
Henry Newman, the most powerful voice in Anglican Oxford, con-
verted to the Roman Catholic Church in 1845, to be followed over the
years by a steady stream of undergraduates. This included Hopkins,
who decided to join the Jesuit order as a priest.*

*On entering the Jesuit community, Hopkins burnt most of his
poems, and for many years wrote nothing. When he finally composed
The Wreck of the Deutschland—a major poem which commemorates
the drowning of a party of nuns—extraordinary new rhythms and
vocabulary were evident. One of his technical innovations was the use
of "sprung rhythm", which borrows from the rhythms of ordinary
speech rather than those of metrical regularity. (It consists of a certain
balance of accented stresses with any number of unstressed syllables in
between.) Hopkins also coined the word "inscape" to describe the
innate and sacred essence of created and natural things and attempted
to capture this in his poems.*

*His poetry was never published in his lifetime, but was fortunately
saved by his friend, Robert Bridges. Initially it was joyous poetry, cele-
brating his love of Christ, whom he saw revealed through nature.
However, as Hopkins became more depressed, his poems reflected his
sense of separation from God. This was worsened by his being sent to
Ireland, where he was bitterly unhappy and finally died of typhoid. His
work, innovative and powerful, is modern years ahead its time.*

Binsey Poplars[1]

Felled 1879

My aspens° dear, whose airy cages quelled, *poplar trees*
Quelled or quenched in leaves the leaping sun
All felled, felled, are all felled;
    Of a fresh and following folded rank
5   Not spared, not one
        That dandled a sandalled
     Shadow that swam or sank
On meadow and river and wind-wandering
    weed-winding bank.

1 *Binsey is a small Thames-side village in
Oxfordshire.*

10   O if we but knew what we do
           When we delve or hew—
           Hack and rack the growing green!
           Since country is so tender
           To touch, her being só slender,
15   That, like this sleek and seeing ball
           But a prick will make no eye at all.
           Where we, even where we mean
             To mend her we end her,
           When we hew or delve:
20 After-comers cannot guess the beauty been.
           Ten or twelve, only ten or twelve
           Strokes of havoc únselve[2]
             The sweet especial scene,
           Rural scene, a rural scene,
25   Sweet especial rural scene.

God's Grandeur

The world is charged with the grandeur of God.
    It will flame out, like shining from shook foil;
    It gathers to a greatness, like the ooze of oil
Crushed. Why do men then now not reck his rod?[3]
5 Generations have trod, have trod, have trod;
    And all is seared with trade; bleared, smeared with toil;
    And wears man's smudge and shares man's smell: the soil
Is bare now, nor can foot feel, being shod.

And for all this, nature is never spent;
10   There lives the dearest freshness deep down things;
And though the last lights off the black West went
    Oh, morning, at the brown brink eastward, springs—
Because the Holy Ghost over the bent
    World broods with warm breast and with ah! bright wings.

2 *Destroy the essential being of the scene.*
3 *Pay heed to. The word "rod", which* *suggests discipline, also recalls the "rood",* *or saving cross of Christ.*

Heaven-Haven

A nun takes the veil

I have desired to go
    Where springs not fail,
To fields where flies no sharp and sided hail
    And a few lilies blow.

5   And I have asked to be
    Where no storms come,
Where the green swell is in the havens dumb,
    And out of the swing of the sea.

Spring

Nothing is so beautiful as spring—
    When weeds, in wheels, shoot long and lovely and lush;
    Thrush's eggs look little low heavens, and thrush
Through the echoing timber does so rinse and wring
5   The ear, it strikes like lightnings to hear him sing;
    The glassy pear-tree leaves and blooms, they brush
    The descending blue; that blue is all in a rush
With richness; the racing lambs too have fair their fling.

What is all this juice and all this joy?
10   A strain of the earth's sweet being in the beginning
In Eden garden.—Have, get, before it cloy,
    Before it cloud, Christ, lord, and sour with sinning,
Innocent mind and Mayday[4] in girl and boy,
    Most, O Maid's child, thy choice and worthy the winning.

4 *The first day of May; a festival celebrating
the arrival of spring in the northern
hemisphere.*

The Windhover

To Christ our Lord

I caught this morning morning's minion,° king-   *favourite*
    dom of daylight's dauphin,⁵ dapple-dawn-drawn Falcon,
    in his riding
    Of the rolling level underneath him steady air, and striding
High there, how he rung upon the rein of a wimpling° wing   *rippling*
5   In his ecstasy! then off, off forth on swing,
    As a skate's heel sweeps smooth on a bow-bend: the hurl
    and gliding
    Rebuffed the big wind. My heart in hiding
Stirred for a bird,—the achieve of, the mastery of the thing!

    Brute beauty and valour and act, oh, air, pride, plume, here
10   Buckle! AND the fire that breaks from thee then, a billion
Times told lovelier, more dangerous, O my chevalier!°   *knight*

    No wonder of it: shéer plód makes plough down sillion°   *furrow*
Shine, and blue-bleak embers, ah my dear,
    Fall, gall themselves, and gash gold-vermilion.°   *brilliant red*

5 *Eldest son of the king of France, that is, the heir apparent.*

A.E. Housman (1859 – 1936)

Housman was born in Fockbury, England, and although he showed early promise as a writer, he became a classical scholar and taught Latin, first in London and then in Cambridge. During his lifetime, he published two volumes of poetry, A Shropshire Lad *and* Last Poems. *Further volumes were published posthumously by his brother, Laurence. Housman's poetry is inclined towards pessimism but he is also capable of lyrical work of great beauty. While this is manifest in "Loveliest of trees", this nostalgic lyric provides evidence of his inherent sombreness.*

"Loveliest of trees"[1]

Loveliest of trees, the cherry now
Is hung with bloom along the bough,
And stands about the woodland ride°   *road*
Wearing white for Eastertide.

5   Now, of my threescore years and ten,
Twenty will not come again,
And take from seventy springs a score,
It only leaves me fifty more.

And since to look at things in bloom
10   Fifty springs are little room,
About the woodlands I will go
To see the cherry hung with snow.

1 *From* A Shropshire Lad.

William Butler Yeats (1865 – 1939)

Yeats was born in Ireland of Protestant Irish parents. He developed an early interest in Irish nationalism at a time when the struggle for Irish independence from British rule was intensifying. The plays he wrote gave expression to that interest, treating subjects from Irish mythology and Irish history. His plays were a significant contribution to the development of a national Irish theatre, and when the Abbey Theatre in Dublin was opened in 1904, the first productions included two plays by Yeats, On Baile's Strand *and* Cathleen ni Houlihan.*

In his poetry, too, expression is given to his preoccupation with Irish nationalism, as well as to his interest in the occult and in the cyclical patterns of history and mythology. This can be seen in such volumes as Responsibilities, The Wild Swans at Coole *and* The Winding Stair and Other Poems. *"The Second Coming" presents the Christian era as a cycle in history, while "A Prayer for my Daughter" blends more general subjects with personal and intimate matters. "Leda and the Swan" considers the significance of the mythological background to the story of the Trojan wars.*

Yeats's achievement brought him considerable recognition in his later years, including a seat in the Irish Senate in 1922, and the Nobel Prize for Literature in 1923. Together with T.S. Eliot, he ranks as one of the foremost poets of the twentieth century.

A Prayer for my Daughter

Once more the storm is howling, and half hid
Under this cradle-hood and coverlid
My child sleeps on. There is no obstacle
But Gregory's wood and one bare hill
5 Whereby the haystack- and roof-levelling wind,
Bred on the Atlantic, can be stayed;
And for an hour I have walked and prayed
Because of the great gloom that is in my mind.

I have walked and prayed for this young child an hour
10 And heard the sea-wind scream upon the tower,
And under the arches of the bridge, and scream
In the elms above the flooded stream;
Imagining in excited reverie
That the future years had come,
15 Dancing to a frenzied drum,
Out of the murderous innocence of the sea.

May she be granted beauty and yet not
Beauty to make a stranger's eye distraught,
Or hers before a looking-glass, for such,
20 Being made beautiful overmuch,
Consider beauty a sufficient end,
Lose natural kindness and maybe
The heart-revealing intimacy
That chooses right, and never find a friend.

25 Helen[1] being chosen found life flat and dull
And later had much trouble from a fool,
While that great Queen,[2] that rose out of the spray,
Being fatherless could have her way
Yet chose a bandy-leggéd smith[3] for man.
30 It's certain that fine women eat
A crazy salad with their meat
Whereby the Horn of Plenty[4] is undone.

In courtesy I'd have her chiefly learned;
Hearts are not had as a gift but hearts are earned
35 By those that are not entirely beautiful;
Yet many, that have played the fool
For beauty's very self, has charm made wise,
And many a poor man that has roved,
Loved and thought himself beloved,
40 From a glad kindness cannot take his eyes.

May she become a flourishing hidden tree
That all her thoughts may like the linnet be,
And have no business but dispensing round
Their magnanimities of sound,
45 Nor but in merriment begin a chase,
Nor but in merriment a quarrel.
O may she live like some green laurel
Rooted in one dear perpetual place.

1 *Helen of Troy, whose beauty "launched a thousand ships".*
2 *Venus, goddess of love, born from the sea; the wife of Vulcan.*
3 *Vulcan, the lame god of fire.*
4 *A magical object, also known as a cornucopia, resembling a large goat's horn, overflowing with flowers, fruit and corn.*

My mind, because the minds that I have loved,
50 The sort of beauty that I have approved,
Prosper but little, has dried up of late,
Yet knows that to be choked with hate
May well be of all evil chances chief.
If there's no hatred in a mind
55 Assault and battery of the wind
Can never tear the linnet from the leaf.

An intellectual hatred is the worst,
So let her think opinions are accursed.
Have I not seen the loveliest woman born[5]
60 Out of the mouth of Plenty's horn,
Because of her opinionated mind
Barter that horn and every good
By quiet natures understood
For an old bellows full of angry wind?

65 Considering that, all hatred driven hence,
The soul recovers radical innocence
And learns at last that it is self-delighting,
Self-appeasing, self-affrighting,
And that its own sweet will is heaven's will;
70 She can, though every face should scowl
And every windy quarter howl
Or every bellows burst, be happy still.

And may her bridegroom bring her to a house
Where all's accustomed, ceremonious;
75 For arrogance and hatred are the wares
Peddled in the thoroughfares.
How but in custom and in ceremony
Are innocence and beauty born?
Ceremony's a name for the rich horn,
80 And custom for the spreading laurel tree.

5 *Maud Gonne, the unattained object of
Yeats's love for many years; for him at this
point the prototype of feminine beauty. Her*
*passionate devotion to the Irish nationalist
cause found a political outlet, while Yeats's
national feeling sought expression in his art.*

The Second Coming[6]

Turning and turning in the widening gyre[7]
The falcon cannot hear the falconer;
Things fall apart; the centre cannot hold;
Mere anarchy is loosed upon the world,
5   The blood-dimmed tide is loosed, and everywhere
The ceremony of innocence is drowned;
The best lack all conviction, while the worst
Are full of passionate intensity.

Surely some revelation is at hand;
10 Surely the Second Coming is at hand.
The Second Coming! Hardly are those words out
When a vast image out of *Spiritus Mundi*[8]
Troubles my sight: somewhere in sands of the desert
A shape with lion body and the head of a man,
15 A gaze blank and pitiless as the sun,
Is moving its slow thighs, while all about it
Reel shadows of the indignant desert birds.
The darkness drops again; but now I know
That twenty centuries of stony sleep
20 Were vexed to nightmare by a rocking cradle,
And what rough beast, its hour come round at last,
Slouches towards Bethlehem[9] to be born?

6 *These words are associated with the second coming of Christ, as anticipated by Christians.*
7 *The conical arc described by the falcon around the falconer; there is a sense of strain on the leash, so that the circumference is collapsing into the centre.*
8 *The universal soul, a storehouse of supernatural images; transcendental realm. Literally, "soul" or "spirit of the world".*
9 *The birthplace of Jesus.*

Leda and the Swan[1]

A sudden blow: the great wings beating still
Above the staggering girl, her thighs caressed
By the dark webs, her nape caught in his bill,
He holds her helpless breast upon his breast.

5 How can those terrified vague fingers push
The feathered glory from her loosening thighs?
And how can body, laid in that white rush,
But feel the strange heart beating where it lies?

A shudder in the loins engenders there
10 The broken wall, the burning roof and tower
And Agamemnon[2] dead.
                    Being so caught up,
So mastered by the brute blood of the air,
Did she put on his knowledge with his power
Before the indifferent beak could let her drop?

---

1 *In the myth to which Yeats alludes, the chief
Olympian god, Zeus, in the guise of a swan,
impregnates Leda, who ultimately gives birth
to the future Helen of Troy. Leda's infant
carries the seeds of the destruction of Troy,
and of Agamemnon.*

2 *King of Mycenae (a kingdom of classical
Greece), brother of Menelaus (husband of
Helen) and commander-in-chief of the Greek
forces in the Trojan War. Treacherously
murdered by his wife Clytemnestra on his
return from Troy.*

Robert Frost (1874 – 1963)

Frost studied at Harvard for two years, hoping to become a college teacher. Instead, he ran a farm in New Hampshire, supplementing his farming income by school-teaching. During his ten years of farming, he also wrote poetry, although his first work, A Boy's Will, *was published only in 1913. Frost won four Pulitzer Prizes for his poetry and was awarded several honorary degrees.*

"Stopping by Woods on a Snowy Evening" reflects Frost's comfortable intimacy with nature. His tone is characteristically meditative and reflective, as if he were communing as much with his surroundings as with the reader. "Out, out—", by contrast, suggests the sounds of the snarling, rattling "buzz saw" which initiates a farm-yard tragedy. This the poet sets out with compassionate understatement.

"Out, out—"

The buzz saw snarled and rattled in the yard
And made dust and dropped stove-length sticks of wood,
Sweet-scented stuff when the breeze drew across it.
And from there those that lifted eyes could count
5   Five mountain ranges one behind the other
Under the sunset far into Vermont.[1]
And the saw snarled and rattled, snarled and rattled,
As it ran light, or had to bear a load.
And nothing happened: day was all but done.
10 Call it a day, I wish they might have said
To please the boy by giving him the half hour
That a boy counts so much when saved from work.
His sister stood beside them in her apron
To tell them "Supper". At the word, the saw,
15 As if to prove saws knew what supper meant,
Leaped out at the boy's hand, or seemed to leap—
He must have given the hand. However it was,
Neither refused the meeting. But the hand!
The boy's first outcry was a rueful laugh,
20 As he swung toward them holding up the hand
Half in appeal, but half as if to keep
The life from spilling. Then the boy saw all—
Since he was old enough to know, big boy
Doing a man's work, though a child at heart—

---

1 *A state in New England, USA.*

25   He saw all spoiled. "Don't let him cut my hand off—
     The doctor, when he comes. Don't let him, sister!"
     So. But the hand was gone already.
     The doctor put him in the dark of ether.°   *anaesthetic*
     He lay and puffed his lips out with his breath.
30   And then—the watcher at his pulse took fright.
     No one believed. They listened at his heart.
     Little—less—nothing!—and that ended it.
     No more to build on there. And they, since they
     Were not the one dead, turned to their affairs.

Stopping by Woods on a Snowy Evening

Whose woods these are I think I know.
His house is in the village though;
He will not see me stopping here
To watch his woods fill up with snow.

5   My little horse must think it queer
    To stop without a farmhouse near
    Between the woods and frozen lake
    The darkest evening of the year.

He gives his harness bells a shake
10 To ask if there is some mistake.
    The only other sound's the sweep
    Of easy wind and downy flake.

The woods are lovely, dark and deep,
But I have promises to keep,
15 And miles to go before I sleep,
    And miles to go before I sleep.

F.C. Slater (1876 – 1958)

The son of parents of 1820-settler stock, Francis Carey Slater was born in Alice in the Eastern Cape, and spent his early life on a number of farms in the district. His close contact with and knowledge of the rural Xhosa people is reflected in poems such as "Lament for a Dead Cow". Slater initially pursued a banking career, which he relinquished in order to concentrate on literature. His many works include two volumes of short stories, The Sunburnt South *and* The Secret Veld, *as well as a novel called* The Shining River, *and an autobiography entitled* Settler's Heritage. *He also wrote several volumes of poetry among which* The Karoo and Other Poems *and* Dark Folk and Other Poems *are significant for both their indigenous and individual qualities. He was also responsible for compiling, in 1925,* The Centenary Book of South African Verse, *the first significant anthology of South African English poetry. Slater's contribution to South African literature was recognized by the University of South Africa in 1947, when he was awarded an honorary doctorate in literature.*

Lament for a Dead Cow

Chant by Xhosa family on the death of Wetu, their only cow

Siyalila, siyalila, inkomo yetu ifile![1]
Beautiful was Wetu as a blue shadow,
That nests on the grey rocks
About a sunbaked hilltop:
5   Her coat was black and shiny
Like an isipingo[2]-berry;
Her horns were as sharp as the horns of the new moon
That tosses aloft the evening star;
Her round eyes were as clear and soft
10 As a mountain-pool,
Where shadows dive from the high rocks.
No more will Wetu banish teasing flies
With her whistling tail;
No more will she face yapping curs
15 With lowered horns and bewildered eyes;
No more will her slow shadow
Comfort the sunburnt veld, and her sweet lowing
Delight the hills in the evening.

---

1 *We weep, we weep, our cow is dead!*   2 *Thorny shrub.*

The fountain that filled our calabashes
20 Has been drained by a thirsty sun;
The black cloud that brought us white rain
Has vanished—the sky is empty;
Our kraal is desolate;
Our calabashes are dry:
25 And we weep.

William Carlos Williams (1883 – 1963)

Williams graduated as MD from the University of Pennsylvania, served an internship in New York City, spent a graduate year in paediatrics in Germany, then set up a practice in Rutherford, New Jersey. His work as an obstetrician and paediatrician provided the material for his plays, while his novels were based on his wife's girlhood and her family. His critical work, In the American Grain, *with its emphasis on the emergence of a distinctive poetry from American speech and culture, was to influence several younger poets such as Robert Lowell and Allen Ginsburg.*

Williams's poetry displays a keen sensitivity to speech-rhythms and an artistic awareness of vivid focal points. In "The Red Wheelbarrow", the conversational opening line invites the reader to consider the placement of each object in a visual composition of contrasting colours and textures. In the strikingly evocative "This is just to say", the title line moves conversationally into the body of the poem, where the omission of punctuation leaves the meaning open-ended.

The Red Wheelbarrow

so much depends
upon

a red wheel
barrow

5 glazed with rain
water

beside the white
chickens.

This is Just to Say

I have eaten
the plums
that were in
the icebox

5   and which
you were probably
saving
for breakfast

Forgive me
they were delicious
so sweet
and so cold

D.H. Lawrence (1885 – 1930)

Born in Nottinghamshire to a poor family, Lawrence was a school-teacher until his contraction of tuberculosis compelled him to abandon the profession. Because of his illness he was excused from military service in the First World War and, finding the ethos of Britain uncongenial, he travelled widely. He visited Australia (his response to which is evoked in the novel, Kangaroo*), and also Mexico, Sicily, Sardinia, Italy and the USA. Lawrence wrote several novels that broke new ground, such as* The Rainbow, Women in Love *and* Lady Chatterley's Lover *(initially banned because of its sexual explicitness).*

As a poet, he is noted for the directness of his tone and views. In "Red Geranium and Godly Mignonette", he stresses the senses rather than the intellect, and provides a somewhat humorous view of God as creator.

Piano

Softly, in the dusk, a woman is singing to me;
Taking me back down the vista of years, till I see
A child sitting under the piano, in the boom of the tingling strings
And pressing the small, poised feet of a mother who smiles as she sings.

5   In spite of myself, the insidious mastery of song
Betrays me back, till the heart of me weeps to belong
To the old Sunday evenings at home, with winter outside
And hymns in the cosy parlour, the tinkling piano our guide.

So now it is vain for the singer to burst into clamour
10   With the great black piano appassionato.[1] The glamour
Of childish days is upon me, my manhood is cast
Down in the flood of remembrance, I weep like a child for the past.

---

1 *A musical term indicating impassioned feeling.*

Red Geranium and Godly Mignonette

Imagine that any mind ever *thought* a red geranium!
As if the redness of a red geranium could be anything but a sensual experience
and as if sensual experience could take place before there were any senses.
We know that even God could not imagine the redness of a red geranium
5   nor the smell of mignonette
when geraniums were not, and mignonette neither.
And even when they were, even God would have to have a nose
to smell at the mignonette.
You can't imagine the Holy Ghost sniffing at cherry-pie heliotrope.[1]
10   Or the Most High, during the coal age, cudgelling his mighty brains
even if he had any brains: straining his mighty mind
to think, among the moss and mud of lizards and mastodons
to think out, in the abstract, when all was twilit green and muddy:
"Now there shall be tum-tiddly-um[2], and tum-tiddly-um,
15   hey-presto! scarlet geranium!"
We know it couldn't be done.

But imagine, among the mud and the mastodons
God sighing and yearning with tremendous creative yearning, in that dark green
         mess
oh, for some other beauty, some other beauty
20   that blossomed at last, red geranium, and mignonette.

1 *A member of the borage family, having*   *flowers.*
   clusters of small, reddish-purple or white   2 *A word used by magicians in conjuring.*

Ezra Pound (1885 – 1972)

*Pound studied at the University of Pennsylvania and taught briefly in
Indiana before leaving for Europe in 1908, where his first volume of
poems was published. He later moved to London, where he lectured in
medieval Romance poetry for a short time, and established his consi-
derable literary reputation.*

*Pound was friend, enthusiastic reviewer and literary advisor to
many of the major literary figures of his time, including James Joyce,
T.S. Eliot, William Carlos Williams, W.B. Yeats, Marianne Moore,
Robert Frost and Ernest Hemingway. Pound has aptly been described
by T.S. Eliot as "more responsible for the twentieth century revolution
in poetry than any other individual". He founded the Imagist school of
poets, a movement away from the neo-Romanticism which flourished
in the early years of the century. Imagists advocated the use of free
rhythms, concrete images rather than modern abstractions, and con-
ciseness in both language and imagery. The usually short poems that
resulted are characterized by precision, simplicity and clarity of image,
and owe much to the Japanese haiku. One such example is "In a
Station of the Metro". Without rhyme or set rhythm, this poem
conveys in only three lines (including the title) the intensity of the
impression the poet receives in a Parisian underground station.*

In a Station of the Metro[1]

The apparition of these faces in the crowd;
Petals on a wet, black bough.

---

1 *The underground railway in Paris.*

Siegfried Sassoon (1886 – 1967)

*In a now famous statement protesting the continuation of the First
World War, Sassoon wrote: "I have seen and endured the sufferings of
the troops, and I can no longer be a party to prolong those sufferings
for ends which I believe to be evil and unjust ...". This statement might
well be seen as a fair reflection of the inspiration for most of his poetry.*

*Born in Kent in England, Sassoon enlisted for the war in 1914.
Wounded in 1917, he refused to return to the front, and cast his
Military Cross ribbon into the Mersey River in protest. Eventually he
did return to the army and was wounded again. He saw battle at its
most intense, including the horror and massive casualties of trench
warfare. This first-hand experience equipped him to write biting, often
satirical poetry as an eloquent and perceptive critic of war. Indeed,
some of his poems were refused publication as they were considered to
be detrimental to the enlistment campaign.*

*Sassoon's poem, "Attack", is typical of his work in that it
expresses his conviction about the injustice and futility of the war. He
writes clearly and directly of the horrors he perceives, and the reader is
made aware of his sympathy and concern for the doomed soldiers, and
of the deep sincerity of his final plea for mercy.*

Attack

At dawn the ridge emerges massed and dun
In the wild purple of the glowering sun,
Smouldering through spouts of drifting smoke that shroud
The menacing scarred slope; and, one by one,
5   Tanks creep and topple forward to the wire.
The barrage roars and lifts. Then, clumsily bowed
With bombs and guns and shovels and battle-gear,
Men jostle and climb to meet the bristling fire.
Lines of grey, muttering faces, masked with fear,
10 They leave their trenches, going over the top,
While time ticks blank and busy on their wrists,
And hope, with furtive eyes and grappling fists,
Flounders in mud. O Jesus, make it stop!

Marianne Moore (1887 – 1972)

Moore, a renowned American poet, was educated at Bryn Mawr and
Carlisle Commercial Colleges and went on to receive acclaim, fellow-
ships and no less than nine doctoral degrees in literature from various
universities. She was awarded the Pulitzer Prize for her Collected
Poems *in 1952. Her work is characterized by an urbane sophistication,*
a conversational tone, accuracy of observation, varied subject matter
and strong visual effects. Her much-acclaimed "Poetry" exemplifies
her conversational style which she herself described as follows: "every-
thing comes in straight order, just as if I had not thought it before, and
were talking to you. Unrestrained and natural".

Poetry

I, too, dislike it: there are things that are important beyond all this fiddle.
    Reading it, however, with a perfect contempt for it, one discovers in
    it after all, a place for the genuine.
        Hands that can grasp, eyes
5   that can dilate, hair that can rise
            if it must, these things are important not because a

high-sounding interpretation can be put upon them but because they are
    useful. When they become so derivative as to become unintelligible,
    the same thing may be said for all of us, that we
10   do not admire what
        we cannot understand: the bat
            holding on upside down or in quest of something to

eat, elephants pushing, a wild horse taking a roll, a tireless wolf under
    a tree, the immovable critic twitching his skin like a horse that feels a flea,
    the base-
15   ball fan, the statistician—
        nor is it valid
            to discriminate against "business documents and

school-books"; all these phenomena are important. One must make a distinction
   however: when dragged into prominence by half poets, the result is not
   poetry,
20   nor till the poets among us can be
             "literalists of
             the imagination"—above
                 insolence and triviality and can present

   for inspection, imaginary gardens with real toads in them, shall we have
25   it. In the meantime, if you demand on the one hand,
         the raw material of poetry in
             all its rawness and
             that which is on the other hand
                 genuine, then you are interested in poetry.

T.S. Eliot (1888 – 1965)

Eliot studied philosophy at Harvard. He married in England, and worked there as a teacher, as a clerk for Lloyd's Bank, and as an editor (eventually, a director) of the publishing firm, Faber and Faber. The Wasteland, which registers the profound loss of belief in traditional religion and society in Europe after the First World War, established Eliot as one of the foremost writers of a new kind of imagist poetry. In similar vein, "The Hollow Men" evokes the spiritual vacuity of human beings devoid of any guiding faith in God or love. "Preludes" evokes the routine that shapes the lives of city-dwellers and this poem also suggests the effects, on the soul, of complacency and despair. In "Journey of the Magi", the Magi who travel to pay tribute to the infant Jesus are, by contrast, capable of commitment and self-sacrifice.

Eliot identifies himself with those who consciously engage themselves spiritually, as opposed to those who merely exist, sunk in thoughtless hedonism. He embraces the more traditional elements of the Anglican Church, insisting on the need for hierarchy and an elite in society.

To make the images in his poetry as evocative as possible, Eliot employs a language derived from an essentially twentieth-century urban existence. It is in his choice of language and theme, which expresses the boredom, horror and ugliness beneath appearances, that Eliot has been most influential. He was awarded the Nobel Prize for Literature in 1948.

The Hollow Men[1]

A penny for the Old Guy[2]

I

We are the hollow men
We are the stuffed men
Leaning together
Headpiece filled with straw. Alas!
5 Our dried voices, when
We whisper together
Are quiet and meaningless
As wind in dry grass
Or rats' feet over broken glass
10 In our dry cellar

Shape without form, shade without colour,
Paralysed force, gesture without motion;

Those who have crossed
With direct eyes, to death's other Kingdom
15 Remember us—if at all—not as lost
Violent souls, but only
As the hollow men
The stuffed men.

II

Eyes I dare not meet in dreams
20 In death's dream kingdom
These do not appear:
There, the eyes are
Sunlight on a broken column
There, is a tree swinging
25 And voices are
In the wind's singing
More distant and more solemn
Than a fading star.

1 *There are three possible sources from which this title is derived:* The Hollow Land *by William Morris;* The Broken Men *by Rudyard Kipling; Shakespeare's* Julius Caesar *(IV, ii): "There are no tricks in plain and simple faith; / But hollow men, like horses hot at hand, / Make gallant show and promise of their mettle."*

2 *The phrase originates from a game of make-believe in which children carried about a stuffed effigy of Guy Fawkes and begged for pennies with which to buy fireworks on November 5 each year.*

Let me be no nearer
30 In death's dream kingdom
Let me also wear
Such deliberate disguises
Rat's coat, crowskin, crossed staves
In a field
35 Behaving as the wind behaves
No nearer—
Not that final meeting
In the twilight kingdom

III

This is the dead land
40 This is cactus land
Here the stone images
Are raised, here they receive
The supplication of a dead man's hand
Under the twinkle of a fading star.

45 Is it like this
In death's other kingdom
Waking alone
At the hour when we are
Trembling with tenderness
50 Lips that would kiss
Form prayers to broken stone.

The eyes are not here
There are no eyes here
In this valley of dying stars
55 In this hollow valley
This broken jaw of our lost kingdoms

In this last of meeting places
We grope together
And avoid speech
60 Gathered on this beach of the tumid river

Sightless, unless
The eyes reappear
As the perpetual star
Multifoliate° rose   *many-leaved*
65 Of death's twilight kingdom
The hope only
Of empty men.

IV

Here we go round the prickly pear
Prickly pear prickly pear
70 *Here we go round the prickly pear*
At five o'clock in the morning.

Between the idea
And the reality
Between the motion
75 And the act
Falls the Shadow
      For Thine is the Kingdom

Between the conception
And the creation
80 Between the emotion
And the response
Falls the Shadow
      Life is very long

Between the desire
85 And the spasm
Between the potency
And the existence
Between the essence
And the descent
90 Falls the Shadow
      For Thine is the Kingdom

For Thine is
Life is
For Thine is the

95 *This is the way the world ends*
This is the way the world ends
This is the way the world ends
Not with a bang but a whimper.

Journey of the Magi[3]

"A cold coming we had of it,
Just the worst time of the year
For a journey, and such a long journey:
The ways deep and the weather sharp,
5 The very dead of winter."
And the camels galled, sore-footed, refractory,
Lying down in the melting snow.
There were times we regretted
The summer palaces on slopes, the terraces,
10 And the silken girls bringing sherbet.
Then the camel men cursing and grumbling
And running away, and wanting their liquor and women,
And the night-fires going out, and the lack of shelters,
And the cities hostile and the towns unfriendly
15 And the villages dirty and charging high prices:
A hard time we had of it.
At the end we preferred to travel all night,
Sleeping in snatches,
With the voices singing in our ears, saying
20 That this was all folly.

Then at dawn we came down to a temperate valley,
Wet, below the snow line, smelling of vegetation;
With a running stream and a water-mill beating the darkness,
And three trees on the low sky,
25 And an old white horse galloped away in the meadow.
Then we came to a tavern with vine-leaves over the lintel,
Six hands at an open door dicing for pieces of silver,
And feet kicking the empty wine-skins.
But there was no information, and so we continued
30 And arrived at evening, not a moment too soon
Finding the place; it was (you may say) satisfactory.

All this was a long time ago, I remember,
And I would do it again, but set down
This set down
35 This: were we led all that way for
Birth or Death? There was a Birth, certainly,
We had evidence and no doubt. I had seen birth and death,

3 *The three wise men who came from the East,*
bringing gifts to the infant Jesus.

But had thought they were different; this Birth was
Hard and bitter agony for us, like Death, our death.
40 We returned to our places, these Kingdoms,
But no longer at ease here, in the old dispensation,
With an alien people clutching their gods.
I should be glad of another death.

Macavity: The Mystery Cat[4]

Macavity's a Mystery Cat: he's called the Hidden Paw—
For he's the master criminal who can defy the Law.
He's the bafflement of Scotland Yard,[5] the Flying Squad's despair:
For when they reach the scene of crime—*Macavity's not there!*

5   Macavity, Macavity, there's no one like Macavity,
He's broken every human law, he breaks the law of gravity.
His powers of levitation[6] would make a fakir[7] stare,
And when you reach the scene of crime—*Macavity's not there!*
You may seek him in the basement, you may look up in the air—
10 But I tell you once and once again, *Macavity's not there!*

Macavity's a ginger cat, he's very tall and thin;
You would know him if you saw him, for his eyes are sunken in.
His brow is deeply lined with thought, his head is highly domed;
His coat is dusty from neglect, his whiskers are uncombed.
15 He sways his head from side to side, with movements like a snake;
And when you think he's half asleep, he's always wide awake.

Macavity, Macavity, there's no one like Macavity,
For he's a fiend in feline shape, a monster of depravity.
You may meet him in a by-street, you may see him in the square—
20 But when a crime's discovered, then *Macavity's not there!*

He's outwardly respectable. (They say he cheats at cards.)
And his footprints are not found in any file of Scotland Yard's.
And when the larder's looted, or the jewel-case is rifled,
Or when the milk is missing, or another Peke's[8] been stifled,
25 Or the greenhouse glass is broken, and the trellis past repair—
Ay, there's the wonder of the thing! *Macavity's not there!*

---

4 *This poem is taken from Eliot's* Old
   Possum's Book of Practical Cats, *on which*
   the well known musical, Cats, *is based.*
5 *Police headquarters in London.*

6 *Rising in the air in opposition to gravity.*
7 *Oriental holy man or wonder-worker.*
8 *Pekin(g)ese: small long-haired breed of dog,*
   originally from the Imperial Palace, Peking.

And when the Foreign Office find a Treaty's gone astray,
Or the Admiralty lose some plans and drawings by the way,
There may be a scrap of paper in the hall or on the stair—
30 But it's useless to investigate—*Macavity's not there!*
And when the loss has been disclosed, the Secret Service say:
"It *must* have been Macavity!"—but he's a mile away.
You'll be sure to find him resting, or a-licking of his thumbs,
Or engaged in doing complicated long division sums.

35 Macavity, Macavity, there's no one like Macavity,
There never was a Cat of such deceitfulness and suavity.
He always has an alibi, and one or two to spare:
At whatever time the deed took place—MACAVITY WASN'T THERE!
And they say that all the Cats whose wicked deeds are widely known
40 (I might mention Mungojerrie, I might mention Griddlebone)
Are nothing more than agents for the Cat who all the time
Just controls their operations: the Napoleon[9] of Crime!

Preludes

I

The winter evening settles down
With smell of steaks in passageways.
Six o'clock.
The burnt-out ends of smoky days.
5 And now a gusty shower wraps
The grimy scraps
Of withered leaves about your feet
And newspapers from vacant lots;
The showers beat
10 On broken blinds and chimney-pots,
And at the corner of the street
A lonely cab-horse steams and stamps.
And then the lighting of the lamps.

II

The morning comes to consciousness
15 Of faint stale smells of beer
From the sawdust-trampled street
With all its muddy feet that press

---

9 *Napoleon I: French emperor (1769-1821).*   *rapaciousness.*
The allusion is to power, audacity and

To early coffee-stands.
With the other masquerades
20   That time resumes,
One thinks of all the hands
That are raising dingy shades
In a thousand furnished rooms.

III

You tossed a blanket from the bed,
25   You lay upon your back, and waited;
You dozed, and watched the night revealing
The thousand sordid images
Of which your soul was constituted;
They flickered against the ceiling.
30   And when all the world came back
And the light crept up between the shutters
And you heard the sparrows in the gutters,
You had such a vision of the street
As the street hardly understands;
35   Sitting along the bed's edge, where
You curled the papers from your hair,
Or clasped the yellow soles of feet
In the palms of both soiled hands.

IV

His soul stretched tight across the skies
40   That fade behind a city block,
Or trampled by insistent feet
At four and five and six o'clock;
And short square fingers stuffing pipes,
And evening newspapers, and eyes
45   Assured of certain certainties,
The conscience of a blackened street
Impatient to assume the world.

I am moved by fancies that are curled
Around these images, and cling:
50   The notion of some infinitely gentle
Infinitely suffering thing.

Wipe your hand across your mouth, and laugh;
The worlds revolve like ancient women
Gathering fuel in vacant lots.

Rhapsody on a Windy Night

Twelve o'clock.
Along the reaches of the street
Held in a lunar synthesis,
Whispering lunar incantations
5 Dissolve the floors of memory
And all its clear relations,
Its divisions and precisions.
Every street lamp that I pass
Beats like a fatalistic drum,
10 And through the spaces of the dark
Midnight shakes the memory
As a madman shakes a dead geranium.

Half-past one,
The street-lamp sputtered,
15 The street-lamp muttered,
The street-lamp said, "Regard that woman
Who hesitates toward you in the light of the door
Which opens on her like a grin.
You see the border of her dress
20 Is torn and stained with sand,
And you see the corner of her eye
Twists like a crooked pin."

The memory throws up high and dry
A crowd of twisted things;
25 A twisted branch upon the beach
Eaten smooth, and polished
As if the world gave up
The secret of its skeleton,
Stiff and white.
30 A broken spring in a factory yard,
Rust that clings to the form that the strength has left
Hard and curled and ready to snap.

Half-past two,
The street-lamp said,
35 "Remark the cat which flattens itself in the gutter,
Slips out its tongue
And devours a morsel of rancid butter."
So the hand of the child, automatic,
Slipped out and pocketed a toy that was running along the quay.
40 I could see nothing behind that child's eye.

I have seen eyes in the street
Trying to peer through lighted shutters,
And a crab one afternoon in a pool,
An old crab with barnacles on his back,
45 Gripped the end of a stick which I held him.

Half-past three,
The lamp sputtered,
The lamp muttered in the dark.
The lamp hummed:
50 "Regard the moon,
La lune ne garde aucune rancune,[1]
She winks a feeble eye,
She smiles into corners.
She smooths the hair of the grass.
55 The moon has lost her memory.
A washed-out smallpox cracks her face,
Her hand twists a paper rose,
That smells of dust and eau de Cologne,[2]
She is alone
60 With all the old nocturnal smells
That cross and cross across her brain."
The reminiscence comes
Of sunless dry geraniums
And dust in crevices,
65 Smells of chestnuts in the streets,
And female smells in shuttered rooms,
And cigarettes in corridors
And cocktail smells in bars.

The lamp said,
70 "Four o'clock,
Here is the number on the door.
Memory!
You have the key,
The little lamp spreads a ring on the stair.
75 Mount.
The bed is open; the tooth-brush hangs on the wall,
Put your shoes at the door, sleep, prepare for life."

The last twist of the knife.

1 *The moon does not bear any grudge.*   2 *A perfume first made in Cologne, Germany.*

John Crowe Ransom (1888 – 1974)

Ransom, a poet and critic of the American South, was educated at Oxford and worked in the English departments of Vanderbilt University and Kenyon College, where he founded the influential Kenyon Review. *Ransom was a strong supporter of the New Criticism, the movement which favoured close textual analysis and which was associated with leading literary figures such as T.S. Eliot, I.A. Richards and Ezra Pound. Ransom is well known for his ballads and elegies. "Bells for John Whiteside's Daughter", contrasts the child's speed, agility and vitality in life with her dead form which is so "primly propped". Through his opposing portraits of this child, Ransom reveals the effective use of imagery and realism, and the depth of feeling for which he is renowned.*

Bells for John Whiteside's Daughter

There was such speed in her little body,
And such lightness in her footfall,
It is no wonder her brown study°   *reverie or daydream*
Astonishes us all.

5   Her wars were bruited in our high window.
We looked among orchard trees and beyond
Where she took arms against her shadow,
Or harried unto the pond

The lazy geese, like a snow cloud
10   Dripping their snow on the green grass
Tricking and stopping, sleepy and proud,
Who cried in goose, Alas,

For the tireless heart within the little
Lady with rod that made them rise
15   From their noon apple-dreams and scuttle
Goose-fashion under the skies!

But now go the bells, and we are ready,
In one house we are sternly stopped
To say we are vexed at her brown study,
20   Lying so primly propped.

Archibald MacLeish (1892 – 1982)

MacLeish was born in Illinois and educated at Yale University. He was Assistant Secretary of State from 1944 to 1945 and won numerous awards for his poetry, including the Pulitzer Prize. Best known for his lyric poetry, MacLeish produced his most noteworthy work after the age of fifty. As its name implies, "Ars Poetica" focuses on his ideas about the art of poetry.

Ars Poetica[1]

A poem should be palpable and mute
As a globed fruit,

Dumb
As old medallions to the thumb,

5   Silent as the sleeve-worn stone
Of casement ledges where the moss has grown—

A poem should be wordless
As the flight of birds.

    *   *   *

A poem should be motionless in time
10 As the moon climbs,

Leaving, as the moon releases
Twig by twig the night-entangled trees,

Leaving, as the moon behind the winter leaves,
Memory by memory the mind—

15 A poem should be motionless in time
As the moon climbs.

    *   *   *

1 *Art of poetry.*

A poem should be equal to:
Not true.

For all the history of grief
20   An empty doorway and a maple leaf.

For love
The leaning grasses and two lights above the sea—

A poem should not mean
But be.

Wilfred Owen (1893 – 1918)

Wilfred Owen was born into a relatively cultivated but financially straitened family in Oswestry, Shropshire. As his family could not afford to send him to university, he was educated at the Shrewsbury Technical College, and sent as a pupil to the Reverend Herbert Wigan, an Anglican vicar. Owen found the experience boring but important in the sense that his social conscience was awakened by the misery he saw among the poor in the parish. On leaving Wigan's establishment, he went to Bordeaux in France, where he was living when the First World War broke out in 1914. At first, he regarded the war as an irritating interruption, but visiting a military hospital changed his outlook. He returned to England, joined the Artists' Rifles, and was fighting in France by the end of 1916.

The horrors of trench warfare, along with the hideous landscape in which he lived during those years, forced him to mature rapidly as a poet. He lost his faith in the conventional concept of Christ, developing instead a more revolutionary vision, depicted in a brotherhood of fighting men whom Owen identified with Christ.

Owen wrote his poems chiefly to shock the British, who he felt were ignorant and uncaring about the truth of the war. In "Anthem for Doomed Youth", he deliberately and graphically emphasizes the number of soldiers killed. In October 1918, he was awarded the Military Cross, and was killed exactly a month later.

Anthem for Doomed Youth

What passing-bells for these who die as cattle?
Only the monstrous anger of the guns.
Only the stuttering rifles' rapid rattle
Can patter out their hasty orisons.°   *prayers*
5   No mockeries now for them; no prayers nor bells,
Nor any voice of mourning save the choirs,
The shrill, demented choirs of wailing shells;
And bugles calling for them from sad shires.

What candles may be held to speed them all?
10   Not in the hands of boys, but in their eyes
Shall shine the holy glimmers of good-byes.
The pallor of girls' brows shall be their pall;
Their flowers the tenderness of patient minds,
And each slow dusk a drawing-down of blinds.

Dulce et decorum est

Bent double, like old beggars under sacks,
Knock-kneed, coughing like hags, we cursed through sludge,
Till on the haunting flares we turned our backs,
And towards our distant rest began to trudge.
5   Men marched asleep. Many had lost their boots,
But limped on, blood-shod. All went lame, all blind;
Drunk with fatigue; deaf even to the hoots
Of tired, outstripped Five-Nines° dropping softly behind.   *gas-shells*

Gas! GAS! Quick, boys!—An ecstasy of fumbling,
10   Fitting the clumsy helmets just in time,
But someone still was yelling out and stumbling
And floundering like a man in fire or lime . . .
Dim through the misty panes and thick green light,
As under a green sea, I saw him drowning.

15   In all my dreams before my helpless sight,
He plunges at me, guttering, choking, drowning.

If in some smothering dreams you too could pace
Behind the wagon that we flung him in,
And watch the white eyes writhing in his face,
20   His hanging face, like a devil's sick of sin;

If you could hear, at every jolt, the blood
Come gargling from the froth-corrupted lungs,
Obscene as cancer, bitter as the cud
Of vile, incurable sores on innocent tongues,—
25 My friend, you would not tell with such high zest
To children ardent for some desperate glory,
The old Lie: Dulce et decorum est
Pro patria mori.[1]

Futility

Move him into the sun—
Gently its touch awoke him once,
At home, whispering of fields unsown.
Always it woke him, even in France,
5 Until this morning and this snow.
If anything might rouse him now
The kind old sun will know.

Think how it wakes the seeds,—
Woke, once, the clays of a cold star.
10 Are limbs, so dear-achieved, are sides,
Full-nerved—still warm—too hard to stir?
Was it for this the clay grew tall?
—O what made fatuous sunbeams toil
To break earth's sleep at all?

1 *A quotation from the Roman poet, Horace:
"It is sweet and fitting to die for one's
country".*

E.E. Cummings (1894 – 1962)

*The son of a Congregational minister, Cummings grew up in
Massachusetts and was educated at Harvard. During the First World
War, he was stationed in France where, as a result of an indiscreet
letter written by a friend, Cummings was incarcerated in a detention
centre. He was released three months later and recorded the experience
in his autobiographical work,* The Enormous Room. *He also published
several volumes of poetry, commencing with* Tulips and Chimneys,
*which contains some of his more conventional poetry written before he
went to France. His* Complete Poems *contains a wide range of work,
from love poetry to satirical verse—the latter an expression of
Cummings's disillusionment with human institutions, following his
term in prison.*

*Cummings is best known for his idiosyncratic typography, for his
preference for the lower type-case and for his eccentric use of punctua-
tion. Clearly non-conformist, Cummings laments the apathetic adhe-
rence to convention by those he labels "mostpeople". His poems cele-
brate, instead, the uniqueness of those who are truly individual.*

"Buffalo Bill's" [1]

Buffalo Bill's
defunct
    who used to
    ride a watersmooth-silver
5   stallion
and break onetwothreefourfive pigeonsjustlikethat
                        Jesus

he was a handsome man
               and what i want to know is
10 how do you like your blueeyed boy
Mister Death

1 *William F. Cody (1846–1917), American
scout, later a Wild West showman.*

"anyone lived in a pretty how town"

anyone lived in a pretty how town
(with up so floating many bells down)
spring summer autumn winter
he sang his didn't he danced his did.

5   Women and men(both little and small)
cared for anyone not at all
they sowed their isn't they reaped their same
sun moon stars rain

children guessed(but only a few
10   and down they forgot as up they grew
autumn winter spring summer)
that noone loved him more by more

when by now and tree by leaf
she laughed his joy she cried his grief
15   bird by snow and stir by still
anyone's any was all to her

someones married their everyones
laughed their cryings and did their dance
(sleep wake hope and then)they
20   said their nevers they slept their dream

stars rain sun moon
(and only the snow can begin to explain
how children are apt to forget to remember
with up so floating many bells down)

25   one day anyone died i guess
(and noone stooped to kiss his face)
busy folk buried them side by side
little by little and was by was

all by all and deep by deep
30   and more by more they dream their sleep
noone and anyone earth by april
wish by spirit and if by yes.

Women and men(both dong and ding)
summer autumn winter spring
35   reaped their sowing and went their came
sun moon stars rain

"the Cambridge ladies who live in furnished souls"

the Cambridge[2] ladies who live in furnished souls
are unbeautiful and have comfortable minds
(also, with the church's protestant blessings
daughters, unscented shapeless spirited)
5   they believe in Christ and Longfellow,[3] both dead,
are invariably interested in so many things—
at the present writing one still finds
delighted fingers knitting for the is it Poles?
perhaps. While permanent faces coyly bandy
10   scandal of Mrs. N and Professor D
. . . . the Cambridge ladies do not care, above
Cambridge if sometimes in its box of
sky lavender and cornerless, the
moon rattles like a fragment of angry candy

---

2 *Cambridge, Massachusetts.*   3 *American poet of the nineteenth century.*

Malvina Reynolds (1900 – 1978)

Reynolds was an American singer, guitarist, composer, lyricist and writer of children's music. She began her career as a writer of protest songs. Her best known works include "What Have They Done to the Rain?", "Turn Around" and "Little Boxes". The latter work appears deceptively simple; in reality it is a complex indictment of the conformity and materialism of modern society.

Little Boxes

Little boxes on the hillside,
Little boxes made of ticky tacky,°   *flimsy construction material*
Little boxes, little boxes, little boxes all the same.
There's a green one and a pink one
5   and a blue one and a yellow one,
And they're all made out of ticky tacky
And they all look just the same.

And the people in the houses all go to the university,
And they all get put in boxes, little boxes all the same.
10   And there's doctors and there's lawyers
     and business executives,
And they're all made out of ticky tacky
And they all look just the same.

And they all play on the golf course
15   And drink their martini[1] dry,
And they all have pretty children
     and the children go to school,
And the children go to summer camp
     and then to the university,
20   And they all get put in boxes,
And they all come out the same.

And the boys go into business
     and marry and raise a family,
And they all get put in boxes, little boxes all the same.
25   There's a green one and a pink
     one and a blue one and a yellow one,
And they're all made out of ticky tacky,
And they all look just the same.

---

1   *Gin and vermouth cocktail.*

Roy Campbell (1901 – 1957)

The son of a doctor, Roy Campbell was born in Durban. His prodigious talent is shown in the long poem, The Flaming Terrapin, *which he wrote when he was twenty-four years old. The poem has a youthful vitality and an exuberance of exotic imagery which is unlike the European poetry of the time. "Autumn" and "The Zulu Girl" are from his* Adamastor *collection of poetry. Written in anti-pastoral vein, "The Zulu Girl" suggests that one day the rural oppressed will rise to govern the country. Clearly non-conformist and highly critical, Campbell also focuses a satirical eye on white South African society and on the English literary fraternity in later volumes. The anti-establishment stance he demonstrates in these works originated from a genuinely Romantic sense of the value of the individual and of the imaginative and intuitive faculties. He hated mediocrity and conventionality.*

Campbell found himself unable to adjust to South African or to English society and settled in Portugal, where he supported his family by working as a bullfighter, a fisherman and a horse-trader. In the poems of this period, published in Flowering Reeds, *a quieter, more spiritual vision is apparent.*

Campbell received an honorary doctorate from the University of Natal in 1954. He died three years later in a motor accident.

Autumn

I love to see, when leaves depart,
The clear anatomy arrive,
Winter, the paragon of art,
That kills all forms of life and feeling
5   Save what is pure and will survive.

Already now the clanging chains
Of geese are harnessed to the moon;
Stripped are the great sun-clouding planes:
And the dark pines, their own revealing,
10 Let in the needles of the noon.

Strained by the gale the olives whiten
Like hoary wrestlers bent with toil
And, with the vines, their branches lighten
To brim our vats where summer lingers
15 In the red froth and sun-gold oil.

Soon on our hearth's reviving pyre
Their rotted stems will crumble up:
And like a ruby, panting fire,
The grape will redden on your fingers
20   Through the lit crystal of the cup.

The Zulu Girl

When in the sun the hot red acres smoulder,
Down where the sweating gang its labour plies,
A girl flings down her hoe, and from her shoulder
Unslings her child tormented by the flies.

5   She takes him to a ring of shadow pooled
By thorn-trees: purpled with the blood of ticks,
While her sharp nails, in slow caresses ruled,
Prowl through his hair with sharp electric clicks,

His sleepy mouth plugged by the heavy nipple,
10   Tugs like a puppy, grunting as he feeds:
Through his frail nerves her own deep languors ripple
Like a broad river sighing through its reeds.

Yet in that drowsy stream his flesh imbibes
An old unquenched unsmotherable heat—
15   The curbed ferocity of beaten tribes,
The sullen dignity of their defeat.

Her body looms above him like a hill
Within whose shade a village lies at rest,
Or the first cloud so terrible and still
20   That bears the coming harvest in its breast.

Langston Hughes (1902 – 1967)

Hughes, an influential black American poet, playwright and translator, was educated at Columbia and Lincoln Universities. He was a key figure in the Harlem Renaissance and an untiring fighter for the rights of his people. Hughes is well known for his literary blues, for jazz and for poetry which employs natural speech patterns to portray black confidence and racial pride. In a letter quoted in Volume 51 of the Dictionary of Literary Biographies, *Hughes expressed his desire to counter that black poetry which was "aimed at the heads of the highbrows, rather than at the hearts of the people"; poetry which served a white-controlled publishing industry, out of the reach of "the great masses of coloured people". "Theme for English B" is typical of his poems depicting the daily lives of black people in America. His militancy is expressed in "As I Grew Older", a poem which portrays the nostalgia and anger of the speaker, who deplores the wall of racial prejudice which stands between himself and his dream.*

As I Grew Older

It was a long time ago.
I have almost forgotten my dream
But it was there then,
In front of me,
5 Bright like a sun—
My dream.

And then the wall rose,
Rose slowly,
Slowly,
10 Between me and my dream.
Rose slowly, slowly,
Dimming,
Hiding,
The light of my dream.
15 Rose until it touched the sky—
The wall.
Shadow.
I am black.

I lie down in the shadow.
20 No longer the light of my dream before me,
Above me.
Only the thick wall.
Only the shadow.

My hands!
25 My dark hands!
Break through the wall!
Find my dream!
Help me to shatter this darkness,
To smash this night,
30 To break this shadow
Into a thousand lights of sun,
Into a thousand whirling dreams
Of sun!

Theme for English B[1]

The instructor said,

> Go home and write
> a page tonight.
> And let that page come out of you—
5 > Then, it will be true.

I wonder if it's that simple?

I am twenty-two, colored, born in Winston-Salem.[2]
I went to school there, then Durham,[3] then here
to this college on the hill above Harlem.[4]
10 I am the only colored student in my class.
The steps from the hill lead down to Harlem,
through a park, then I cross St. Nicholas,[5]
Eighth Avenue, Seventh,[6] and I come to the Y,[7]
the Harlem Branch Y, where I take the elevator
15 up to my room, sit down, and write this page:

It's not easy to know what is true for you or me
at twenty-two, my age. But I guess I'm what
I feel and see and hear. Harlem, I hear you:
hear you, hear me—we two—you, me talk on this page.
20 (I hear New York, too.) Me—who?

---

1 *English B language class is usually taught at the lower level.*
2 *City in North Carolina, USA.*
3 *Site of the University of New Hampshire, USA.*
4 *New York suburb populated mainly by black people.*
5 & 6 *Like Harlem, these sites of New York city are situated near Columbia University.*
7 *Abbreviation for YMCA, the Young Men's Christian Association, which provides inexpensive board and lodging.*

Well, I like to eat, sleep, drink, and be in love.
I like to work, read, learn, and understand life.
I like a pipe for a Christmas present,
or records—Bessie,[8] bop, or Bach.[9]

25   I guess being colored doesn't make me not like
the same things other folks like who are other races.
So will my page be colored when I write?
Being me, it will not be white.
But it will be

30   a part of you, instructor.
You are white—
yet a part of me, as I am a part of you.
That's American.
Sometimes perhaps you don't want to be a part of me.

35   Nor do I often want to be part of you.
But we are, that's true!
As I learn from you,
I guess you learn from me—
although you're older—and white—

40   and somewhat more free.

This is my page for English B.

---

8 *American Jazz singer, Bessie Smith*
   (1898–1937).

9 *The German composer, Johann Sebastian*
   Bach (1685–1750).

Stevie Smith (1902 – 1971)

From the time her father abandoned the family, when she was three
years old, Florence Margaret (Stevie) Smith spent her life in London in
the care of an aunt. She worked for the British Broadcasting
Corporation as a freelance broadcaster for thirty years. During those
years, she published a novel entitled Novel on Yellow Paper; or, Work
It Out for Yourself *and a volume of poetry called* A Good Time was
had by All. *Her* Selected Poems, *illustrated by herself, were published*
in 1962. Although Smith's writing is humorous and playful, it never-
theless confronts the terrors of isolation and reveals an enduring preoc-
cupation with death. "Not Waving but Drowning" illustrates both
these aspects of her insight.

Not Waving but Drowning

Nobody heard him, the dead man,
But still he lay moaning:
I was much further out than you thought
And not waving but drowning.

5 Poor chap, he always loved larking
And now he's dead
It must have been too cold for him his heart gave way,
They said.

Oh, no no no, it was too cold always
10 (Still the dead one lay moaning)
I was much too far out all my life
And not waving but drowning.

H.I.E. Dhlomo (1903 – 1956)

*Dhlomo, who occasionally used the pen-names "Busy B" and "X",
was born in Natal and educated at a mission school. He worked
successively as teacher, journalist and librarian. In the 1940s, he
worked in Durban for his brother, R.R. Dhlomo, as assistant editor on
a newspaper featuring both Zulu and English writing. In addition to a
number of plays, both historical and contemporary, Dhlomo wrote
poetry and essays, which include critical writings on African literature.
The essay, "Zulu Life and Thought" and the long poem,* Valley of a
Thousand Hills, *focus on the tension between the traditional African
way of life and the civilization introduced by western colonizers.
Dhlomo's* Collected Works *were published in 1985.*

Not for Me

Not for me the Victory[1] celebrations!
Not for me,
Ah! not for me.
I who helped and slaved in the protection
5   Of their boasted great civilization;
Now sit I in tears 'mid celebrations
Of a war I won to lose,
Of a peace I may not choose.
Before me lies
10 Grim years of strife,
Who gave my life
To gain—what prize?
In land and sea my brothers buried lie;
The message came; they answered and they fell.
15 With blood and toil our rights they thought to buy,
And by their loyal stand Race fires to quell.
Now that the War is ended,
Begins my war!
I rise to fight unaided
20 The wrongs I abhor!
I see the flags of peace in joy unfurled,
And think of my position in the world
They say will come.
And I stand dumb

1 *A reference to the celebrations marking the
Allied victory in 1945, at the end of the
Second World War. Many black people
served with the South African forces, but
received little recognition for their
contribution.*

25 With wrath! Not victory in the battle field
Those precious things we crave for life will yield.
I see them gathered to decide on peace,
For War, they know, will lead to Man's surcease.
But, Lord, I am not represented:
30 My presence there is still resented.
Yet where I'm not,
There Christ is not!
For Jesus died and lives for all;
To Him no race is great or small.
35 And if they meet without the Lord to guide,
They cannot build a Peace that will abide.
The cause of war are Greed, Race, Pride and Power,
Yet these impostors sway peace-talks this hour.
How long O Lord before they learn the art
40 Of peace demands a change in their own heart!
I'll fight! but pray, 'Forgive them Father,
Despite their boast and pomp they know not what they do.'

I hate them not; believe I rather
My battle will lead them to discover Christ anew.
45 This is the irony,
This is the agony:
As long as those in power repentance need,
I sit upon the spikes of Wrong and bleed!
Not for me,
50 Ah! not for me
The celebrations,
The peace orations.
Not for me,
Yes, not for me
55 Are victory
And liberty!
Of the Liberty I died to bring in need;
And this betrayal wounds and sears my soul. I bleed.

L.R. (no dates available)

These initials represent an anonymous writer on the staff of the newspaper, Umteteli wa Bantu, which featured the poem, "'Civilised' Labour Policy", on 29 October 1932. The poem (a parody of Psalm 23) is set against a background of poverty which, springing from the Great Depression, was exacerbated by the governmental policy of reserving jobs for whites.

"Civilised" Labour Policy

Hertzog[1] is my shepherd; I am in want.
He maketh me to lie down on park benches,
He leadeth me beside still factories,
He arouseth my doubt of his intention.
5 He leadeth me in the path of destruction for his Party's sake.
Yea, I walk through the valley of the shadow of destruction
And I fear evil, for thou art with me.
The Politicians and the Profiteers, they frighten me;
Thou preparest a reduction in my salary before me,
10 In the presence of mine enemies.
Thou anointest mine income with taxes,
My expense runneth over.
Surely unemployment and poverty will follow me
All the days of this Administration,
15 And I shall dwell in a mortgaged house forever.

1 *General James Barry Munnik Hertzog (1866–1942) was Prime Minister of South* *Africa from 1924 to 1939.*

William Plomer (1903 – 1973)

*Born in Pietersburg in the Transvaal, Plomer was educated in Rugby,
England. He returned to Zululand for a short while, where he edited
the satirical journal,* Voorslag, *together with Roy Campbell. However,
after a sojourn in Japan, Plomer settled in England. Like Campbell,
Plomer developed a critical attitude towards South African society,
which found early expression in the novel* Turbott Wolfe, *published in
1925.*

*Despite his departure from the country of his birth, South Africa
had a lasting influence on his writing, as "The Wild Doves at Louis
Trichardt" and "Namaqualand after Rain" testify.*

*Plomer's literary talent spans the genres, ranging from a biography
of Cecil John Rhodes to operatic librettos. Two of his many novels—*
The Invaders *and* Museum Pieces—*were published by Jonathan Cape,
with whom he was associated as Director and, later, as Reader. He was
awarded the Queen's Gold Medal for Poetry in 1963 and the CBE in
1968.*

Namaqualand after Rain[1]

Again the veld revives,
Imbued with lyric rains,
And sap re-sweetening dry stalks
Perfumes the quickening plains;

5 Small roots explode in strings of stars,
Each bulb gives up its dream,
Honey drips from orchid throats,
Jewels each raceme;°   *flower cluster*

The desert sighs at dawn—
10 As in another hemisphere
The temple lotus breaks her buds
On the attentive air—

A frou-frou° of new flowers,   *rustling*
Puff of unruffling petals,
15 While rods of sunlight strike pure streams
From rocks beveined with metals;

1 *Namaqualand is an area in the north-
western Cape where, after good winter rains,* *wild daisies blossom and carpet the normally
arid landscape.*

Far in the gaunt karroo
That winter dearth denudes,
Ironstone caves give back the burr
20   Of lambs in multitudes;

Grass waves again where drought
Bleached every upland kraal,
A peach-tree shoots along the wind
Pink volleys through a broken wall,

25   And willows growing round the dam
May now be seen
With all their traceries of twigs
Just hesitating to be green,

Soon to be hung with colonies
30   All swaying with the leaves
Of pendant wicker love-nests
The pretty loxia² weaves.

The Wild Doves at Louis Trichardt³

Morning is busy with long files
Of ants and men, all bearing loads.
The sun's gong beats, and sweat runs down.
A mason-hornet shapes his hanging house.
5   In a wide flood of flowers
Two crested cranes are bowing to their food.
From the north today there is ominous news.

Midday, the mad cicada-time.⁴
Sizzling from every open valve
10   Of the overheated earth
The stridulators° din it in—   *noisy insects*
Intensive and continuing praise
Of the white-hot zenith, shrilling on
Toward a note too high to bear.

2 *Bird of the finch family.*   *chiefly devoted to cattle-farming.*
3 *Town in the northern Transvaal. The climate*   4 *A cicada is an insect characterized by its*
   is intensely hot and dry, and the area is   *loud, chirping sound.*

15 Oven of afternoon, silence of heat.
    In shadow, or in shaded rooms,
    This face is hidden in folded arms,
    That face is now a sightless mask,
    Tree-shadow just includes those legs.
20 The people have all lain down, and sleep
    In attitudes of the sick, the shot, the dead.

    And now in the grove the wild doves begin,
    Whose neat silk heads are never still,
    Bubbling their coolest colloquies.
25 The formulae they liquidly pronounce
    In secret tents of leaves imply
    (Clearer than man-made music could)
    Men being absent, Africa is good.

Herman Charles Bosman (1905 – 1951)

One of South Africa's foremost writers, Bosman was born in the small town of Kuils River, in the Cape, and was educated chiefly in Potchefstroom and Johannesburg. A brief spell in the teaching profession was terminated by a four-year term in Pretoria Central Prison for killing his step-brother, an experience which was later described in the largely autobiographical work, Cold Stone Jug. *Shortly after his release in 1930, Bosman took up the journalistic career that was to be his principal means of support for the rest of his life. His main contribution to South African literature is a large collection of short stories set in the Marico, a drought-stricken farming area in the western Transvaal. Bosman wrote a good deal of poetry (some of which is collected in the volume* The Earth is Waiting), *as well as a great number of essays and articles, and two novels. Although his attitude to art was largely influenced by Edgar Allan Poe and the French Symbolists, Bosman insisted that South African writing should not be a tame imitation of western models, but should reflect the country of its origin. The poem "Seed" bears witness to this stance.*

Seed

The farmer ploughs into the ground
More than the wheat-seed strewn on the ground
The farmer ploughs into the ground
The plough and the oxen and his body
5　He ploughs into the ground the farmstead and the cattle
And the pigs and the poultry and the kitchen utensils
And the afternoon sunlight shining into the window panes of the voorhuis
And the light entangled in the eyes of the children
He ploughs into the ground his wife's brown body
10　And the windmill above the borehole
And the borehole and the wind driving the windmill.
The farmer ploughs the blue clouds into the ground;
And as a tribute to the holocaust of the ploughshare—
To the sowing that was the parting of the Juggernaut—
15　The earth renders the farmer in due season
Corn

W.H. Auden (1907 – 1973)

After discovering his vocation as a poet, Auden read English at Oxford, spent a year in Berlin and began travelling widely. After visiting the USA, he decided to become a naturalized American citizen. This decision was taken just before the outbreak of war in Europe and incurred some criticism. From 1956 to 1961 he was Professor of Poetry at Oxford.

The poetry Auden wrote in the 1930s was an attempt at moral enlightenment in an age which saw both the rise of totalitarianism and the undermining of capitalism as a credible social system.In 1937 he published a number of poems which deal with England as an island fortress, open to attack from beyond its frontier and susceptible to an internal failure of the imagination. For Auden, frontier-consciousness is the equivalent of self-consciousness in human relationships: a symptom of the opposition between instinctive self and official self which is responsible for our failure to come to terms with our own fallibility.

Musée des Beaux Arts[1]

About suffering they were never wrong,
The Old Masters: how well they understood
Its human position; how it takes place
While someone else is eating or opening a window or just walking dully along;
5   How, when the aged are reverently, passionately waiting
For the miraculous birth, there always must be
Children who did not specially want it to happen, skating
On a pond at the edge of the wood:
They never forgot
10 That even the dreadful martyrdom must run its course
Anyhow in a corner, some untidy spot
Where the dogs go on with their doggy life, and the torturer's horse
Scratches its innocent behind on a tree.

In Brueghel's *Icarus*, for instance: how everything turns away
15 Quite leisurely from the disaster; the ploughman may
Have heard the splash, the forsaken cry,
But for him it was not an important failure; the sun shone

1 *Museum of Fine Arts, Brussels, where Auden had seen the painting entitled* The Fall of Icarus *by the Flemish painter Pieter Brueghel (1520-69). Icarus was the son of the mythical Daedalus who, trapped in Crete,* *devised wings for himself and for Icarus. The father flew safely across the Aegean Sea, but Icarus flew too close to the sun and the wax fastening the wings to his body melted. He plunged into the sea and was drowned.*

As it had to on the white legs disappearing into the green
Water; and the expensive delicate ship that must have seen
20   Something amazing, a boy falling out of the sky,
Had somewhere to get to and sailed calmly on.

The Unknown Citizen

(To JS/07/M/378
This Marble Monument
Is Erected by the State)

He was found by the Bureau of Statistics to be
One against whom there was no official complaint,
And all the reports on his conduct agree
That, in the modern sense of an old-fashioned word, he was a saint,
5   For in everything he did he served the Greater Community.
Except for the War till the day he retired
He worked in a factory and never got fired,
But satisfied his employers, Fudge Motors Inc.
Yet he wasn't a scab or odd in his views,
10   For his Union reports that he paid his dues,
(Our report on his Union shows it was sound)
And our Social Psychology workers found
That he was popular with his mates and liked a drink.
The Press are convinced that he bought a paper every day
15   And that his reactions to advertisements were normal in every way.
Policies taken out in his name prove that he was fully insured,
And his Health-card shows he was once in hospital but left it cured.
Both Producers Research and High-Grade Living declare
He was fully sensible to the advantages of the Instalment Plan
20   And had everything necessary to the Modern Man,
A phonograph,² a radio, a car and a frigidaire.
Our researchers into Public Opinion are content
That he held the proper opinions for the time of year;
When there was peace, he was for peace; when there was war, he went.
25   He was married and added five children to the population,
Which our Eugenist says was the right number for a parent of his generation,
And our teachers report that he never interfered with their education.
Was he free? Was he happy? The question is absurd:
Had anything been wrong, we should certainly have heard.

2   *An early form of gramophone, or record*
player, using cylinders.

R.N. Currey (1907 –)

Currey was born in Mafikeng in South Africa, and educated at Oxford. He now lives in England, where he served as Senior English Master at Colchester's Royal Grammar School. Currey has several volumes of poetry to his name: Tiresias and Other Poems, This Other Planet, Indian Landscape: A Book of Descriptive Poems *and* The Africa We Knew. *Currey's poetry reflects his life in South Africa (including the experience of exile, as in "Durban Revisited") and in England. It focuses, too, on his service during the Second World War.*

Currey was awarded the Viceroy's Poetry Prize in 1945 and, together with Anthony Delius, the South African Poetry Prize in 1959.

Durban Revisited

After these weeks at sea, my native land:
I stand and stare at the remembered Bluff;
Enough that long green skyline for a boy,
The joy of those high breakers, their huge roar
5   Upon the shore, the lift-in of the tide.

A forefather in eighteen-forty-eight
In state landed his family here; his blood
Has flowed up almost every fertile valley;
But many of his sons, through circumstance,
10 Lost his intense and civilized tolerance.

By chance we ride at anchor in the Bay
A day or two, and may not go ashore;
Once more between me and this lovely land
There stands a barrier; it used to be
15 My childhood, now it's my maturity.

Louis Macneice (1907 – 1963)

*Born in Belfast, Northern Ireland, MacNeice went to Oxford
University and lectured in Greek at the University of London. He
wrote most of his poetry during the 1930s and there is an underlying
sadness in much of his work, which seems to emerge from his vision of
the transience of life.*

Snow

The room was suddenly rich and the great bay-window was
Spawning snow and pink roses against it
Soundlessly collateral and incompatible:
World is suddener than we fancy it.

5   World is crazier and more of it than we think,
Incorrigibly plural. I peel and portion
A tangerine and spit the pips and feel
The drunkenness of things being various.

And the fire flames with a bubbling sound for world
10 Is more spiteful and gay than one supposes—
On the tongue on the eyes on the ears in the palms of one's hands—
There is more than glass between the snow and the huge roses.

Theodore Roethke (1908 – 1963)

Roethke's father was a greenhouse gardener who died when his son was fourteen. This loss led to Roethke's suffering a series of mental breakdowns, but also gave rise to some of his most delightful poetry, such as "My Papa's Waltz". At its best, his style is simple, vigorous and controlled. He has a gift for evoking physical sensations and emotional experience rather than approaching his material intellectually. The freshness and wonder of childhood are present in much of his work, and although his focus is relatively narrow, commenting little on the outside world, he explores deeply the nature of human experience, the psyche and psychological integration.

My Papa's Waltz

The whiskey on your breath
Could make a small boy dizzy;
But I hung on like death:
Such waltzing was not easy.

5   We romped until the pans
Slid from the kitchen shelf;
My mother's countenance
Could not unfrown itself.

The hand that held my wrist
10 Was battered on one knuckle;
At every step you missed
My right ear scraped a buckle.

You beat time on my head
With a palm caked hard by dirt,
15 Then waltzed me off to bed
Still clinging to your shirt.

Elizabeth Bishop (1911 – 1979)

*Born in Worcester, Massachusetts, Elizabeth Bishop was raised in
Nova Scotia and educated at Vassar. After some time in Key West, an
island off the coast of Florida, she spent many years in Brazil, return-
ing to the USA in 1969, where she took up a teaching post at Harvard.
The poem "The Fish" focuses on the values of resourcefulness and
endurance in a hostile environment. In different vein, "In the Waiting
Room" tells how, in the overheated room adjoining a dentist's surgery,
the seven-year-old persona loses her sense of self, fusing her identity
with her aunt in the dentist's chair, with the occupants of the waiting
room and with the diverse and strange beings whose pictures fill the
National Geographic magazine she has been reading. Both poems are
noteworthy for their simplicity of language, their minutely observed
detail and their controlled emotion.*

The Fish

    I caught a tremendous fish
    and held him beside the boat
    half out of the water, with my hook
    fast in a corner of his mouth.
5   He didn't fight.
    He hadn't fought at all.
    He hung a grunting weight,
    battered and venerable
    and homely. Here and there
10 his brown skin hung in strips
    like ancient wallpaper,
    and its pattern of darker brown
    was like wallpaper:
    shapes like full-blown roses
15 stained and lost through age.
    He was speckled with barnacles,
    fine rosettes of lime,
    and infested
    with tiny white sea-lice,
20 and underneath two or three
    rags of green weed hung down.
    While his gills were breathing in
    the terrible oxygen
    —the frightening gills,
25 fresh and crisp with blood,
    that can cut so badly—
    I thought of the coarse white flesh
    packed in like feathers,

the big bones and the little bones,
30 the dramatic reds and blacks
of his shiny entrails,
and the pink swim-bladder
like a big peony.
I looked into his eyes
35 which were far larger than mine
but shallower, and yellowed,
the irises backed and packed
with tarnished tinfoil
seen through the lenses
40 of old scratched isinglass.
They shifted a little, but not
to return my stare.
—It was more like the tipping
of an object toward the light.
45 I admired his sullen face,
the mechanism of his jaw,
and then I saw
that from his lower lip
—if you could call it a lip—
50 grim, wet and weaponlike,
hung five old pieces of fish-line,
or four and a wire leader
with the swivel still attached,
with all their five big hooks
55 grown firmly in his mouth.
A green line, frayed at the end
where he broke it, two heavier lines,
and a fine black thread
still crimped from the strain and snap
60 when it broke and he got away.
Like medals with their ribbons
frayed and wavering,
a five-haired beard of wisdom
trailing from his aching jaw.
65 I stared and stared
and victory filled up
the little rented boat,
from the pool of bilge
where oil had spread a rainbow
70 around the rusted engine
to the bailer rusted orange,
the sun-cracked thwarts,
the oarlocks on their strings,
the gunnels—until everything
75 was rainbow, rainbow, rainbow!
And I let the fish go.

In the Waiting Room

In Worcester, Massachusetts,
I went with Aunt Consuelo
to keep her dentist's appointment
and sat and waited for her
5   in the dentist's waiting room.
It was winter. It got dark
early. The waiting room
was full of grown-up people,
arctics and overcoats,
10   lamps and magazines.
My aunt was inside
what seemed like a long time
and while I waited I read
the *National Geographic*°   *a magazine*
15   (I could read) and carefully
studied the photographs:
the inside of a volcano,
black, and full of ashes:
then it was spilling over
20   in rivulets of fire.

Osa and Martin Johnson
dressed in riding breeches,
laced boots, and pith helmets.
A dead man slung on a pole
25   —"Long Pig," the caption said.
Babies with pointed heads
wound round and round with string:
black, naked women with necks
wound round and round with wire
30   like the necks of light bulbs.
Their breasts were horrifying.
I read it right straight through.
I was too shy to stop.
And then I looked at the cover:
35   the yellow margins, the date.

Suddenly, from inside,
came an *oh*! of pain
—Aunt Consuelo's voice—
not very loud or long.
40   I wasn't at all surprised;
even then I knew she was
a foolish, timid woman.
I might have been embarrassed,
but wasn't. What took me

45   completely by surprise
was that it was *me*:
my voice, in my mouth.
Without thinking at all
I was my foolish aunt,
50   I—we—were falling, falling,
our eyes glued to the cover
of the *National Geographic*,
February, 1918.

I said to myself: three days
55   and you'll be seven years old.
I was saying it to stop
the sensation of falling off
the round, turning world
into cold, blue-black space.
60   But I felt: you are an *I*,
you are an *Elizabeth*,
you are one of *them*.
Why should you be one, too?
I scarcely dared to look
65   to see what it was I was.
I gave a sidelong glance
—I couldn't look any higher—
at shadowy gray knees,
trousers and skirts and boots
70   and different pairs of hands
lying under the lamps.
I knew that nothing stranger
had ever happened, that nothing
stranger could ever happen.
75   Why should I be my aunt,
or me, or anyone?
What similarities—
boots, hands, the family voice
I felt in my throat, or even
80   the *National Geographic*
and those awful hanging breasts—
held us all together
or made us all just one?
How—I didn't know any
85   word for it—how "unlikely" . . .
How had I come to be here,
like them, and overhear
a cry of pain that could have
got loud and worse but hadn't?

90 The waiting room was bright
and too hot. It was sliding
beneath a big black wave,
another, and another.

Then I was back in it.
95 The War was on. Outside,
in Worcester, Massachusetts,
were night and slush and cold,
and it was still the fifth
of February, 1918.

Charles Madge (1912 –)

*Madge was born in Johannesburg and educated in Oxford. He was a
Professor of Sociology at the University of Birmingham from 1950
until 1970. His poetry has been published in* Poems, The Disappearing
Castle *and* The Father Found. *He was Director of the Pilot Press and
has participated in a number of UN and UNESCO projects. Madge
was married for a time to the poet and critic, Kathleen Raine.*

*In "Apocalypse", Madge's preoccupation with literature is evident:
the self is presented in terms of a literary device.*

Apocalypse[1]

My horses are metaphors; they have been known
As reason, passion, imagination
And there is a fourth, obscure, who gallops alone.

I hold the metaphorical reins of these
5 Shadowy, fiery creatures and if I please
Give one or the other his head or bring him to his knees.

This is the fable but I am no longer sure
If they are horses and if there are only four
Or if at times they are five, six or more.

---

1 *Reference to the "Four Horsemen of the
Apocalypse". In* The Revelation of St John
the Divine *(ch. 6), they are the four agents of*
*destruction, two being agents of war and
two of famine and pestilence.*

10 Once pastured in my breast and stabled in my brains
They reared transparent heads and shook invisible manes,
They were me, they were mine, it was I who held the reins,

The symbol strong, the atavistic° horses   *ancestral*
Careering in heights and depths on changing courses,
15 The animal form of powers, the shape of mental forces.

Who knows how much longer the horses will ever appear
As horses, or if even now they are plunging near
To the edge of disembodiment, the sheer

Precipice of reduction? I can see
20 My horses locked in cylinder heads; and we
Driving on, screaming and groaning, helplessly.

But I still look into the abyss and find
Among the printed circuits of the mind
A trace of hoofs, a whinnying on the wind.

George Barker (1913 –)

George Barker was born in Essex, England, and has taken up visiting professorships in Japan, New York, York and Florida. He has always been an isolated and individual writer who produces poems with comic wit and honest simplicity. His poetry includes the long autobiographical work called The True Confession of George Barker. *He has also written plays and novels.*

To my Mother

Most near, most dear, most loved and most far,
Under the window where I often found her
Sitting as huge as Asia, seismic° with laughter,   *shaking like an earthquake*
Gin and chicken helpless in her Irish hand,
5 Irresistible as Rabelais,[1] but most tender for
The lame dogs and hurt birds that surround her,—
She is a procession no one can follow after
But be like a little dog following a brass band.

She will not glance up at the bomber,[2] or condescend
10 To drop her gin and scuttle to a cellar,
But lean on the mahogany table like a mountain
Whom only faith can move, and so I send
O all my faith, and all my love to tell her
That she will move from mourning into morning.

1 *Francois Rabelais, sixteenth-century satirist and humorist, noted for his ribald, coarse ("Rabelaisian") humour.*

2 *This refers to the air raids in London during the Second World War.*

Modikwe Dikobe (1913 –)

Dikobe was born in the Northern Transvaal and went to school in Johannesburg. His employment as newspaper vendor, clerk and night-watchman possibly accounts for the concern with class differences that he expresses in his novel, The Marabi Dance. *His volume of poetry,* Dispossessed, *focuses on black oppression. "Counter 14" describes a scene in a "pass office" under the system of apartheid. "Passes", or identity documents, served largely to control the movements of black South Africans.*

Counter 14

Around Albert Street
Are faces pale, haggard and desperate
Lips cracked with cavities
Scrambling over job-seeking

5   In a yard
Twenty feet high
Bounded from sightseeing many more
Seated, shifting, yawning

Not even a bazaar
10 Would have so many customers
Queueing
Their fate
On a white face

"Escort"
15 72 hours grace
Out of the urban area
To starve, rob, steal
In own homeland.

Dylan Thomas (1914 – 1953)

Born in Swansea in Wales, Thomas had no formal education beyond grammar school. He devoted himself to writing poetry which became noted for its lyrical eloquence and musicality. In "Fern Hill", the poet's evocation of carefree youth—where time poured forth its blessings and was expansive and merciful—is rhapsodic. In "Do not go gentle into that good night", the poet passionately urges all who are faced with death, particularly his father, to "rage against the dying of the light", as if such strategies might outwit death, of whose threat Thomas seems intensely aware.

"Do not go gentle into that good night"

Do not go gentle into that good night,
Old age should burn and rave at close of day;
Rage, rage against the dying of the light.

Though wise men at their end know dark is right,
5   Because their words have forked no lightning they
Do not go gentle into that good night.

Good men, the last wave by, crying how bright
Their frail deeds might have danced in a green bay,
Rage, rage against the dying of the light.

10 Wild men who caught and sang the sun in flight,
And learn, too late, they grieved it on its way,
Do not go gentle into that good night.

Grave men, near death, who see with blinding sight
Blind eyes could blaze like meteors and be gay,
15 Rage, rage against the dying of the light.

And you, my father, there on the sad height,
Curse, bless me now with your fierce tears, I pray.
Do not go gentle into that good night.
Rage, rage against the dying of the light.

Fern Hill

Now as I was young and easy under the apple boughs
About the lilting house and happy as the grass was green,
    The night above the dingle° starry,   *valley*
    Time let me hail and climb
5   Golden in the heydays of his eyes,
And honoured among wagons I was prince of the apple towns
And once below a time I lordly had the trees and leaves
    Trail with daisies and barley
Down the rivers of the windfall light.

10 And as I was green and carefree, famous among the barns
About the happy yard and singing as the farm was home,
    In the sun that is young once only,
    Time let me play and be
Golden in the mercy of his means,
15 And green and golden I was huntsman and herdsman, the calves
Sang to my horn, the foxes on the hills barked clear and cold,
    And the sabbath rang slowly
In the pebbles of the holy streams.

All the sun long it was running, it was lovely, the hay
20 Fields high as the house, the tunes from the chimneys, it was air
    And playing, lovely and watery
    And fire green as grass.
And nightly under the simple stars
As I rode to sleep the owls were bearing the farm away,
25 All the moon long I heard, blessed among stables, the nightjars
    Flying with the ricks, and the horses
    Flashing into the dark.

And then to awake, and the farm, like a wanderer white
With the dew, come back, the cock on his shoulder: it was all
30   Shining, it was Adam and maiden,[1]
    The sky gathered again
    And the sun grew round that very day.
So it must have been after the birth of the simple light
In the first, spinning place, the spellbound horses walking warm
35   Out of the whinnying green stable
    On to the fields of praise.

1 *Adam and Eve; the first human beings*   *tradition. (See Genesis 2:15-19.)*
  created, according to the Judaeo-Christian

And honoured among foxes and pheasants by the gay house
Under the new made clouds and happy as the heart was long,
   In the sun born over and over,
40   I ran my heedless ways,
   My wishes raced through the house high hay
And nothing I cared, at my sky blue trades, that time allows
In all his tuneful turning so few and such morning songs
   Before the children green and golden
45   Follow him out of grace,

Nothing I cared, in the lamb white days, that time would take me
Up to the swallow thronged loft by the shadow of my hand,
   In the moon that is always rising,
      Nor that riding to sleep
50   I should hear him fly with the high fields
And wake to the farm forever fled from the childless land.
Oh as I was young and easy in the mercy of his means,
   Time held me green and dying
      Though I sang in my chains like the sea.

Anthony Delius (1916 – 1989)

*Delius was born in Simonstown in the Cape Province, and educated at
Rhodes University. He was a journalist, working for a time as a parlia-
mentary correspondent and leader-writer in Cape Town. He later
moved to London, where he was a broadcaster for the BBC. In addi-
tion to his satirical look at white South African values in the long
poem, "The Last Division", and the prose work,* The Day Natal Took
Off, *Delius has written three volumes of poetry:* An Unknown Border,
A Corner of the World *and* Black South Easter. *In 1959, Delius (with
R.N. Currey) was awarded the South African Poetry Prize, and in
1976 he received the CNA Prize for* Border, *a novel about the 1820
Settlers.*

*In "The Gamblers", Delius presents a sustained metaphor which
pictures the sea as Nature's casino. Implicit in the poem is the recogni-
tion of human frailty and vulnerability—especially in those whom soci-
ety has forced into a precarious existence.*

The Gamblers

The Coloured long-shore fishermen unfurl
their nets beside the chilly and unrested sea,
and in their heads the little dawn-winds whirl
some scraps of gambling, drink and lechery.

5   Barefoot on withered kelp and broken shell,
they toss big baskets on the brittle turf,
then with a gambler's bitter patience still
slap down their wagering boat upon the surf.

Day flips a golden coin—but they mock it.
10   With calloused, careless hands they reach
deep down into the sea's capacious pocket
and pile their silver chips upon the beach.

Guy Butler (1918 –)

Guy Butler was born in Cradock, Cape Province, and raised in the Karoo. He was educated at Rhodes University, and was Professor of English there from 1952 until 1983. He was awarded the SABC Prize for his book of poems, Stranger to Europe *(the title-poem appears below) and the CNA Prize for* Selected Poems. *Other volumes of his poetry are* South of the Zambezi: Poems from South Africa, On First Seeing Florence *and* 24 Songs and Ballads. *Among his many other publications are several plays and the autobiographical works* Karoo Morning, Bursting World *and* A Local Habitation.

Butler spent some time in Europe during the Second World War, and a good deal of his writing is concerned with the relationship between western and South African culture. The poem "Myths", explores the crisis of identity experienced by many white English-speaking South Africans.

Stranger to Europe

Stranger to Europe, waiting release,
My heart a torn-up, drying root
I breathed the rain of an Irish peace
That afternoon when a bird or a tree,
5   Long known as an exiled name, could cease
As such, take wing and trembling shoot
Green light and shade through the heart of me.

Near a knotty hedge we had stopped.
"This is an aspen." "Tell me more."
10 Customary veils and masks had dropped.
Each looked at the hidden other in each.
Sure, we who could never kiss had leapt
To living conclusions long before
Golden chestnut or copper beech.

15 So, as the wind drove sapless leaves
Into the bonfire of the sun,
As thunderclouds made giant graves
Of the black, bare hills of Kerry,[1]
In a swirl of shadow, words, one by one
20 Fell on the stubble and the sheaves;
"Wild dog rose this; this, hawthorn berry."

1 *A county of Ireland, in the province of Munster.*

But there was something more you meant,—
As if the trees and clouds had grown
Into a timeless flame that burnt
25 All worlds of words and left them dust
Through stubble and sedge by the late wind blown:
A love not born and not to be learnt,
But given and taken, an ultimate trust.

Now, between my restless eyes
30 And the scribbled wisdom of the ages
Black hills meet moving skies
And through rough hedges a late wind blows;
And in my palm through all the rages
Of lust and love now, always, lie
35 Brown hawthorn berry, red dog rose.

Myths

Alone one noon on a sheet of igneous rock
I smashed a five-foot cobra's head to pulp;
Then, lifting its cool still-squirming gold
In my sweating ten separate fingers, suddenly
5   Tall aloes were also standing there,
Lichens were mat-red patches on glinting boulders,
Clouds erupted white on the mountain's edge,
And, all insisting on being seen.
Familiar, and terribly strange, I felt the sun
10 Gauntlet my arms and cloak my growing shoulders.

Never quite the same again
Poplar, oak or pine, no, none
Of the multifarious shapes and scents that breed
About the homestead, below the dam, along the canal,
15 Or any place where a European,
Making the most of a fistful of water, splits
The brown and grey with wedges of daring green—
Known as invaders now, alien,
Like the sounds on my tongue, the pink on my skin;

20 And, like my heroes, Jason,[2] David,[3] Robin Hood,[4]
Leaving tentative footprints on the sand between
The aloe and the rock, uncertain if this
Were part of their proper destiny. Reading
Keats's *Lamia* and *Saint Agnes' Eve*
25 Beneath a giant pear tree buzzing with bloom
I glanced at the galvanised windmill turning
Its iron sunflower under the white-hot sky
And wondered if a Grecian or Medieval dream
Could ever strike root away from our wedges of green.

30 Could ever belong down there
Where the level sheen on new lucerne stops short:
Where aloes and thorns thrust roughly out
Of the slate-blue shales and purple dolerite.

2 *In Greek mythology, Jason, leader of the Argonauts, was sent to fetch the Golden Fleece.*
3 *The second king of Israel succeeding Saul. He was the boy slayer of the Philistine giant Goliath, player of the harp, and the beloved*

companion of Saul's son Jonathan.
4 *Leader of a band of robbers in medieval times whose aim was to bring about a more equitable distribution of wealth by robbing the rich to help the poor.*

Yet sometimes the ghosts that books had put in my brain
35 Would slip from their hiding behind my eyes
To take on flesh, the sometimes curious flesh
Of an African incarnation.

One winter dusk when the livid snow
On Swaershoek Pass[5] went dull, and the grey
40 Ash-bushes grew dim in smudges of smoke,
I stopped at the outspan place to watch,
Intenser as the purple shades drew down,

A little fire leaping near a wagon,
Sending its acrid smoke into the homeless night.
45 Patient as despair, eyes closed, ugly,
The woman stretched small hands towards the flames;
But the man, back to an indigo boulder,
Face thrown up to the sky, was striking
Rivers of sorrow into the arid darkness
50 From the throat of a battered, cheap guitar.

It seemed that in an empty hell
Of darkness, cold and hunger, I had stumbled on
Eurydice,[6] ragged, deaf forever,
Orpheus playing to beasts that would or could not hear,
55 Both eternally lost to news or rumours of spring.

5 A mountain-pass in the Karoo, between
Cradock and Somerset East, so called
because the families in the area are related to
each other. ("Swaer" means brother-in-law.)
6 Wife of Orpheus, who followed her into
Hades (an equivalent of hell) after her death,
and who won her back with his music.
When he disregarded one of the terms of her
release to the upper world, she vanished for
ever.

Lawrence Ferlinghetti (1919 –)

Ferlinghetti is an American poet, playwright and editor who was a
major figure in the Beat poetry movement of the 1950s. This group of
poets aimed to make their writing relevant to ordinary people by using
language that was close to ordinary speech, and by writing about topi-
cal political and social issues. Ferlinghetti's work has been described in
Volume 3 of Contemporary Authors *as "a deft, rapid-paced, whirling*
performance. He has a wonderful eye for meaning in the common-
place". Ferlinghetti's "Constantly risking absurdity" demonstrates that
he regards poetry in this light.

"Constantly risking absurdity"

    Constantly risking absurdity
                    and death
        whenever he performs
               above the heads
5   of his audience
    the poet like an acrobat
            climbs on rhyme
                to a high wire of his own making
    and balancing on eyebeams
10   above a sea of faces
          paces his way
              to the other side of day
        performing entrechats
             and sleight-of-foot tricks
15   and other high theatrics
             and all without mistaking
      any thing
         for what it may not be

    For he's the super realist
20   who must perforce perceive
        taut truth
           before the taking of each stance or step
    in his supposed advance
           toward that still higher perch
25   where Beauty stands and waits
             with gravity
             to start her death-defying leap

And he
    a little charleychaplin[1] man
                who may or may not catch
      her fair eternal form
          spreadeagled in the empty air
  of existence

30

1 *Charlie (Charley) Chaplin, an English comedian who won international fame with*   *his portrayal in silent films of a pathetic yet comic little tramp.*

Ruth Miller (1919 – 1969)

Ruth Miller was born in Uitenhage, Cape Province, and educated in
Pietersburg, Transvaal. She married the writer, Wolfe Miller, but they
later separated. Ruth Miller worked first as a shorthand typist and
then, from 1961 to 1964, as an English teacher. In 1966, she was
awarded the Ingrid Jonker Memorial Prize for her volume of poetry,
Floating Island, the title poem of which is reproduced below. A second
book of poetry, Selected Poems, was published in 1968. She also wrote
radio plays and short stories. She died of cancer at the age of fifty. A
collected edition of her poems, plays and prose writings, edited by
Lionel Abrahams, appeared in 1990.

Miller's poetry owes much to her South African heritage and to the
inspiration and mysteries of nature.

The Floating Island

Down the glutted river's throat
Jut the jagged trunks of trees,
Giddily the bubbles float;
The dead drowned buck have wounded knees.
5 The basket nests ooze mud in sodden trees.

Swirling in a giddy gyre
Down the brown Zambesi[1] flood
Comes an island—torn entire
With tendon reeds and brackish blood,
10 Prised from its moorings in the silent mud.

Bearing on its swinging arc
A herd of buck, alive, aground,
With anguished eyes, their wet flanks dark
With sweat. The water gabbles round.
15 Their sucking hoofprints moon the mud with sound.

The sliding scenery repeats
The gliding greenery of fear.
A newborn buck gropes for the teats;
Green to terror, he does not hear
20 The lipping tongues around his mother's feet.

---

1 *The Zambesi (Zambezi) is a river running*   Indian Ocean.
   from Zambia, through Mozambique, to the

Head back flat, with seashell horns
Against the wind the leader strains.
Around him lean the does and fawns;
They can remember summer rains—
25 But not like these. Not these obliterated plains.

Do they smell the tumbling doom
Scarved in silken spray that slides
To the falling ledge, that looms
But one nightfall on? Their sides
30 Bulge and flatten. Their eyes darken and grow wide.

Along the gorged Zambesi swims
In a slow insensate dance
Frieze of buck with dervish° limbs   *whirling*
Frozen in a dreamer's trance.
35 Anarchy has leapt beyond mischance.

A nightfall on the Smoke that Thunders[2]
Will spring to gun their leaping sides.
Wrenched from our continent, we blunder
And lacking weather-sense for guide
40 *Our* green uncharted islands sink in ravelled floods, blind-eyed.

Penguin on the Beach

Stranger in his own element,
Sea-casualty, the castaway manikin
Waddles in his tailored coat-tails. Oil

Has spread a deep commercial stain
5 Over his downy shirtfront. Sleazy, grey,
It clogs the sleekness. Far too well

He must recall the past, to be so cautious;
Watch him step into the waves. He shudders
Under the froth, slides, slips, on the wet sand,

10 Escaping to dryness, dearth, in a white cascade,
An involuntary shouldering off of gleam.
Hands push him back into the sea. He stands

2 *The Victoria Falls in Zimbabwe.*

In pained and silent expostulation.
Once he knew a sunlit, leaping smoothness,
15 But close within his head's small knoll, and dark

He retains the image; oil on sea,
Green slicks, black lassos of sludge
Sleaving° the breakers in a stain-spread scarf.   *cleaving, splitting*

He shudders now from the clean flinching wave,
20 Turns and plods back up the yellow sand,
Ineffably weary, triumphantly sad.

He is immensely wise: he trusts nobody. His senses
Are clogged with experience. He eats
Fish from his Saviour's hands, and it tastes black.

Submarine

Icarus² swaggered into his dandelion death
Knowing the wings were strong, being his seed-maker's.
When he plunged, the crumpled sea was deathless.

But within depths so dense that even fishes
5 Abandon the domelid pressure to slow, dark
Lumpish things, or reeling threads
Lamped with a million moons in the seasonless weather—
Atom on atom, fathom on fathom, the lords
Of the earth and sky in their sleek phallus ram
10 Through forests of throttled night and rubber weed,
Packed with steel on steel, to hang there driftless.

The sea humps, thick and crammed.
Itself upon itself pressed in coiled weight;
Gathers a muscled push, one huge Laocoon³ heave.
15 Rivets melt like motes, bulwarks sway gelid,°   *frozen*

2 *Son of the mythical Daedalus who, trapped
in Crete, devised wings for himself and for
Icarus. The father flew safely across the
Aegean Sea, but Icarus flew too close to the
sun and the wax fastening the wings to his
body melted. He plunged into the sea and
was drowned.*

3 *A priest of Apollo who, while sacrificing to
Neptune, was crushed, with his two sons, by
two huge sea serpents. This was in
punishment for having tried to dissuade the
Trojans from bringing into the city the
"wooden horse" in which their enemies, the
Greeks, were hidden.*

The steel is mothed and butterflied. There are no more men.
The swaying list in the impacting solid
Thins, miles high, onto a white beach
Where Heaven is always Up

20 While the persistent tides
Wait secretly to smash
Those whom dark hells in privacy corrupt.

Pete Seeger (1919 –)

*Seeger is an American folk singer, poet, and songwriter. He has
appeared in three motion pictures and recorded over eighty record
albums. During his military service in the US Army Special Services, he
entertained troops in the USA and the South Pacific. Seeger is
renowned for his children's songs, folk ballads and freedom songs.
Titles which are particularly well known are "If I Had a Hammer" and
"Kisses are Sweeter than Wine". "Where Have all the Flowers Gone",
an anti-war song, was written during the Vietnam War; it laments the
waste of human life, beauty and potential.*

"Where have all the flowers gone?"

Where have all the flowers gone?
Long time passing.
Where have all the flowers gone?
Long time ago.
5 Where have all the flowers gone?
Young girls picked them every one.
When will they ever learn?
When will they ever learn?

Where have all the young girls gone?
10 Long time passing.
Where have all the young girls gone?
Long time ago.
Where have all the young girls gone?
Gone to young men every one.
15 When will they ever learn?
When will they ever learn?

Where have all the young men gone?
Long time passing.
Where have all the young men gone?
20   Long time ago.
Where have all the young men gone?
Gone as soldiers every one.

Where have all the soldiers gone?
Long time passing.
25   Where have all the soldiers gone?
Long time ago.
Where have all the soldiers gone?
Gone to graveyards every one.

Where have all the graveyards gone?
30   Long time passing.
Where have all the graveyards gone?
Long time ago.
Where have all the graveyards gone?
Gone to flowers every one.
35   When will they ever learn?
When will they ever learn?

D.J. Enright (1920 –)

Born in Leamington in Warwickshire, England, Enright has taught in universities in Egypt, Japan, Germany, Thailand, and in Singapore where he served as Professor of English from 1960 to 1970. He is now resident in London. He was awarded the Queen's Gold Medal for Poetry in 1981 and edited The Oxford Book of Contemporary Verse 1945–1980 *and* The Oxford Book of Death.

The Word   *'In the beginning there was the word.'* — *St. John's Gospel*

The sage° said: We are all books   *wise man*
In the great Library of God.
(He was a bookish person.)

One asked: Does He ever   *Will man ever live again after death?*
5   Take us out?
We spend our years as a tale that is told.   *Once ended – no one interested any more.*

The sage said: His will be done   *(Prayer – His will be done in Heaven)*
In the Library as it is Elsewhere.   *(As on Earth. God's will rules. If He wants to give life again it is up to Him.)*

One asked: But perhaps   *Worried that God will only give attention to upper-class – different perhaps less valua-*
10   He is only interested in first editions,   *ble 'books'. People. Reprints – copies of*
Not in reprints, abridgements, strip cartoon   *those who have* — *shorter versions*   *(gone before them.*
Or other adaptations;   *light-hearted*   *different in any way. Short lives – lives – no depth*

The sage said: His love speaks volumes.   *continuation of metaphor.*
He is a speed reader. He is no respecter   *understands us much better & much faster than we understand ourselves*
15   Of Bestseller lists.   *Takes no notice of other people's opinions*
He suffers the little magazines to come unto Him.   *"suffered the little children to come unto him" even unsubstantial seeming magazines have a place in His library.*
Some hoped their jackets would be clean   *concerned with superficial / outward appearance*
And well pressed when the call was heard,
Their loins girded° about and their lights burning.   *ready for the return of the messiah, each in their own way.*   *prepared for action*

20   God thought: I wrote all the books,   *Irony if God is creator of all man-kind (i.e. author of books) He need not*
Now they expect Me to read them.   *read them to know their content – strength & weakness, good ect. No need to take them off the shelf once placed there !!!*

METAPHOR – WE ARE ALL BOOKS IN GOD'S LIBRARY.

Edwin Morgan (1920 –)

Born in Glasgow, Edwin Morgan has remained in Scotland, where he has taught at various universities. He has written several types of poetry but is best known for his light-hearted permutations. This is demonstrated in the poem "Opening the Cage", in which he tries to define poetry and himself by means of variations on a theme. He is also known for his interest in science and technology, evident in his poems dealing with space exploration.

Opening the Cage

14 variations on 14 words
I have nothing to say and I am saying it and that is poetry.
John Cage

I have to say poetry and is that nothing and am I saying it
I am and I have poetry to say and is that nothing saying it
I am nothing and I have poetry to say and that is saying it
I that am saying poetry have nothing and it is I and to say
5   And I say that I am to have poetry and saying it is nothing
I am poetry and nothing and saving it is to say that I have
To have nothing is poetry and I am saying that and I say it
Poetry is saying I have nothing and I am to say that and it
Saying nothing I am poetry and I have to say that and it is
10 It is and I am and I have poetry saying say that to nothing
It is saying poetry to nothing and I say I have and am that
Poetry is saying I have it and I am nothing and to say that
And that nothing is poetry I am saying and I have to say it
Saying poetry is nothing and to that I say I am and have it

David Wright (1920 –)

Wright, who has been deaf from childhood, was born in Johannesburg and educated at the Northampton School for the Deaf in England. He left South Africa at the age of fourteen. His volumes of poetry include Poems, Moral Stories, Monologue of a Deaf Man, Nerve Ends *and* Selected Poems. *Notwithstanding his domicile, Wright's sustained interest in South Africa is seen in his book of poems entitled* A South African Album. *He has received numerous literary awards, among them the 1950 Atlantic Award for literature and the 1958 and 1960 Guinness Poetry Prizes. Wright's poem, "Swift", reveals a close and sympathetic regard for nature.*

Swift

A peculiar dropout, a small fledgling swift,
Stayed with us for a while as a kind of guest.
Voracious, he sat on his belly all day
Squeaking as high as a bat, except when fed.

5   Streamlined for flight, yet too topheavy to fly
Or take to the air in which he was meant to live,
How might he leave the ground, though designed for the sky?
Happy to squeak and eat, he made no attempt.

Feet like talons, powerful to cling and grip,
10   The hooded greedy face of a predator,
He gobbled his meat like a dragon, remained fat,
Satisfied and demanding, until one day

The scimitar wings for no reason suddenly
Beat ten times to the second. He upended
15   Himself with furious flutters; keeled half over
Battering with black feathers at the level

Tabletop he'd been squatting on, and almost
Stood on his head. Nothing would keep him quiet,
Having made clear to us that his time had come
20   He was ready to go, our pensioner of a fortnight.

We fetched him out to a field, carried in the palm
Of a hand; bowled the soft body like a ball
Into the air, which received him falling, but
His wings found their element, then scissoring

25 With panic sleight, bore the surprised and able
Creature to his inheritance; who sank,
Lifted and sank, with fear and confidence
Exulting into the distance, out of our sight.

Tatamkulu Afrika (1921 –)

*Little is known about Tatamkulu Afrika. He is over 70 years old,
works as a book-keeper and writes under this* nom de plume *to pre-
serve his privacy. He began writing poetry only in 1988. His poems
embody a remarkable capacity to face violence and pain calmly. In
1990 he won the Sydney Clouts Memorial Prize for his poem "The
Funeral of Anton Fransch", and his first volume of poetry,* Nine Lives,
*was awarded the English Academy's Olive Schreiner Prize for 1992.
The poem "Waiting for Lazarus", written in 1991, evokes the anticipa-
tion of a crowd of South Africans who are waiting for the return of a
political exile. The poem traces the speaker's response to both the
returning exile, and to the policeman whose task it is to monitor the
excited crowd.*

Waiting for Lazarus[1]

We begin to think he might not come.
Planes land and leak
grey dribbles of grey people onto tarmac, leave
us staring at a runway plunged
5 back into the heart of darkness of our fears.
More of us come, cram
into the airport lounge,
overflow it into the parking area, strain
against those of us inside.

1 *Biblical figure who rose from the dead (see
John 11).*

10 The police are everywhere: they smile
    as though they know something we still only fear,
    their walking through us with their walkie-talkies°   *two-way radios*
    the truculence° of those who dare.   *aggression*
    Someone whispers they have sneaked him through the other door,

15 have spirited him away.
    The whisper touches fire to the straw:
    we droop our heads and sway,
    and stomp, and sing, and bellow like a maddened bull,
    heavy as a woman from the rape of rage,
20 bones too narrowed for the head to batter through
    and screech in the inarticulate
    agony of the betrayed.

    We dance, we sway.
    I catch a blond young policeman's glance:
25 he is watching me, wide-eyed,
    wondering if I am the serpent in
    his sanitised° shell-hole.   *hygienic*
    And yet his foot is tapping too:
    the merest tremor, but it's there.
30 Perhaps he dragged at some black nursemaid's dugs
    and sucked her milk into his blood
    and became an African before an alien,
    shrinking from the glistening, wet snakeskin
    of this, his dancing, black, buck-nigger kin.

35 And then he's there,
    suddenly, as though he had always been,
    suit and tie, neat as a pin,
    improbably full-toothed, wide, white grin,
    and I think: "O-my-god,
40 he looks like a public relations man!"
    But then the AK47's° blaze   *automatic weapons*
    in the rolling thunder of our clapping hands
    (or so we like to see ourselves,
    dreaming of a people's mecca² under people's tsars),³
45 and I am swept along and onto him,
    hand thrust out, chin tucked in,
    but he embraces me, ear nestling on my ear,
    and I know this is a dark side of the moon man.

2 *Literally, Mohammed's birthplace and a*   3 *Russian emperors; here, rulers chosen by the*
   shrine; here, the place of one's aspirations.   *people.*

His name is Lazarus and he comes in
50 from the cold and bitter water of the Bay,
shells tangling in the tendrils of his hair,
cerements° beneath the suit and tie,   *grave clothes*
gulls screaming in his water-stopped ears,
his leaden body seeking proof
55 that he lives again,
has purpose, meaning, name.

Philip Larkin (1922 – 1985)

Philip Larkin was born in Warwickshire, England, and educated at
Oxford. He is one of the most significant British poets to have emerged
after 1950. Larkin was the most prominent member of a group of
poets who called themselves "The Movement", and who aimed to
write lucid and technically ordered poetry. To a certain extent, they
were reacting against the irrationalism of poets such as Dylan Thomas
and the excesses of free-form poetry that Modernism inspired. As is
evident from "Mr Bleaney", Larkin conforms to the tight structure of
an ordered rhyme scheme. He also felt that poetry should be brought
back to its readers, and thus tends to take his imagery from the experi-
ences of everyday life.

Mr Bleaney

"This was Mr Bleaney's room. He stayed
The whole time he was at the Bodies,[1] till
They moved him." Flowered curtains, thin and frayed,
Fall to within five inches of the sill,

5 Whose window shows a strip of building land,
Tussocky, littered. "Mr Bleaney took
My bit of garden properly in hand."
Bed, upright chair, sixty-watt bulb, no hook

Behind the door, no room for books or bags—
10 "I'll take it." So it happens that I lie
Where Mr Bleaney lay, and stub my fags
On the same saucer-souvenir, and try

1 *Motor car plant.*

Stuffing my ears with cotton-wool, to drown
The jabbering set he egged her on to buy.
15 I know his habits—what time he came down,
His preference for sauce to gravy, why

He kept on plugging at the four aways[2]—
Likewise their yearly frame: the Frinton[3] folk
Who put him up for summer holidays,
20 And Christmas at his sister's house in Stoke.[4]

But if he stood and watched the frigid wind
Tousling the clouds, lay on the fusty bed
Telling himself that this was home, and grinned,
And shivered, without shaking off the dread

25 That how we live measures our own nature,
And at his age having no more to show
Than one hired box should make him pretty sure
He warranted no better, I don't know.

---

2 *Section of British football pool which
requires competitors to gamble on a
prediction of four Association Football
teams winning matches "away" from their*
home grounds.
3 *English coastal holiday resort.*
4 *Village in Nottinghamshire, in England's
east midlands.*

Daniel P. Kunene (1923 –)

Born in Edenville, Orange Free State, Kunene has been Professor of African Languages and Literature at the University of Wisconsin in the USA since 1986. In addition to his critical study, Heroic Poetry of the Basotho, *and his collection of short stories,* From the Pit of Hell to the Spring of Life, *Kunene has written two volumes of poetry:* Pirates Have Become Our Kings *and* A Seed Must Seem to Die. *The latter examines the troubles experienced by blacks in Johannesburg's Soweto township.*

Do Not Ask Me

Do not ask me, mother, if they're gone
I fear to tell you
they left in the middle of the night
turned their backs on the warmth of the hearth
5   and for the last time
heard the home rooster crowing

Do not ask me, mother, where they went
Tracks on watery dew-bells
as puny feet brushed the morning grass
10   have evaporated in the heat of the sun's kindness
and the hunting bloody-snouted hounds
have lost the trail

But to you I will whisper:
Look where the willows weep
15   The willows of the Mohokare River[1]
have seen the forbidden sight
tiny feet in a mad choreographer's dance
from shore to shore
wading on the sandy bed
20   And the waters washed and levelled up the sands
Nor will the willows point their drooping limbs
to say where they've gone

Do not ask me, mother, why they left
Need I tell you
25   They took the amasi° bird out of the forbidden pot   *milk*
and bade it fill their clay-bowls to the very
brim they'd been so hungry
so long

---

1 *Caledon River, south-eastern Cape.*

Then an army with giant boots
30 came towering over them
Brand new guns
made to silence little children who cry
glinting in the African sun
The gun-toters threw the amasi bird
35 back into the pot
and wrote on it with the government's ink
   For white children only
and henceforth it was guarded night and day
by one hundred bayoneted soldiers

40 And the children raised their fists
and shouted:
Amasi! Amasi! We demand the amasi bird!
Amandla°! Amandla! Ngawethu!°   *Power! Ours!*

Now they've been gathered up
45 in the wings of the Giant Bird
to the place of circumcision
far, far away

And the village waits
for the day of their return
50 to conquer

Dennis Brutus (1924 –)

Dennis Brutus was born in Salisbury, Rhodesia (now Harare, Zimbabwe). He was a teacher and the President of the South African Non-Racial Olympic Committee before he left South Africa in 1966 after political imprisonment. He has travelled and lectured extensively, and was appointed Professor of English at Northwestern University, Illinois. He has published several volumes of poetry, including Letters to Martha and Other Poems from a South African Prison *and* Thoughts Abroad. *"On The Island" is based on the poet's experience of imprisonment on Robben Island, near Cape Town.*

On The Island[1]

1

Cement-grey floors and walls
cement-grey days
cement-grey time
and a grey susurration°   *whispering*
5   as of seas breaking
winds blowing
and rains drizzling

A barred existence
so that one did not need to look
10   at doors or windows
to know that they were sundered by bars
and one locked in a grey gelid° stream   *frozen*
of unmoving time.

2

When the rain came
15   it came in a quick moving squall
moving across the island
murmuring from afar
then drumming on the roof
then marching fading away.

---

1 *The title refers to Robben Island, site of a former political prison, visible from the* shoreline of Cape Town.

20   And sometimes one mistook
the weary tramp of feet
as the men came shuffling from the quarry
white-dust-filmed and shambling
for the rain
25   that came and drummed and marched away.

3

It was not quite envy
nor impatience
nor irritation
but a mixture of feelings
30   one felt
for the aloof deep-green dreaming firs
that poised in the island air
withdrawn, composed and still.

4

On Saturday afternoons we were embalmed in time
35   like specimen moths pressed under glass;
we were immobile in the sunlit afternoon
waiting;
visiting time:
until suddenly like a book snapped shut
40   all possibilities vanished as zero hour passed
and we knew another week would have to pass.

Sydney Clouts (1926 – 1982)

Born in Cape Town and educated in the Cape Province, Clouts moved to London in 1961, where he worked as a librarian. His poetry is published in One Life *(which was awarded the Ingrid Jonker Prize in 1967 and the Olive Schreiner Prize in 1968) and in the posthumous volume,* Sydney Clouts: Collected Poems, *which was published in 1984.*

"After the Poem" bears witness to Clouts's literary interests, showing an acute awareness of the poem as a literary artefact. His concern with the unique essence of things and of persons is manifest both here and in "The Sleeper".

After the Poem

After the poem the coastline took
its place with a forward look
toughly disputing the right of a poem to possess it

It was not a coast that couldn't yet be made
5   the subject of a poem don't mistake me
nothing to do with "literary history"

But the coast flashed up—flashed, say, like objections
up to the rocky summit of the Sentinel[1]
that sloped into the sea
10   such force in it that every line was broken

    and the sea came by
    the breaking sea came by

The Sleeper

For Marge

When you awake
Gesture will waken
To decisive things.
Asleep, you have taken

---

1 *Mountain peak adjacent to Table Mountain, formerly used as a lookout post. (There are various Sentinels in South Africa and* *Namibia. Clouts presumably refers to the one in Cape Town.)*

5   Motion and tenderly laid it
Within, deeply within you.
Your shoulders are shining
With your own clear light.
I should be mistaken
10 To touch you even softly,
To disturb your bold
And entirely personal devotion
To the self that sleeps,
And is your very self,
15 Crucial as when you hasten
In the house and hasten through the street,
Or sit in the deep yellow chair
And breathe sweet air.

Unaware of the stars
20 Outside your window
That do not know they shine;
As well as of the wild sea
That can have no care;
As well as of the wind
25 That blows unaware
Of its motion in the air,
Sound be your rest
And gentle the dreaming
Of your silent body
30 Passionately asleep.
Can a cloud stay so still?
Can a bird be so lonely?

It seems you have found
Great patience in your breath:
35 It moves with life,
It rehearses death.

John Ashbery (1927 –)

Born near Rochester, New York, John Ashbery was educated at
Harvard and Columbia Universities in the USA. He spent ten years in
Paris, during which he worked as an art critic for various journals. The
works reproduced below show a preoccupation with art and the artist.
While Ashbery's poems cannot be confined to single meanings, the
poem "Crazy Weather" suggests a nostalgic evocation of young love
and its "simple unconscious dignity". "The Painter" records the fate of
the artist who, overawed by the immensity of the ocean he wishes to
capture in paint, invites the sea to "usurp the canvas" instead.
Conversational in tone, these works are characterized by simple diction
and flexibility of structure.

Crazy Weather

It's this crazy weather we've been having:
Falling forward one minute, lying down the next
Among the loose grasses and soft, white, nameless flowers.
People have been making a garment out of it,
5   Stitching the white of lilacs together with lightning
At some anonymous crossroads. The sky calls
To the deaf earth. The proverbial disarray
Of morning corrects itself as you stand up.
You are wearing a text. The lines
10   Droop to your shoelaces and I shall never want or need
Any other literature than this poetry of mud
And ambitious reminiscences of times when it came easily
Through the then woods and ploughed fields and had
A simple unconscious dignity we can never hope to
15   Approximate now except in narrow ravines nobody
Will inspect where some late sample of the rare,
Uninteresting specimen might still be putting out shoots, for all we know.

The Painter

Sitting between the sea and the buildings
He enjoyed painting the sea's portrait.
But just as children imagine a prayer
Is merely silence, he expected his subject
5   To rush up the sand, and, seizing a brush,
Plaster its own portrait on the canvas.

So there was never any paint on his canvas
Until the people who lived in the buildings
Put him to work: "Try using the brush
10   As a means to an end. Select, for a portrait,
Something less angry and large, and more subject
To a painter's moods, or, perhaps, to a prayer".

How could he explain to them his prayer
That nature, not art, might usurp the canvas?
15   He chose his wife for a new subject,
Making her vast, like ruined buildings,
As if, forgetting itself, the portrait
Had expressed itself without a brush.

Slightly encouraged, he dipped his brush
20   In the sea, murmuring a heartfelt prayer:
"My soul, when I paint this next portrait
Let it be you who wrecks the canvas".
The news spread like wildfire through the buildings:
He had gone back to the sea for his subject.

25   Imagine a painter crucified by his subject!
Too exhausted even to lift his brush,
He provoked some artists leaning from the buildings
To malicious mirth: "We haven't a prayer
Now, of putting ourselves on canvas,
30   Or getting the sea to sit for a portrait!"

Others declared it a self-portrait.
Finally all indications of a subject
Began to fade, leaving the canvas
Perfectly white. He put down the brush.
35   At once a howl, that was also a prayer,
Arose from the overcrowded buildings.

They tossed him, the portrait, from the tallest of the buildings;
And the sea devoured the canvas and the brush
As though his subject had decided to remain a prayer.

Charles Tomlinson (1927 –)

Tomlinson began his career as an artist, remains fascinated by modern art (Cezanne in particular) and still alternates periods of poetic composition with periods of painting, of which he is a recognized master. A poem such as "Paring the Apple" shows something of his mastery of both crafts. Visual intensity and intellectual curiosity, often exploring the relationship of his reader to the object or landscape described, are combined in many of his poems. His painterly eye imparts to his writing a precision, a respect for the details of language and sentence structure, which demands that the reading of his poetry should be pursued slowly and carefully.

Paring the Apple

There are portraits and still-lives.

And there is paring the apple.

And then? Paring it slowly,
From under cool-yellow
5   Cold-white emerging. And . . .?

The spring of concentric peel
Unwinding off white,
The blade hidden, dividing.

There are portraits and still-lives
10   And the first, because "human"
Does not excel the second, and
Neither is less weighted
With a human gesture, than paring the apple
With a human stillness.

15   The cool blade
Severs between coolness, apple-rind
Compelling a recognition.

Maya Angelou (1928 –)

Maya Angelou was born in St Louis, Missouri, and grew up in Arkansas. When she was a young child, the shock of being sexually assaulted by one of her mother's male friends rendered her mute for some time. She teaches American Studies at Wake Forest University in North Carolina, and is best known for her volumes of autobiography, the first of which is entitled I Know Why the Caged Bird Sings. *Her poetry communicates both the problems and the optimism of the black American working class.*

Still I Rise

You may write me down in history
With your bitter, twisted lies,
You may trod me in the very dirt
But still, like dust, I'll rise.

5   Does my sassiness° upset you?   *cheekiness*
Why are you beset with gloom?
'Cause I walk like I've got oil wells
Pumping in my living room.

Just like moons and like suns,
10   With the certainty of tides,
Just like hopes springing high,
Still I'll rise.

Did you want to see me broken?
Bowed head and lowered eyes?
15   Shoulders falling down like teardrops,
Weakened by my soulful cries.

Does my haughtiness offend you?
Don't you take it awful hard
'Cause I laugh like I've got gold mines
20   Diggin' in my own back yard.

You may shoot me with your words,
You may cut me with your eyes,
You may kill me with your hatefulness,
But still, like air, I'll rise.

25 Does my sexiness upset you?
 Does it come as a surprise
 That I dance like I've got diamonds
 At the meeting of my thighs?

 Out of the huts of history's shame
30 I rise
 Up from a past that's rooted in pain
 I rise
 I'm a black ocean, leaping and wide,
 Welling and swelling I bear in the tide.

35 Leaving behind nights of terror and fear
 I rise
 Into a daybreak that's wondrously clear
 I rise
 Bringing the gifts that my ancestors gave,
40 I am the dream and the hope of the slave.
 I rise
 I rise
 I rise.

Woman Work

 I've got the children to tend
 The clothes to mend
 The floor to mop
 The food to shop
5 Then the chicken to fry
 The baby to dry
 I got company to feed
 The garden to weed
 I've got the shirts to press
10 The tots to dress
 The cane to be cut
 I gotta clean up this hut
 Then see about the sick
 And the cotton to pick.

15 Shine on me, sunshine
 Rain on me, rain
 Fall softly, dewdrops
 And cool my brow again.

Storm, blow me from here
20 With your fiercest wind
Let me float across the sky
'Til I can rest again.

Fall gently, snowflakes
Cover me with white
25 Cold icy kisses and
Let me rest tonight.

Sun, rain, curving sky
Mountain, oceans, leaf and stone
Star shine, moon glow
30 You're all that I can call my own.

Anne Sexton (1928 – 1974)

Sexton married at sixteen after a brief career as a fashion model. The birth of her first child was followed by a series of nervous breakdowns and long hospitalizations, and eventually she took her own life. Her poetry has been seen by some critics as autobiographical: it expresses deeply personal feelings and treats mental illness, women's experience and religious questions (as explored in "The Starry Night") with courage and honesty. It could be argued that her writing began as "therapy", but her controlled employment of language and of poetic structures raises her work above the level of simply case history.

The Starry Night

> *That does not keep me from having a terrible need*
> *of—shall I say the word—religion. Then I go out at*
> *night to paint the stars.*
> Vincent van Gogh:[1] In a letter to his brother

The town does not exist
except where one black-haired tree slips
up like a drowned woman into the hot sky.
The town is silent. The night boils with eleven stars.
5   Oh starry starry night! This is how
I want to die.

It moves. They are all alive.
Even the moon bulges in its orange irons
to push children, like a god, from its eye.
10   The old unseen serpent swallows up the stars.
Oh starry starry night! This is how
I want to die:

into that rushing beast of the night,
sucked up by that great dragon, to split
15   from my life with no flag,
no belly,
no cry.

---

1 *The Dutch painter, Vincent van Gogh*
(1853-1890).

Thom Gunn (1929 –)

Born in Gravesend, England, Gunn studied English at Trinity College, Cambridge, after completing his national service. While still an under-graduate he completed his first collection of poetry, Fighting Terms *(1954). In the same year he moved to California and enrolled for post-graduate study at Stanford University. Four years later he was appointed as a teacher at Berkeley and he remained there until 1966. He settled in San Francisco, where he became interested in mysticism and the "flower-power" counter-culture.*

Thom Gunn's earlier poetry displays an interest in violence, both in nature and in social life, while his more recent work, The Passages of Joy *(1982) and* The Man with Night Sweats *(1992), commemorates friendship and loss.*

Memory Unsettled[1]

Your pain still hangs in air,
Sharp motes of it suspended;
The voice of your despair—
That also is not ended:

5   When near your death a friend
Asked you what he could do,
"Remember me", you said.
We will remember you.

Once when you went to see
10   Another with a fever
In a like hospital bed,
With terrible hothouse cough
And terrible hothouse shiver
That soaked him and then dried him,
15   And you perceived that he
Had to be comforted,

You climbed in there beside him
And hugged him plain in view,
Though you were sick enough,
20   And had your own fears too.

---

1 *This poem from the volume* The Man with   *result of AIDS.*
Night Sweats *concerns a friend's death as a*

Adrienne Rich (1929 –)

Adrienne Rich is an influential American poet and critic whose mature vision has been exclusively devoted to women. Her own life has been a rich and diverse one, ranging from marriage and motherhood to widowhood, lesbianism and feminism. One of the chief problems with which Rich wrestles in her poetry and prose is the difficulty of writing about the oppressed and marginalized while using the language of the dominant group. Another paradox she addresses is the apparent impossibility of women acquiring power without using the violence that characterizes patriarchy. "Your Small Hands", a love poem to another woman, deals with this problem by drawing attention to the constructive (rather than the destructive) potential of a woman's hands.

From 21 LOVE POEMS *(extract)*

6

Your small hands, precisely equal to my own—
only the thumb is larger, longer—in these hands
I could trust the world, or in many hands like these,
handling power-tools or steering-wheel
5 or touching a human face . . . . Such hands could turn
the unborn child rightways in the birth canal
or pilot the exploratory rescue-ship
through icebergs, or piece together
the fine, needle-like sherds° of a great krater-cup°   *shards / wine-vessel*
10 bearing on its sides
figures of ecstatic women striding
to the sibyl's den or the Eleusinian[1] cave—
such hands might carry out an unavoidable violence
with such restraint, with such a grasp
15 of the range and limits of violence
that violence ever after would be obsolete.

1 *Eleusinian rites took place at Eleusis, near Athens, in honour of Demeter, the Greek goddess of fruit and grain. They also focused on the return of Demeter's daughter, Persephone, after she was taken into the underworld by Hades (Pluto).*

Ted Hughes (1930 –)

Ted Hughes was born in Yorkshire, England, and educated at Cambridge. In 1956 he married the American poet, Sylvia Plath. He is one of the most influential British poets to emerge since the 1950s.

There is a profusion of creatures in Hughes's work. However, he is certainly not a sentimental animal-poet. His creatures are used as central emblems or metaphors for the human condition. Hughes is a typically modern poet who seeks to go beyond the conscious, rational self, into the unconscious, and to explore vital, natural, non-human forces. In his early poetry, Hughes makes much use of animal metaphors to express the immediacy of the primary struggles between vitality and death. His poetry is directed at making the reader aware of the life forces, both violent and beautiful, underlying the familiar world of common perception.

In "Pike", Hughes uses the presentation of nature for the purpose of exploring basic dualities, such as beauty and horror, peace and violence, and the seen and unseen. In a different vein, "The Thought Fox", while sensitively portraying the animal's characteristic movements, explores the workings of the poet's mind in the process of creation.

From CROW[1] *(extract)*

Two Legends

I

Black was the without eye
Black the within tongue
Black was the heart
Black the liver, black the lungs
5 Unable to suck in light
Black the blood in its loud tunnel
Black the bowels packed in furnace
Black too the muscles
Striving to pull out into the light
10 Black the nerves, black the brain

---

1 Crow *is Ted Hughes's reworking of the Creation myth. It is based on the idea of the folk tale in which God, having created the world, has a nightmare. In this nightmare a voice tells God that Man wants God to take life back since his creation has been such a* terrible muddle. God challenges the nightmare to do better and the nightmare produces Crow. God shows Crow around the universe, giving Crow the opportunity to comment on creation.

With its tombed visions
Black also the soul, the huge stammer
Of the cry that, swelling, could not
Pronounce its sun.

II

15 Black is the wet otter's head, lifted.
Black is the rock, plunging in foam.
Black is the gall lying on the bed of the blood.

Black is the earth-globe, one inch under,
An egg of blackness
20 Where sun and moon alternate their weathers

To hatch a crow, a black rainbow
Bent in emptiness
                    over emptiness
But flying

Nightjar

The tree creeps on its knees
The dead branch aims, in the last light.
The cat-bird is telescopic.

The sun's escape
5 Shudders, shot
By wings of ashes.

The moon falls, with all its moths,
Into a bird's face.

Stars spark
10 From the rasp of its cry.

Till the moon-eater, cooling,
Yawns dawn
And sleeps bark.

Pike

Pike, three inches long, perfect
Pike in all parts, green tigering the gold.
Killers from the egg: the malevolent aged grin.
They dance on the surface among the flies.

5   Or move, stunned by their own grandeur,
Over a bed of emerald, silhouette
Of submarine delicacy and horror.
A hundred feet long in their world.

In ponds, under the heat-struck lily pads—
10 Gloom of their stillness:
Logged on last year's black leaves, watching upwards.
Or hung in an amber cavern of weeds

The jaws' hooked clamp and fangs
Not to be changed at this date;
15 A life subdued to its instrument;
The gills kneading quietly, and the pectorals.

Three we kept behind glass,
Jungled in weed: three inches, four,
And four and a half: fed fry to them—
20 Suddenly there were two. Finally one

With a sag belly and the grin it was born with.
And indeed they spare nobody.
Two, six pounds each, over two feet long,
High and dry and dead in the willow-herb—

25 One jammed past its gills down the other's gullet:
The outside eye stared: as a vice locks—
The same iron in this eye
Though its film shrank in death.

A pond I fished, fifty yards across,
30 Whose lilies and muscular tench
Had outlasted every visible stone
Of the monastery that planted them—

Stilled legendary depth:
It was as deep as England. It held
35 Pike too immense to stir, so immense and old
That past nightfall I dared not cast

But silently cast and fished
With the hair frozen on my head
For what might move, for what eye might move.
40 The still splashes on the dark pond,

Owls hushing the floating woods
Frail on my ear against the dream
Darkness beneath night's darkness had freed,
That rose slowly towards me, watching.

The Thought-Fox

I imagine this midnight moment's forest:
Something else is alive
Beside the clock's loneliness
And this blank page where my fingers move.

5 Through the window I see no star:
Something more near
Though deeper within darkness
Is entering the loneliness:

Cold, delicately as the dark snow,
10 A fox's nose touches twig, leaf;
Two eyes serve a movement, that now
And again now, and now, and now

Sets neat prints into the snow
Between trees, and warily a lame
15 Shadow lags by stump and in hollow
Of a body that is bold to come

Across clearings, an eye,
A widening deepening greenness,
Brilliantly, concentratedly,
20 Coming about its own business

Till, with a sudden sharp hot stink of fox
It enters the dark hole of the head.
The window is starless still; the clock ticks,
The page is printed.

Thrushes

Terrifying are the attent° sleek thrushes on the lawn,   *attentive*
More coiled steel than living—a poised
Dark deadly eye, those delicate legs
Triggered to stirrings beyond sense—with a start, a bounce, a stab
5   Overtake the instant and drag out some writhing thing.
No indolent procrastinations and no yawning stares.
No sighs or head-scratchings. Nothing but bounce and stab
And a ravening second.

Is it their single-minded-sized skulls, or a trained
10   Body, or genius, or a nestful of brats
Gives their days this bullet and automatic
Purpose? Mozart's[1] brain had it, and the shark's mouth
That hungers down the blood-smell even to a leak of its own
Side and devouring of itself: efficiency which
15   Strikes too streamlined for any doubt to pluck at it
Or obstruction deflect.

With a man it is otherwise. Heroisms on horseback,
Outstripping his desk-diary at a broad desk,
Carving at a tiny ivory ornament
20   For years: his act worships itself—while for him,
Though he bends to be blent in the prayer, how loud and above what

Furious spaces of fire do the distracting devils
Orgy and hosannah, under what wilderness   *shout praises*
Of black silent waters weep.

---

1 *The Austrian composer, Wolfgang Amadeus
Mozart (1756–1791).*

Douglas Livingstone (1932 –)

One of South Africa's major contemporary poets, Livingstone was born in Kuala Lumpur, Malaya, and moved to South Africa with his parents when he was ten. He was educated at Kearsney College, Natal, and the Pasteur Institute in Salisbury, Rhodesia (now Harare, Zimbabwe). He heads the marine bacteriology research centre at the Council for Scientific and Industrial Research in Durban.

Livingstone has written several volumes of poetry, including Sjambok and Other Poems from Africa, Eyes Closed Against the Sun *and* The Anvil's Undertone, *which successively focus, inter alia, on animals, urbanization and cultural transition, all in an African context. He received the BBC Federal Broadcasting Corporation Prize in 1964, the Guinness and the Cholmondeley Poetry Prizes in 1965 and 1970 respectively, the Olive Schreiner Prize in 1975 and the CNA Award in 1985.*

Gentling a Wildcat

Not much wild life, roared Mine leonine Host
from the fringe of a forest of crackles
round an old dome-headed steam radio,
between hotel and river—a mile of bush—
5   except for the wildcats and jackals.

And he, of these parts for years, was right.
That evening I ventured with no trepidations
and a torch, towed by the faculty
I cannot understand, that has got me
10   into too many situations.

Under a tree, in filtered moonlight,
a ragged heap of dusty leaves stopped moving.
A cat lay there, open from chin to loins;
lower viscera missing: truncated tubes
15   and bitten-off things protruding.

Little blood there was, but a mess of
damaged lungs; straining to hold its breath
for quiet; claws fixed curved and jutting,
jammed open in a stench of jackal meat;
20   it tried to raise its head hating the mystery, death.

The big spade skull with its lynx-fat cheeks
aggressive still, raging eyes hooked in me, game;
nostrils pulling at a tight mask of anger
and fear; then I remembered hearing
25 they are quite impossible to tame.

Closely, in a bowl of unmoving roots,
an untouched carcass, unlicked, swaddled and wrapped
in trappings of birth, the first of a litter stretched.
Rooted out in mid-confinement: a time
30 when jackals have courage enough for a wildcat.

In some things too, I am a coward,
and could not here punch down with braced thumb,
lift the nullifying stone or stiff-edged hand
to axe with mercy the nape of her spine.
35 Besides, I convinced myself, she was numb.

And oppressively, something felt wrong:
not her approaching melting with earth,
but in lifetimes of claws, kaleidoscopes:
moon-claws, sun-claws, teeth after death,
40 certainly both at mating and birth.

So I sat and gentled her with my hand,
not moving much but saying things, using my voice;
and she became gentle, affording herself
the influent luxury of breathing—
45 untrammelled, bubbly, safe in its noise.

Later, calmed, despite her tides of pain,
she let me ease her claws, the ends of the battle,
pulling off the trapped and rancid flesh.
Her miniature limbs of iron relaxed.
50 She died with hardly a rattle.

I placed her peaceful ungrinning corpse
and that of her firstborn in the topgallants[1]
of a young tree, out of ground reach, to grow: restart
a cycle of maybe something more pastoral,
55 commencing with beetles, then maggots, then ants.

---

1 Literally, the top rigging on a sailing vessel.

Stormshelter

Under the baobab tree, treaded
death, stroked in by the musty cats,
scratches silver on fleshy earth.
Threaded flame has unstitched and sundered
5 hollow thickets of bearded branches
blanched by a milk-wired ivy. Choleric°   *angry*
thunder staggers raging overhead.

"Never stand under trees in a storm."
Old saws° have an ancient rhythm   *proverbial sayings*
10 in them, but these dry, far from bold
norms and maxims are scalpel severed
by the sharp, needle-thin lightning,
frightening reason behind the eye,
slivered into lank abstract forms.

15 Steel spears, slim, yielding and stained
lightly with water, rattle their points.
Jointed the hafts swing, tufted brightly,
maiming invisibly. The shafts reel
through the streaked Impi² from Nowhere.
20 There is only one thing to do—
wheel, stamping, into that brittle rain.

Sunstrike

A solitary prospector
staggered, locked in a vision
of slate hills that capered
on the molten horizon.

5 Waterless, he came to where
a river had run, now a band
flowing only in ripples
of white unquenchable sand.

Cursing, he dug sporadically
10 here, here, as deep as his arm,
and sat quite still, eyes thirstily
incredulous on his palm.

2 *Unit of Zulu warriors.*

A handful of alluvial
diamonds leered back, and more: mixed
15 in the scar, glinted globules
of rubies, emeralds, onyx.

And then he was swimming in fire
and drinking, splashing hot halos
of glittering drops at the choir
20 of assembled carrion crows.

There are Times

There are times almost free from
certainties of disaster;
from awareness of mangling

by men and machines of men;
5 from knowledge of domestic
cruelties and suppressions.

There are times I benignly
walk the afternoon sunlight
balancing constellations

10 in the peaceable kingdom
of my spiritual and
temporal lack of success.

There are times, sometimes, these days
when for one minute or two
15 I am not even in love.

Casey Motsisi (1932 – 1977)

Casey Motsisi was a short-story writer and worked as a journalist for
Drum *magazine, a well-known black publication which launched the*
careers of several South African writers. "The Efficacy of Prayer" is a
heavily ironic poem about a couple's prayer that their daughter may
escape the fate of "Dan the Drunk". The prayer is granted, but the
poet's tone encourages the reader to question this "miracle".

The Efficacy of Prayer

They called him Dan the Drunk.
The old people refuse to say how old he was,
Nobody knows where he came from—but they all
Called him Dan the Drunk.
5   He was a drunk, but perhaps his name was not really Dan.
Who knows, he might have been Sam.
But why brother, he's dead, poor Dan.
Gave him a pauper's funeral, they did.
Just dumped him into a hole to rest in eternal drunkenness.
10   Somehow the old people are glad that Dan the Drunk is dead.
Ghastly!
They say he was a bad influence on the children.
But the kids are sad that Dan the Drunk is no more.
No more will the kids frolic on the music that used to flow out
15   of his battered concertina. Or listen to the tales he used to tell.
All followed him into that pauper's hole.
How the kids used to worship Dan the Drunk!
He was just one of them grown older too soon.
"I'm going to be just like Dan the Drunk," a little girl said to her parents
20   of a night cold while they crowded around a sleepy brazier.
The parents looked at each other and their eyes prayed.
"God Almighty, save our little Sally."
God heard their prayer.
He saved their Sally.
25   Prayer. It can work miracles.
Sally grew up to become a nanny . . .

Sylvia Plath (1932 – 1963)

*Born in Boston, Sylvia Plath was educated at Smith College in the
USA, and at Cambridge University in England, which she attended on
a Fulbright Scholarship. While at Cambridge she met the British poet,
Ted Hughes, whom she married in 1956. On completion of her degree,
Plath returned to Smith College, where she taught from 1957 to 1959.
She returned to England and lived there until her suicide in 1963.*

*In addition to four volumes of poetry—*The Colossus, Ariel,
Crossing the Water *and* Winter Trees, *Plath wrote an autobiographical
novel,* The Bell Jar. *Much of Plath's poetry explores an inner psycho-
logical world of anger and despair. "Black Rook in Rainy Weather"
and "Sheep in Fog" depict a mood of sombre depression, but Plath's
other poems are more optimistic, revealing the range of her poetic
talent. "You're" is a joyous celebration of an unborn child, while
"Balloons" describes a small child's perception of something he does
not understand, and his mother's vision of the delight children bring to
the stark realities of life.*

Balloons

Since Christmas they have lived with us,
Guileless and clear,
Oval soul-animals,
Taking up half the space,
5   Moving and rubbing on the silk

Invisible air drifts,
Giving a shriek and pop
When attacked, then scooting to rest, barely trembling.
Yellow cathead, blue fish—
10   Such queer moons we live with

Instead of dead furniture!
Straw mats, white walls
And these travelling
Globes of thin air, red, green,
15   Delighting

The heart like wishes or free
Peacocks blessing
Old ground with a feather
Beaten in starry metals.
20   Your small

Brother is making
His balloon squeak like a cat.
Seeming to see
A funny pink world he might eat on the other side of it,
25 He bites,

Then sits
Back, fat jug
Contemplating a world clear as water,
A red
30 Shred in his little fist.

Black Rook in Rainy Weather

On the stiff twig up there
Hunches a wet black rook
Arranging and rearranging its feathers in the rain.
I do not expect miracle
5 Or an accident

To set the sight on fire
In my eye, nor seek
Any more in the desultory weather some design,
But let spotted leaves fall as they fall,
10 Without ceremony, or portent

Although, I admit, I desire,
Occasionally, some backtalk
From the mute sky, I can't honestly complain:
A certain minor light may still
15 Leap incandescent

Out of the kitchen table or chair
As if a celestial burning took
Possession of the most obtuse objects now and then—
Thus hallowing an interval
20 Otherwise inconsequent

By bestowing largesse, honor,
One might say love. At any rate, I now walk
Wary (for it could happen
Even in this dull, ruinous landscape); sceptical,
25 Yet politic; ignorant

Of whatever angel may choose to flare
Suddenly at my elbow. I only know that a rook
Ordering its black feathers can so shine
As to seize my senses, haul
30   My eyelids up, and grant

A brief respite from fear
Of total neutrality. With luck,
Trekking stubborn through this season
Of fatigue, I shall
35   Patch together a content

Of sorts. Miracles occur,
If you care to call those spasmodic
Tricks of radiance miracles. The wait's begun again,
The long wait for the angel.
40   For that rare, random descent.[1]

Sheep in Fog

The hills step off into whiteness.
People or stars
Regard me sadly, I disappoint them.

The train leaves a line of breath.
5   O slow
Horse the colour of rust,

Hooves, dolorous bells—
All morning the
Morning has been blackening,

10   A flower left out.
My bones hold a stillness, the far
Fields melt my heart.

They threaten
To let me through to a heaven
15   Starless and fatherless, a dark water.

1 *At Pentecost, the Holy Ghost descended*   *form of tongues of flame.*
   upon Christ's disciples (Acts 2:1–4) in the

You're

Clownlike, happiest on your hands,
Feet to the stars, and moon-skulled,
Gilled like a fish. A common-sense
Thumbs-down on the dodo's mode.
5 Wrapped up in yourself like a spool,
Trawling your dark as owls do.
Mute as a turnip from the Fourth
Of July² to All Fools' Day,³
O high-riser, my little loaf.

10 Vague as fog and looked for like mail.
Farther off than Australia.
Bent-backed Atlas,⁴ our travelled prawn.
Snug as a bud and at home
Like a sprat in a pickle jug.
15 A creel of eels, all ripples.
Jumpy as a Mexican bean.
Right, like a well-done sum.
A clean slate, with your own face on.

2 *American Day of Independence.*
3 *1st April, a festival of misrule.*
4 *In Greek mythology, the Titan, Atlas, was* *compelled to carry the heavens on his* *shoulders. He is often pictured as bearing the* *earth on his shoulders.*

Sipho Sepamla (1932 –)

Sepamla was born in Krugersdorp and has worked as a teacher, a personnel officer and an editor of literary magazines. He has also been involved in training programmes for black artists and writers. His own literary output includes drama, poems, short stories and novels. His poetry has been described as a weapon which hits hard at a system that tries to dehumanize and reduce people to reference numbers. Together with writers such as Mtshali and Serote, Sepamla has taken his place as one of the new black poets of the 1970s.

With Lionel Abrahams, Sepamla received a Pringle Award in 1976.

The Blues is You in Me

When my heart pulsates a rhythm
off-beat with God's own scintillating pace
and I can trace only those thoughts
that mar the goodness of living with you
5   then I know I've got the blues for howling

        yeah I've been howling
        clouds have been muffling
        and the rain has come
        and washed away
10   these blues of mine

        the blues is you in me

I want to say it louder now
I want to holler my thoughts now
for I never knew the blues until I met you

15   the blues is you in me

the blues is the clicks of my tongue
agitated by the death I live

the blues is my father's squeals
every Friday in a week

20   the blues is you in me
        I never knew the blues until I met you

the blues is the screeches of the censor's pen
as he scribbles lamentations on my sensitized pad

the blues is the shadow of a cop
25 dancing the Immorality Act jitterbug

the blues is the Group Areas Act and all its jive

the blues is the Bantu Education Act[1] and its improvisations

    the blues is you in me
    I never knew the blues until I met you

30 the blues is people huddled on a bench
eating of their own thoughts

the blues is those many words said to repair
yesterdays felled again and again by today's promises
the blues is the long shadow I count
35 measured by moments dragging the sun

the blues is the ratting of my brother
for opportunities he gets which he ought to have had

    the blues is you in me
    I never knew the blues until I met you

40 I want to holler the how-long blues
because we are the blues people all
the whiteman bemoaning his burden
the blackman offloading the yoke

    the blues is you in me
45   I never knew the blues until I met you.

---

1 *The Immorality Act, Group Areas Act and
Bantu Education Act, which prohibited
racially mixed marriages, living areas and*
*education, were part of the apartheid
apparatus.*

Come Duze Baby[2]

Hela baby!	*Hi baby!*
Zwakala daarso	*Come over here [there]*
Of hoe sê ek?	*Or how shall I put it?*

Jy moet my notch	*You must look at me*
5 Kyk my mooi sweetie	*Look my pretty sweetie*
Ek is nie een van hulle	*I am not one of those*
Jy ken mos	*You know*
Die Hillbrow[3] type.	*The Hillbrow type.*

Hela Sisi!	*Hi Sister!*
10 Look sharp	*Look sharp*
Otherwise jy val	*Otherwise you'll fall*
Met my "M",	*I swear by my mother*
Jy val soos 'n sak kool.	*You'll fall like a sack of coal.*

Ek wil jou weedie	*I want to tell you*
15 Of praat jy net met situations	*Or do you talk only with those who*
	think they're superior
Die manne met 'n ntanjana	*The men with collar and tie*
Die Stetson oukies	*The Stetson guys*
Die Mpala-mpala outies	*The guys with large, black American cars*
Wat jou rwa	*Who cheat you*
20 Met Manyeledi[4]	*With offers of Manyeledi*
And Mgababa[5]	*And Mgababa*
Of hoe sê ek?	*Or how shall I put it?*

Baby jy's 'n washout	*Baby you're a washout*
Hulle vang jou	*They'll catch you*
25 Sluit jou toe	*Shut you up*
For Immorality[6]	*For Immorality*
'Strue met my "P"	*I swear by my father*
Jy's 'n has-been	*You're a has-been.*

---

2   *The poem is in "tsotsitaal", or the language of tsotsis, a popular black culture with its own norms, speech, dress, gait and interests. The operations of thugs and of street gangs have promoted a negative view of tsotsis.*

3   *Also known as flatland, Hillbrow is a densely populated suburb immediately north of Johannesburg's city centre.*

4   *& 5 Holiday resorts.*

6   *See "The Blues is You in Me", footnote 1.*

Kyk, ek mca jou baby	*Look, I like you baby*
30 Ek is serious	*I am serious*
My hart maak shandies	*My heart is behaving strangely*
Jy ken mos	*You know*
Die downtown beat	*The downtown beat*
Van Jimmy Smith se mojo.[7]	*Of Jimmy Smith's mojo.*
35 Ek praat die real ding	*I'm saying the real thing*
Moenie dink	*Don't think*
Ek wala-wala net stof	*I'm talking nonsense*
Ek wil jou cover	*I want to hug you*
Ek wil jou smekana	*I want to kiss you*
40 Jy ken mos	*You know*
Die movie-star ding.	*The movie-star thing.*
Jy's my number one mbuzana	*You're my number one girlfriend*
Die neneweet	*The whole truth*
Jy's my eie ding	*You're my very own*
45 Met my ma!	*I swear by my mother.*
Baby come duze!	*Baby come closer!*
Come duze baby!	*Come closer baby!*

7 *The allusion is to a song, popular among
tsotsis, by Jimmy Smith.*

Abdullah Ibrahim (1934 –)

The jazz musician Abdullah Ibrahim, formerly known as Dollar Brand, was born in Cape Town and lived for many years in Europe and the USA. He took his present name after converting to Islam. He has published poetry in The Journal of the New South African Literature and Arts, The Classic *and Cosmo Pieterse's* Seven South African Poets. *The poem "blues for district six" shows both Ibrahim's Cape heritage and his passion for music. (District Six was formerly a lively and densely populated "coloured" area which was evacuated and demolished under the Group Areas Act.)*

From AFRICA, MUSIC AND SHOW BUSINESS *(extract)*

VI

blues for district six

early one new year's morning
when the emerald bay waved its clear waters against the noisy dockyard
a restless south easter skipped over slumbering lion's head[1]
danced up hanover street
5   tenored a bawdy banjo
strung an ancient cello
bridged a host of guitars
tambourined through a dingy alley
into a scented cobwebbed room
10   and crackled the sixth sensed district
into a blazing swamp fire of satin sound

early one new year's morning
when the moaning bay mourned its murky water against the deserted dockyard
a bloodthirsty south easter roared over hungry lion's head
15   and ghosted its way up hanover street
empty
forlorn
and cobwebbed with gloom

---

1   *Lion's Head is the name of the mountain*
peak west of Table Mountain in Table Bay,
Cape Town.

Marge Piercy (1936 –)

*Born in Detroit, Michigan, Marge Piercy has been poet-in-residence at
the University of Kansas, Professor of Letters at Buffalo State
University of New York and Professor of Poetry at the University of
Cincinnati. Piercy has written ten novels as well as numerous volumes
of poetry. She has always tried to make her writing both accessible and
meaningful, insisting that a coherent poem can speak through rich and
complex imagery. In "A Story Wet as Tears", Piercy uses a traditional
fairy story to make a comment on human relationships.*

A Story Wet as Tears

Remember the princess who kissed the frog
so he became a prince? At first they danced
all weekend, toasted each other in the morning
with coffee, with champagne at night
5   and always with kisses. Perhaps it was
in bed after the first year had ground
around she noticed he had become cold
with her. She had to sleep
with heating pad and down comforter.
10   His manner grew increasingly chilly
and damp when she entered a room.
He spent his time in water sports,
hydroponics, working on his insect
collection.
         Then in the third year
15   when she said to him one day, my dearest,
are you taking your vitamins daily,
you look quite green, he leaped
away from her.
         Finally on their
fifth anniversary she confronted him.
20   "'My precious, don't you love me any
more?" He replied, "Rivet. Rivet."[1]
Though courtship turns frogs into princes,
marriage turns them quietly back.

---

1 *Indicates the sound made by a frog.*

Roger Mc Gough (1937 –)

McGough is a British poet and playwright. He was born into a work-ing-class home and became a school teacher. His anthology, In the Glassroom, *is based on his teaching experiences and is dedicated to "all those who gaze out of windows when they should be paying atten-tion". The image of glass also features in "A Brown Paper Carrierbag", a shocking portrayal of the destruction caused by a bomb explosion. The poem owes its effect not only to the typographical devices used, but also to the appalling contrast between a seemingly commonplace item—a brown paper bag—and the devastation caused when the bomb inside it is detonated.*

A Brown Paper Carrierbag

IN THE TIME . . .
  a spider's web woven across
  the plateglass° window shivers snaps   *thick, clear glass*
  and sends a shimmering haze of lethal stars
5 across the crowded restaurant

IN THE TIME IT TAKES . . .
  jigsaw pieces of shrapnel[1]
  glide gently towards children
  tucking in   to the warm flesh
10 a terrible hunger sated°   *satisfied*

IN THE TIME IT TAKES TO PUT DOWN . . .
  on the pavement
  people come apart   slowly
  at first
15 only the dead not screaming

IN THE TIME IT TAKES TO PUT DOWN A BROWN PAPER CARRIERBAG

---

1 *Fragments of metal from an explosive device.*

Margaret Atwood (1939 –)

Margaret Atwood is a Canadian poet and novelist. The daughter of an entomologist, Atwood puts people and relationships—rather than insects—under the microscope. This intense scrutiny is a feature of both her poetry and her novels. She is also a valuable contributor to the body of feminist writing.

The two poems printed below illustrate the range of Atwood's interests. "Habitation" explores the power politics of marriage in a series of explosive metaphors which reject romantic myths. "Earth" reflects her apprehensions regarding the future of our planet.

Earth

It isn't winter that brings it
out, my cowardice,
but the thickening summer I wallow in
right now, stinking of lilacs, green
5   with worms & stamens duplicating themselves
each one the same

I squat among rows of seeds & imposters
and snout my hand into the juicy dirt:
charred chicken bones, rusted nails,
10 dogbones, stones, stove ashes.
Down there is another hand, yours, hopeless,
down there is a future

in which you're a white white picture
with a name I forgot to write
15 underneath, and no date,

in which you're a suit
hanging with its stubs of sleeves
in a cupboard in a house
in a city I've never entered,

20 a missed beat in space
which nevertheless unrolls itself
as usual. As usual:
that's why I don't want to go on with this.

(I'll want to make a hole in the earth
25   the size of an implosion°, a leaf, a dwarf   *bursting inwards*
  star, a cave
  in time that opens back & back into
  absolute darkness and at last
  into a small pale moon of light
30   the size of a hand,
  I'll want to call you out of the grave
  in the form of anything at all)

Habitation

Marriage is not
a house or even a tent

it is before that, and colder:

the edge of the forest, the edge
5   of the desert
           the unpainted stairs

at the back where we squat
outside, eating popcorn

the edge of the receding glacier

where painfully and with wonder
10   at having survived even
  this far

we are learning to make fire

Geoffrey Haresnape (1939 –)

*Haresnape was born in Durban and educated at the University of Cape
Town, where he is now Professor in the Department of English. In
addition to a critical assessment of the work of Pauline Smith,
Haresnape has published two volumes of poetry:* Drive of the Tide,
which deals with family relationships, and New-born Images. *He has
edited a collection of South African pioneering prose entitled* The
Great Hunters, *and has also served as editor of the journal,* Contrast.
*He has won several awards for creative writing. "The Necklace", with
its ironic allusion to Henry Vaughan's poem, "The World", describes a
gruesome form of mob-execution that arose in South Africa during the
1980s. (The so-called necklace is a burning rubber tyre placed around
the victim's shoulders.)*

The Necklace

    I saw eternity the other night[1]
like a great ring—but not of pure and endless light,
    not calm, as it was bright.
And round about it, crowds with grins, gibes, leers,
5   driven by their fears,
    like a vast shadow moved.

    Yet some who tried to weep and cling;
and cling and weep, were pinioned in the ring;
    but most could do nothing.
10   Poor fools—I thought—here to be decorated so
    and made to go,
    leaving the quiet day.

    At once the fire roared,
and they (first live, them limp) were quickly charred.
15   When I, who saw them, felt dismay,
one with an angry gesture seemed to say:
    "This ring we do for none provide
    who're on our side."

1 *The opening line of Haresnape's poem alerts
us to the relationship with Vaughan's "The
World" (see p. 39). Instead of the possibility
of redemption and grace suggested in
Vaughan's poem, "The Necklace" creates
images of hell and torment.*

242 / Seamus Heaney

Seamus Heaney (1939 –)

Heaney is a Catholic, born in Northern Ireland to farming parents.
Heaney's work refers not only to his rural origins, but also to the poli-
tical conflict that has divided his country for so long. Heaney's poetry
must be seen against the background of Irish history and Irish lore. His
imagination was greatly stirred by the discovery in the Irish boglands
of perfectly preserved Iron Age people who had been ritually slaugh-
tered. Heaney commented: "The unforgettable photographs of these
victims blended in my mind with photographs of atrocities, past and
present, in the long rites of Irish political and religious struggles".
  Heaney won several awards for the collection entitled North, *from*
which "Act of Union" is taken.

Act of Union

To-night, a first movement, a pulse,
As if the rain in bogland gathered head
To slip and flood: a bog-burst,
A gash breaking open the ferny bed.
5   Your back is a firm line of eastern coast
And arms and legs are thrown
Beyond your gradual hills. I caress
The heaving province where our past has grown.
I am the tall kingdom over your shoulder
10 That you would neither cajole nor ignore.
Conquest is a lie. I grow older
Conceding your half-independent shore
Within whose borders now my legacy
Culminates inexorably.

15 And I am still imperially
Male, leaving you with the pain,
The rending process in the colony,
The battering ram, the boom burst from within.
The act sprouted and obstinate fifth column°   *collaborators*
20 Whose stance is growing unilateral.
His heart beneath your heart is a wardrum
Mustering force. His parasitical
And ignorant little fists already
Beat at your borders and I know they're cocked
25 At me across the water. No treaty
I foresee will salve completely your tracked
And stretchmarked body, the big pain
That leaves you raw, like opened ground, again.

Wopko Jensma (1939 –)

Jensma was born in Middelburg in the Cape Province. Sculptor, painter and poet, Jensma pursued a career as an artist in Botswana before returning to South Africa in 1971. His poetry is concerned with apartheid and racial issues, as is clear from the titles of some of his anthologies: Sing for our Execution, Where White is the Colour Where Black is the Number *and* I Must Show you my Clippings. *His contribution to South African poetry was recognized in 1983, when he received an award from the English Academy of Southern Africa. "Misto 3" is one of a group of three poems in* Sing for our Execution. *"Misto" is a Portuguese word meaning "mixed" or "confused".*

Misto 3

```
      lets
      spit
      lets
      spill our names on blank walls
 5    lets
      spell it out: we have no future
      lets
      bolt
      lets
10    howl for their waste blood, yes
      lets
      slit our throbbin human vein—
      guts
      guts
15    guts
      (big boss, my lord, may i vomit,
      i mean, my bitter, bleedin heart
      flippin fool)
      drum
20    guts
      drums, hear our drippin pleadin
      when will our black christ die
      guts
```

Mbuyiseni Oswald Mtshali (1940 –)

Mtshali was born in Vryheid in Natal. His first volume of poetry,
Sounds of a Cowhide Drum, *is about life in South Africa's black town-
ships. Published in 1971, it was widely acclaimed, and triggered an
explosion in black poetry during the 1970s: it was that rare thing in
South Africa—a poetry best-seller. Mtshali studied at Columbia
University, USA, for four years and, on his return to South Africa in
1979, worked first as art critic and then as an English teacher and vice-
principal of a college in Soweto, Johannesburg. His second volume of
poetry,* Fireflames, *which heralds radical political change in South
Africa, was published in 1980. His profound insight into, and empathy
with, the plight of urbanized blacks in South Africa is reflected in both
"An Abandoned Bundle" and "The Master of the House". In different
vein, "The Moulting Country Bird" uses bird imagery to explore a
rural boy's desire to be accepted in the city.*
    Mtshali received the Olive Schreiner Prize for literature in 1975.

An Abandoned Bundle

The morning mist
and chimney smoke
of White City Jabavu[1]
flowed thick yellow
5   as pus oozing
from a gigantic sore.

It smothered our little houses
like fish caught in a net.

Scavenging dogs
10 draped in red bandanas of blood
fought fiercely
for a squirming bundle.

I threw a brick;
they bared fangs
15 flicked velvet tongues of scarlet
and scurried away,
leaving a multilated corpse—

---

1 *A black township near Johannesburg.*

an infant dumped on a rubbish heap—
"Oh! Baby in the Manger[2]
20 sleep well
on human dung."

Its mother
had melted into the rays of the rising sun,
her face glittering with innocence
25 her heart as pure as untrampled dew.

The Moulting Country Bird

I wish
I was not a bird
red and tender of body
with the mark of the tribe
5 branded on me as a fledgling
hatched in the Zulu grass hut.

Pierced in the lobe of the ear
by the burning spike of the elderman;
he drew my blood like a butcher bird
10 that impales the grasshopper on the thorn.

As a full fledged starling
hopping in the city street,
scratching the building corridor,
I want to moult
15 from the dung-smeared down
tattered like a fieldworker's shirt,
tighter than the skin of a snake
that sleeps as the plough turns the sod.

Boots caked with mud,
20 wooden stoppers flapping from earlobes
and a beaded little gourd dangling on a hirsute° chest,   *hairy*
all to stoke the incinerator.

2 *This is a reference to the new-born Jesus, for
whom a manger had to serve in place of a
cradle.*

I want to be adorned
by a silken suit so scintillating° in sheen,   *sparkling*
25 it pales even the peacock's plumage,
and catches the enchanted eye
of a harlot hiding in an alley:
"Come! my moulten bird,
I will not charge you a price!"

The Master of the House

Master, I am a stranger to you,
but will you hear my confession?

I am a faceless man
who lives in the backyard
5   of your house.

I share your table
so heavily heaped with
bread, meat and fruit
it huffs like a horse
10 drawing a coal cart.

As the rich man's to Lazarus,[3]
the crumbs were swept to my lap
by my Lizzie:
"Sweetie! eat and be satisfied now,
15 To-morrow we shall be gone."

So nightly I run the gauntlet,
wrestle with your mastiff, Caesar,[4]
for the bone pregnant with meat
and wash it down with Pussy's milk.

20 I am the nocturnal animal
that steals through the fenced lair
to meet my mate,
and flees at the break of dawn
before the hunter and the hounds
25 run me to ground.

3 *Beggar who was denied crumbs from the rich man's table (Luke 16).*
4 *Julius Caesar, who was virtual dictator of Rome at the height of his power (about half a century before the birth of Jesus). His name is synonymous with imperial authority.*

Jeni Couzyn (1942 –)

Jeni Couzyn was born in South Africa and educated at Natal University, Durban. She moved to London in 1966. Founder member of the Poet's Conference and the Poet's Union, she has also been chairperson of the National Poetry Secretariat from the time of its inception in 1973, and has worked in the Department of Creative Writing at the Canadian University of Victoria, in British Columbia. In addition to poetry readings, she has been commissioned to work for films and art festivals, and has appeared on radio and television. Her volumes of poetry include Flying, Monkey's Wedding, Christmas in Africa, House of Changes *and* Life by Drowning.

Spell for Birth

God the mother
God the daughter
God the holy spirit

5   Triune° of love   trinity, trio
     Triune of grace

Stream take you
Current aid you
Wind escort you
Earth receive you

10 God the mother
     God the daughter
     God the holy spirit

Triune of grace
Triune of power.

Arthur Nortje (1942 – 1970)

Born in Oudtshoorn in the Cape Province, Nortje was educated at the
University of the Western Cape and at Oxford. After teaching for two
years in Canada, he returned to Oxford, where he died in 1970. Two
volumes of his poetry were published posthumously in 1973: Dead
Roots *and* Lonely against the Light. *With Dennis Brutus, Nortje was*
awarded the Mbari Poetry Prize in 1962. "Waiting" records the experi-
ence of exile.

Waiting

The isolation of exile is a gutted
warehouse at the back of pleasure streets:
the waterfront of limbo stretches panoramically—
night the beautifier lets the lights
5 dance across the wharf.
I peer through the skull's black windows
wondering what can credibly save me.
The poem trails across the ruined wall
a solitary snail, or phosphorescently
10 swims into vision like a fish
through a hole in the mind's foundation, acute
as a glittering nerve.

Origins trouble the voyager much, those roots
that have sipped the waters of another continent.
15 Africa is gigantic, one cannot begin
to know even the strange behaviour furthest
south in my xenophobic° department.   *hating strangers*
Come back, come back mayibuye°   *come back*
cried the breakers of stone and cried the crowds
20 cried Mr Kumalo¹ before the withering fire
mayibuye Afrika²

Now there is the loneliness of lost
beauties at Cabo de Esperancia°, Table Mountain: *Cape of Good Hope*
all the dead poets who sang of spring's
25 miraculous recrudescence° in the sandscapes of Karoo   *eruption*
sang of thoughts that pierced like arrows, spoke
through the strangled throat of multi-humanity
bruised like a python in the maggot-fattening sun.

1 *Possibly an allusion to a central character in*   2 *Let Africa come back.*
Alan Paton's Cry, the Beloved Country.

You with your face of pain, your touch of gaiety,
30   with eyes that could distil me any instant
have passed into some diary, some dead journal
now that the computer, the mechanical notion
obliterates sincerities.
The amplitude of sentiment has brought me no nearer
35   to anything affectionate,
new magnitude of thought has but betrayed
the lustre of your eyes.

You yourself have vacated the violent arena
for a northern life of semi-snow
40   under the Distant Early Warning System:[3]
I suffer the radiation burns of silence.
It is not cosmic immensity or catastrophe
that terrifies me:
it is solitude that mutilates,
45   the night bulb that reveals ash on my sleeve.

3 *System of protection against nuclear attack.*

Nikki Giovanni (1943 –)

Nikki Giovanni is one of the most noted poets of the black renaissance which began in the USA in the 1960s. Her poetry ranges from angry, aggressive, revolutionary verse to expressions of sensitive warmth and depth. She is now a folk-heroine and has become known as the "Princess of Black Poetry". She has served as Professor of English at Rutgers University and Professor of Black Studies at Queens College, New York.

Nikki Rosa

childhood memories are always a drag
if you're Black
you always remember things like living in Woodlawn
with no inside toilet
5 and if you become famous or something
they never talk about how happy you were to have
your mother
all to yourself and
how good the water felt when you got your bath
10 from one of those
big tubs that folk in chicago barbeque in
and somehow when you talk about home
it never gets across how much you
understood their feelings
15 as the whole family attended meetings about Hollydale
and even though you remember
your biographers never understand
your father's pain as he sells his stock
and another dream goes
20 And though you're poor it isn't poverty that
concerns you
and though they fought a lot
it isn't your father's drinking that makes any difference
but only that everybody is together and you
25 and your sister have happy birthdays and very good
Christmases
and I really hope no white person ever has cause
to write about me
because they'll never understand
30 Black love is Black wealth and they'll
probably talk about my hard childhood
and never understand that
all the while I was quite happy.

Dorian Haarhoff (1944 –)

Dorian Haarhoff was born in Kimberley and since 1979 has lived in Windhoek, where he teaches at the University of Namibia. His poetry draws on his knowledge of the history and myths of his adopted country. His doctoral thesis, The Wild South West: Frontier Myths and Metaphors in Literature *set in Namibia, was published in 1991. Haarhoff has also written plays, children's stories, and published two collections of poetry.*

Trader on the Namib Edge[1]

he unyards[2] a bolt of cloth,
canvas deep in dialect,
v-neck smile
for the transit riders
5   with mica[3] dust in travel creases.
his store is a wheel-slumped wagon
under a Damara[4] mother tree
with his bivouac° blacks,   *open-air camp*
dried tubers, dog pack, oxen
10 and a windmill
for hand-pump petrol.
the traveller sucks a drink
San[5] like, from a straw
and scans the backdrop stock—
15 a herd of tin-bright buckets,
tumbleweeds of sweets,
last year's dress lengths,
leopard hats, cotton reel beads
and spits of tobacco near
20 a card of MacNab pipes—
Scottish Rehoboth[6]—
then buys from a box
near the paraffin,
a bright blaze of T-shirt: UCLA.[7]

1 *The coastal, desert area of Namibia.*
2 *A yard is an imperial measure, slightly shorter than a metre.*
3 *Scaly mineral containing silicate of aluminium.*
4 *Central Namibia.*
5 *Indigenous Namibian people.*
6 *Namibian group of mixed African and European ancestry.*
7 *University of California, Los Angeles.*

Mongane Wally Serote (1944 –)

Serote was born in Sophiatown, Johannesburg, and spent four years studying fine art at Columbia University, USA. He is one of the leading poets to have emerged in South Africa in the 1970s. In his poetry, he fuses elements of African tradition with those of western culture. "City Johannesburg" is a criticism of the establishment, evoking the heartlessness of the concrete city. In "Alexandra", the poet describes the township as a "mother" who elicits love from her children in spite of her cruelty. The presence of violent death is felt in this poem, but it becomes the central subject of "The Clothes", which evokes the "death-life lives" of many black people.

In addition to his poetry, Serote has written a number of short stories and a novel entitled To Every Birth Its Blood. *He received the Ingrid Jonker Prize in 1973 and a Creative Writing Award in 1983.*

Alexandra¹

Were it possible to say,
Mother, I have seen more beautiful mothers,
A most loving mother,
And tell her there I will go,
5 Alexandra, I would have long gone from you.

But we have only one mother, none can replace,
Just as we have no choice to be born,
We can't choose mothers;
We fall out of them like we fall out of life to death.

10 And Alexandra,
My beginning was knotted to you,
Just like you knot my destiny.
You throb in my inside silences
You are silent in my heart-beat that's loud to me.
15 Alexandra often I've cried.
When I was thirsty my tongue tasted dust,
Dust burdening your nipples.
I cry Alexandra when I am thirsty.
Your breasts ooze the dirty waters of your dongas,
20 Waters diluted with the blood of my brothers, your children,
Who once chose dongas for death-beds.
Do you love me Alexandra, or what are you doing to me?

---

1 *A black township near Johannesburg.*

You frighten me, Mama,
You wear expressions like you would be nasty to me,
25 You frighten me, Mama,
When I lie on your breast to rest, something tells me,
You are bloody cruel.
Alexandra, hell
What have you done to me?
30 I have seen people but I feel like I'm not one,
Alexandra what are you doing to me?

I feel I have sunk to such meekness!
I lie flat while others walk on me to far places.
I have gone from you, many times,
35 I come back.
Alexandra, I love you;
I know
When all these worlds became funny to me,
I silently waded back to you
40 And amid the rubble I lay,
Simple and black.

Burning Cigarette

This little black boy
Is drawn like a cigarette from its box,
Lit.
He looks at his smoke hopes
5 That twirl, spiral, curl
To nothing.
He grows like cigarette ashes
As docile, as harmless;
Is smothered.

City Johannesburg

This way I salute you:
My hand pulses to my back trousers pocket
Or into my inner jacket pocket
For my pass, my life
5 Jo'burg City.
My hand like a starved snake rears my pockets
For my thin, ever lean wallet,
While my stomach groans a friendly smile to hunger,
Jo'burg City.

10 My hand like a starved snake tears my pockets
Don't you know?
Jo'burg City, I salute you;
When I run out or roar in a bus to you,
I leave behind me, my love,
15 My comic houses and people, my dongas and my ever whirling dust,
My death,
That's so related to me as a wink to the eye.
Jo'burg City
I travel on your black and white robotted roads,
20 Through your thick iron breath that you inhale,
At six in the morning and exhale from five noon.
Jo'burg City
That is the time when I come to you,
When your neon flowers flaunt from your electrical wind,
25 That is the time when I leave you,
When your neon flowers flaunt their way through the falling darkness
On your cement trees.
And as I go back, to my love,
My dongas, my dust, my people, my death,
30 Where death lurks in the dark like a blade in the flesh,
I can feel your roots, anchoring your might, my feebleness
In my flesh, in my mind, in my blood,
And everything about you says it,
That, that is all you need of me.
35 Jo'burg City, Johannesburg,
Listen when I tell you,
There is no fun, nothing, in it,
When you leave the women and men with such frozen expressions,
Expressions that have tears like furrows of soil erosion,
40 Jo'burg City, you are dry like death,
Jo'burg City, Johannesburg, Jo'burg City.

The Clothes

I came home in the morning.
There on the stoep,
The shoes I knew so well
Dripped water like a window crying dew;
5 The shoes rested the first time
From when they were new.
Now it's forever.

I looked back,
On the washing line hung
10 A shirt, jacket and trousers
Soaked wet with pity,
Wrinkled and crying reddish water, perhaps also salty;
The pink shirt had a gash on the right,
And stains that told the few who know
15 An item of our death-life lives.

The colourless jacket still had mud,
Dropping lazily from its body
To join the dry earth beneath.

The over-sized black-striped trousers,
20 Dangled from one hip,
Like a man from a rope 'neath his head,
Tired of hoping to hope.

For Don M.—Banned[1]

it is a dry white season
dark leaves don't last, their brief lives dry out
and with a broken heart they dive down gently headed for the earth
not even bleeding.
5 it is a dry white season brother,
only the trees know the pain as they still stand erect
dry like steel, their branches dry like wire,
indeed, it is a dry white season
but seasons come to pass.

1 *Don Mattera, a "black consciousness" poet, was banned during the 1970s. Banning was a form of house arrest the apartheid government used to isolate and silence dissident artists and activists.*

Prelude

When i take a pen,
my soul bursts to deface° the paper   *mar, disfigure*
pus spills—
spreads
5 deforming a line into a figure that violates° my love,   *dishonours or defiles*
when i take a pen,
my crimson heart oozes into the ink,
dilutes it
spreads the gem of my life
10 makes the word i utter a gasp to the world,—
my mother, when i dance your eyes won't keep pace
look into my eyes,
there, the story of my day is told.

Alice Walker (1944 –)

*Alice Walker grew up among the cotton fields in Georgia, USA, but
left the rural south to attend Spelman College in Atlanta. Although she
has written a great deal of poetry, she is better known for her novel,*
The Color Purple. *Since the mid-1970s Walker's work has concentrated
on feminist concerns and, as an editor of* Ms *magazine, she writes
essays and reviews confronting issues that particularly affect women.
Her poetry communicates its message by means of a simple speaking
voice which seems to address its readers directly.*

On Sight

I am so thankful I have seen
The Desert
And the creatures in The Desert
And the desert Itself.

5   The Desert has its own moon
Which I have seen
With my own eye

There is no flag on it.

Trees of the desert have arms
10   All of which are always up
That is because the moon is up
The sun is up
Also the sky
The stars
15   Clouds
None with flags.

If there were flags, I doubt
The trees would point.
Would you?

Lynne Bryer (1946 –)

*Lynne Bryer was born in Port Elizabeth and has been writing poems
for much of her life. After working in publishing in London for a
period, she returned to Cape Town, where she now runs a small pub-
lishing house. In 1990 she was joint winner, with Fiona Zerbst, of the
AA Life/Arthur Nortje Award for Poetry. In her first collection,* A Time
in the Country, *Bryer approaches historical events with compassion
and imbues them with a sense of intimacy.*

Our One

*Sooner or later
every trek becomes a funeral procession*
—Amy Clampitt

They were farmers.
Bearded men, not always gentle,
smelling of tobacco, and ill-tanned leather.
Their women wore black
5   because there was always
something to mourn: a child died,
a father failed to come back
from a cattle-raid commando.
They were always ready to be widows.

10   In fact I think it may not have been
the men who carried it through,
who set the sea of wagon tents in motion.
More likely it was they, the women,
weary of being left alone at night
15   with a small wind tugging at the wooden shutters,
the hearth long cold, the children
muttering warm cries in their sleep, and she alone
awake and listening.
                Fear shuffled
in her like the beasts in the kraal:
20   long before the jackal's howl
they stamp and huddle, salt clogs their hides;
they've smelled the reddish scent, the musk
that now for hours will reek
above the iron tide of blood.

25 These were women weary
of a frontier where their lives
were barricades, where dark
could move in dark,
invisibly.

30 It was they who packed the wakis,[1]
putting in the candlestick, tin plates,
whatever might be called for, one day,
in another cottage, somewhere where you saw
no smoke of neighbour's chimney—
35 a good day's ride from company.

Did they see how they were pushing out
the frontier as they went?
Driving it before them
as surely as the oxen, stung by whips.

40 I think they knew all this
and still went, grimly, putting in
the linen, herbs, the home apothecary°—   *medicine chest*
knowing now at least they were all
slung together, nights, upon the thonged katel,°   *bed*
45 while days they swung through kloof and
poort[2] together in one wagon, under stiffened calico,
bent on the interior,
paradise, the fields
all Africa would not prevent them finding—

50 going now with hope
and with the seeds of hate.

1 *Storage chest in ox-wagon.*   2 *Natural passage through mountain.*

Charles Mungoshi (1947 –)

Mungoshi was born at Manyene, near Enkeldoorn, Rhodesia (now Chivhu, Zimbabwe.) He has worked on the editorial staff of the Zimbabwe Literature Bureau, as a director of Zimbabwe Publishing House and as Writer-in-Residence at the University of Zimbabwe. His poetry has appeared in Staffrider *and in the anthology,* Zimbabwe Poetry in English. *He has also written novels, including* Waiting for Rain, *and a collection of short stories,* Coming of a Dry Season. *Mungoshi received a PEN Award in 1976 and again in 1981.*

Burning Log

   i am
a burning log
my history being reduced
to ashes
5   what i remember
of yesterday
is the ashy taste
of defeat
my hope
10 for tomorrow
is the fire.

Solly Kaplinski (1948 –)

The son of Holocaust survivors, Solly Kaplinski was educated at the Universities of Cape Town and South Africa and also at the Hebrew University in Jerusalem. He is at present headmaster of Herzlia High School in Cape Town. As is indicated by the title of his volume of poetry, Lost and Found: a Polish Experience: a Second Generation Response to the Holocaust *(1992), his poems are about the extermination of Jews by the Nazis during the Second World War. The Majdanek concentration camp was situated about three kilometres from the centre of the city of Lublin, in Poland. It was in this camp that 18 000 Jews were exterminated on 4 November 1943, a day which the S.S. (Nazi officers) named their "harvest festival". This is the horror alluded to in "Lublin—4th November 1943—2.30 p.m.".*

Kaplinski writes about the frailties of humankind and the need to exercise control over potentially destructive primal instincts.

In the Shoe Shop

I went to a shoe shop
today
in
Majdanek
5   800 000 pairs on display
but
no
body
to fill them

10 How easy it must've been
to be ambitious
in
those days

It didn't take long
15 to fill a dead man's shoes.

Lublin—4th November 1943—2.30 p.m.

They told us (they still do)
that they never
heard anything
saw anything
5   knew anything
okay—so let's give them the benefit of the doubt
for a moment
but just for a moment.

They can never say
10   they smelt nothing
Surely human flesh and bone
baking in those ovens
surely
battered bodies barbecued on pyres
15   must've aroused
some new sensations?

Let's make another assumption
for a moment
but just for a moment
20   that those who enjoy a hearty steak
can't tell the difference between man and beast
—even without seasoning

Okay
but how to explain away
25   the blanket of human ashes
so lovingly conveyed by the gentle breezes
on to the city?

They say the most popular item
in the store that day was soap—
30   Shades of Lady Macbeth?[1]

The gardens in the Spring of '44
were the finest ever
rich, lush and an array of spangled colours
so many beautiful flowers in full bloom
35   and tantalising scents

The winter compost made a perfect fertilizer.

1 *In Shakespeare's play,* Macbeth, *Lady Macbeth, her mind disturbed, tries vainly to wash her hands clean after the murder of King Duncan.*

Njabulo Ndebele (1948 –)

Ndebele, who spent his formative years in Charterston Location, Nigel, in the Transvaal, was educated at Cambridge and in the USA before going on to lecture in literature at the University of Lesotho. His volume, Fools and Other Stories, *won the Noma Award for Publishing in Africa in 1984, and a collection of critical essays,* Rediscovery of the Ordinary, *appeared in 1991. He is currently President of the Congress of South African Writers (COSAW) and Vice-Chancellor of the University of the North.*

Written in the context of racial oppression under apartheid, "The Revolution of the Aged" was composed after the black student uprisings of 1976.

The Revolution of the Aged

my voice is the measure of my life
it cannot travel far now,
small mounds of earth already bead my open grave,
so come close
5   lest you miss the dream.

grey hair has placed on my brow
the verdict of wisdom
and the skin-folds of age
bear tales wooled in the truth of proverbs:
10 if you cannot master the wind,
flow with it
letting know all the time that you are resisting.

that is how i have lived
quietly
15 swallowing both the fresh and foul
from the mouth of my masters;
yet i watched and listened.

i have listened too
to the condemnations of the young
20 who burned with scorn
      loaded with revolutionary maxims
        hot for quick results.

they did not know
that their anger
25 was born in the meekness
with which i whipped myself:
it is a blind progeny
that acts without indebtedness to the past.

listen now,
30 the dream:
i was playing music on my flute
when a man came and asked to see my flute
and i gave it to him,
but he took my flute and walked away.
35 i followed this man, asking for my flute;
he would not give it back to me.
how i planted vegetables in his garden!
        cooked his food!
how i cleaned his house!
40 how i washed his clothes!
        and polished his shoes!

but he would not give me back my flute,
yet in my humiliation
i felt the growth of strength in me
45 for i had a goal
as firm as life is endless,
while he lived in the darkness of his wrong

now he has grown hollow from the grin of his cruelty
he hisses death through my flute

50 which has grown heavy, too heavy
for his withered hands,
and now i should smite him:
in my hand is the weapon of youth.

do not eat an unripe apple
55 its bitterness is a tingling knife.
suffer yourself to wait
and the ripeness will come
and the apple will fall down at your feet.

now is the time
60   pluck the apple
and feed the future with its ripeness

Motshile wa Nthodi (1948 –)

Nthodi was born in Lady Selborne township near Pretoria. From the Calabash: Poems and Woodcuts *is a volume which focuses on life in an African village and is illustrated by the author. Nthodi has also exhibited his graphic art widely in South Africa and is represented in collections overseas. "Standard Fifty-eight" focuses on the disparate lifestyles of South Africans under apartheid.*

Standard Fifty-eight

Born on Saturday,
nineteen forty-eight.
After eight years,
my mother bought me a
5   cheap slate for eight pence
and took me to school.

Monday to Friday
in black and white,
from eight to two o'clock,
10   we planted tomatoes
and played football.

At the age of eighteen,
I passed standard eight
and became Baas Groen's
15   good garden boy.

Today I'm twenty-eight
   years old,
   reading form fourteen,
   working in a garage,
20   easy job—
     petrol attendant
for eight rands per month,
   easy job.

I wish I could pass standard
25   fifty-eight,
        in cooking
and become Mrs Beach's
careless kitchen boy,
for eight cents per week.

30 Oh!
What an easy job.

Shabbir Banoobhai (1949 –)

Born in Durban, Shabbir Banoobhai was employed as a lecturer in accountancy at the University of Durban-Westville before qualifying in 1983 as a Cost and Management Accountant. He is now a consultant with the Small Business Development Corporation. His first volume of poems, echoes of my other self, *contains poems of intense social concern. A second volume,* shadows of a sun-darkened land, *appeared in 1984.*

The Border

the border

is as far
as the black man
who walks alongside you

5 as secure
as your door
against the unwanted knock

Ingrid de Kok (1951 –)

Ingrid de Kok was educated at the University of the Witwatersrand, the University of Cape Town and at Queen's University in Canada. She has worked for Khanya College in Cape Town and presently works for the Adult Education Unit at the University of Cape Town. She has published widely in poetry journals both in South Africa and abroad, sometimes under her married name of Fiske. She lived for some years in Canada, and many of the poems in her collection, Familiar Ground, reflect her sense of exile and her mixed feelings on homecoming. The poem "Small Passing" suggests that women are united across colour lines in their universal experience of motherhood.

Small Passing

For a woman whose baby died stillborn, and who was told by a man to stop mourning, "because the trials and horrors suffered daily by black women in this country are more significant than the loss of one white child".

1

In this country you may not
suffer the death of your stillborn,
remember the last push into shadow and silence,
the useless wires and cords on your stomach,
5   the nurse's face, the walls, the afterbirth in a basin.
Do not touch your breasts
still full of purpose.
Do not circle the house,
pack, unpack the small clothes.
10 Do not lie awake at night hearing
the doctor say "It was just as well"
and "You can have another."
In this country you may not
mourn small passings.

15 See: the newspaper boy in the rain
will sleep tonight in a doorway.
The woman in the busline
may next month be on a train
to a place not her own.
20 The baby in the backyard now
will be sent to a tired aunt,

grow chubby, then lean,
return a stranger.
Mandela's daughter tried to find her father
25   through the glass. She thought they'd let her touch him.[1]

And this woman's hands are so heavy when she dusts
the photographs of other children
they fall to the floor and break.
Clumsy woman, she moves so slowly
30   as if in a funeral rite.

On the pavements the nannies meet.
These are legal gatherings.
They talk about everything, about home,
while the children play among them,
35   their skins like litmus,[2] their bonnets clean.

2

Small wrist in the grave.
Baby no one carried live
between houses, among trees.
Child shot running,
40   stones in his pocket,
boy's swollen stomach
full of hungry air.
Girls carrying babies
not much smaller than themselves.
45   Erosion. Soil washed down to the sea.

3

I think these mothers dream
headstones of the unborn.
Their mourning rises like a wall
no vine will cling to.
50   They will not tell you your suffering is white.
They will not say it is just as well.
They will not compete for the ashes of infants.
I think they may say to you:

1 *For most of Nelson Mandela's long incarceration, his family, when visiting, were permitted only to see him with a plate-glass barrier between them.*

2 *Litmus is a soluble powder which turns red under acid conditions. The poet here suggests sensitive white skins which sunburn easily.*

Come with us to the place of mothers.
55   We will stroke your flat empty belly,
let you weep with us in the dark,
and arm you with one of our babies
to carry home on your back.

Farouk Asvat (1952 –)

Asvat is a Johannesburg medical practitioner who also works part-time as a journalist and a critic. His first volume of poetry, The Time of our Lives, *has a political focus and sometimes combines English with the patois called "tsotsitaal" (see also Sepamla's "Come Duze Baby",* p. 234). *Asvat won the AA Mutual Life/ Ad Donker Literary Award for his second collection of poems, A* Celebration of Flowers, *published in 1987. His stories, essays and poems have been published locally and overseas.*

Possibilities for a Man Hunted by SBs[1]

There's one of two possibilities
Either they find you or they don't
If they don't it's ok
But if they find you
5 There's one of two possibilities
Either they let you go or they ban you
If they let you go it's ok
But if they ban you
There's one of two possibilities
10 Either you break your ban or you don't
If you don't it's ok
But if you break your ban
There's one of two possibilities
Either they find out or they don't
15 If they don't it's ok
But if they find out
There's one of two possibilities
Either they find you guilty or not guilty
If they find you not guilty it's ok
20 But if they find you guilty
There's one of two possibilities
Either they suspend your sentence or they jail you
If they suspend your sentence it's ok
But if they jail you
25 There's one of two possibilities
Either they release you
Or you fall from the tenth floor

1 *Security Branch policemen.*

Oupa Thando Mthimkulu (1953 –)

While at high school, Oupa Mthimkulu began writing poetry in
English, Zulu and Southern Sotho. In a brief biographical note written
at the age of twenty-five, his poetry is described as existential rather
than political. The poem "Nineteen Seventy-six" appeared in the first
(banned) issue of Staffrider *in 1978, and refers to his experience in*
detention.

Nineteen Seventy-six

Go nineteen seventy-six
We need you no more
Never come again
We ache inside.
5   Good friends we have
Lost.
Nineteen seventy-six
You stand accused
Of deaths
10   Imprisonments
Exiles
And detentions.
You lost the battle
You were not revolutionary
15   Enough
We do not boast about you
Year of fire, year of ash.

Sujata Bhatt (1956 –)

Born in Ahmedabad, India, Sujata Bhatt studied in the USA and now works as a freelance writer in Germany, translating Gujerati poetry into English. Her poem "Muliebrity" (womanhood) evokes a tender vision of a simple peasant scene in India in which a girl gathering cow-dung is particularized and remains unstereotyped.

Muliebrity

I have thought so much about the girl
who gathered cow-dung in a wide, round basket
along the main road passing by our house
and the Radhavallabh[1] temple in Maninagar.[2]
5 I have thought so much about the way she
moved her hands and her waist
and the smell of cow-dung and road-dust and wet canna lilies,
the smell of monkey breath and freshly washed clothes
and the dust from crows' wings which smells different—
10 and again the smell of cow-dung as the girl scoops
it up, all these smells surrounding me separately
and simultaneously—I have thought so much
but have been unwilling to use her for a metaphor,
for a nice image—but most of all unwilling
15 to forget her or to explain to anyone the greatness
and the power glistening through her cheekbones
each time she found a particularly promising
mound of dung—

---

1 *Radhavallabh is the name of a temple, and means, in essence, a devotee of Krishna.*

2 *A place in Gujarat, India.*

Fhazel Johennesse (1956 –)

Born in Johannesburg, Fhazel Johennesse has published a volume of poetry, The Rainmaker. *The short, ironic poem below conveys only briefly the evocative creative power of the poet and the versatility of his vision. The poem draws attention to political disparity by using the whiteness usually associated with snow at Christmas to refer also to the festive season as an exclusively "white" affair in South Africa.*

thinking about a white christmas

overseas they have white christmas
snow burying everything in sight
and making it all seem soft and lovely
while down here in the south
5   christmas is celebrated in driving heat
i try to connect snow and christmas
i fail and then i laugh
because as i think about it
i realise that christmas down here
10 is really a very white affair

Christopher van Wyk (1957 –)

Van Wyk was born in Johannesburg and edited the journal Staffrider
*for several years. He has written a number of short stories, and a
volume of poems entitled* It is Time to Go Home, *for which he was
awarded (with Patrick Cullinan) the 1980 Olive Schreiner Prize. He
received a Maskew Miller award for children's literature in 1981. "A
Riot Policeman" focuses on racial oppression under apartheid and
looks forward to liberation.*

A Riot Policeman

The sun has gone down
with the last doused flame.
Tonight's last bullet
has singed the day's last victim
5 an hour ago.
It is time to go home.

The hippo° crawls   *armoured vehicle*
in a desultory air of triumph
through, around fluttering
10 shirts and shoes full of death.
Teargas is simmering.
Tears have been dried by heat
or cooled by death.
Buckshot fills the space
15 between the maimed and the mourners.
It is time to go home.

A black man surrenders
a stolen bottle of brandy
scurries away with his life
20 in his hands.
The policeman rests the oasis
on his lips
wipes his mouth on a camouflaged
cuff.
25 It is time to go home.

Tonight he'll shed his uniform.
Put on his pyjamas.
Play with his children.
Make love to his wife.
30 Tomorrow is pay-day.
But it is time to go home now,
It is time to go home.

Gcina Mhlophe (1958 –)

Gcina Mhlophe has worked as a journalist for Learn and Teach *(an educational magazine committed to democracy) and for foreign radio; and served as resident director at the Market Theatre, Johannesburg, during 1989 and 1990. She has won awards for her acting, poetry and other writing, including the plays,* Have You Seen Zandile? *and* Born in the RSA. *Her one-woman performances and her promotion of the art of story-telling are among Mhlophe's talents. "The Dancer" was written in the years of upheaval preceding the release of Nelson Mandela, when many people died in the townships of South Africa, and funerals became the focus of intense political activity.*

The Dancer

Mama,
they tell me you were a dancer
they tell me you had long
beautiful legs to carry your graceful body
5   they tell me you were a dancer

Mama,
they tell me you sang beautiful solos
they tell me you closed your eyes
always when the feeling of the song
10   was right, and lifted your face up to the sky
they tell me you were an enchanting dancer

Mama
they tell me you were always so gentle
they talk of a willow tree
15   swaying lovingly over clear running water
in early Spring when they talk of you
they tell me you were a slow dancer

Mama
they tell me you were a wedding dancer
20   they tell me you smiled and closed your eyes
yours arms curving outward just a little
and your feet shuffling in the sand;
tshi tshi tshitshitshitha, tshitshi tshitshitshitha
o hee! how I wish I was there to see you
25   they tell me you were a pleasure to watch

Mama
they tell me I am a dancer too
but I don't know . . .
I don't know for sure what a wedding dancer is
30   there are no more weddings
but many, many funerals
where we sing and dance
running fast with the coffin
of a would-be bride or would-be groom
35   strange smiles have replaced our tears
our eyes are full of vengeance, Mama

Dear, dear Mama,
they tell me I am a funeral dancer.

Ndaleni Radebe (1960 –)

Ndaleni Radebe lives in Sebokeng, a township near Pretoria. She is the mother of two children. She has been writing poetry since 1983. In the poem below, Radebe celebrates the triumphs and strength of women.

Woman

You bring peace to earth
You bring reconciliation
Woman
You are magnificent
5   You are mother.

At the Inn there was no room
You were between life and death
You went to the stable
You brought forth your seed
10   You are woman.

You have been despised
You have been hated
You know what it is to fear
To worry, to hunger and thirst
15   Woman
And still you know what it is to be triumphant.

Cry out for joy
For your seed has multiplied
Shout out with great joy
20   For you have grown strong
Woman
You will bring everything to pass

Index